THE MONEY PRIMARY

THE MONEY PRIMARY
The New Politics of the Early Presidential Nomination Process

Michael J. Goff

JK
521
.G64
2004
West

ROWMAN & LITTLEFIELD PUBLISHERS, INC.
Lanham • Boulder • New York • Toronto • Oxford

ROWMAN & LITTLEFIELD PUBLISHERS, INC.

Published in the United States of America
by Rowman & Littlefield Publishers, Inc.
A wholly owned subsidiary of The Rowman & Littlefield Publishing Group, Inc.
4501 Forbes Boulevard, Suite 200, Lanham, MD 20706
www.rowmanlittlefield.com

P.O. Box 317, Oxford OX2 9RU, UK

Copyright © 2004 by Rowman & Littlefield Publishers, Inc.

All rights reserved. No part of this publication may be reproduced, stored in a retrieval
system, or transmitted in any form or by any means, electronic, mechanical,
photocopying, recording, or otherwise, without the prior permission of the publisher.

British Library Cataloguing in Publication Information Available

Library of Congress Cataloging-in-Publication Data

Goff, Michael J., 1953–
   The money primary : the new politics of the early presidential
nomination process / Michael J. Goff.
      p. cm.
   Includes bibliographical references and index.
   ISBN 0-7425-3567-3 (cloth : alk. paper)
1. Presidents—United States—Nomination. 2. Campaign funds—United
States. 3. Primaries—United States. I. Title.
   JK521.G64 2004
   324.273'15—dc22

                                                      2004000310

Printed in the United States of America

∞™ The paper used in this publication meets the minimum requirements of American
National Standard for Information Sciences—Permanence of Paper for Printed Library
Materials, ANSI/NISO Z39.48-1992.

To
my mother
Anna Marie Goff
and my daughter
Marie-Therese Goff

Contents

Tables

Online Appendices

All appendices are available online at www.loyola.edu/moneyprimarystudy.

Preface

THE 2004 PRESIDENTIAL NOMINATION CAMPAIGN was well underway by mid-2002, having commenced even earlier than the previous record-setting 2000 presidential nomination campaign. The list of reputed Democratic presidential aspirants, "the mentioned," numbered ten or more by fall 2002 and was still growing. By December 2002, two years before election day, presumed Democratic front-runner Al Gore already had placed himself on the sidelines, and just a month later Senate Minority Leader Thomas Daschle did the same. These dramatic changes in the Democratic candidate field, occurring at an unprecedented early juncture, opened the way for the widest field of Democratic nomination contenders since 1988 and perhaps ever. By early in the pre-election year of 2003, eight candidates—former Gov. Howard Dean, Sen. John Edwards, Rep. Richard Gephardt, Sen. John Kerry, Rep. Dennis Kucinich, Sen. Joseph Lieberman, former Sen. Carol Moseley Braun, and Rev. Al Sharpton—had officially launched presidential nomination bids. A ninth contender—Sen. Bob Graham—joined the official Democratic presidential candidate field in February 2003, albeit for just seven months, and a tenth Democratic candidate—Gen. Wesley Clark—officially joined the race in fall 2003. Other possible contenders, including Sen. Joseph Biden, Sen. Christopher Dodd, former Sen. Gary Hart, and perhaps even Sen. Hillary Rodham Clinton, spent most of 2003 waiting in the wings, poised to join the race if the opportunity presented itself. And just as the Democratic presidential candidate field came together earlier than ever in the pre-election year of 2003, additional early withdrawals by announced candidates—such as Moseley Braun's on the eve of the nomination process and Gephardt's following the Iowa caucuses—occurred as well.

Early candidate fund-raising and the attendant media coverage, powerful factors that comprise what is termed "the money primary," tracked this early presidential nomination campaign. In fact, virtually the entire field of early Democratic presidential contenders and even potential contenders signaled their interest in a presidential race well in advance. Active candidate leadership political action committees (PACs) certainly were harbingers of these nascent and unfolding presidential candidacies. In fact, five of the eight Democratic candidates with announced presidential candidacies as of January 2003— Dean, Edwards, Gephardt, Kerry, and Lieberman—had active pre-candidacy leadership PACs, several with impressive early fund-raising totals, two or more years in advance of the formal nomination campaign. By January 2004, the eve of the formal nomination process, Dean had eclipsed his competitors in early fund-raising, exceeding $40 million in contributions for 2003, with Kerry raising over $19 million, Edwards almost $16 million, Gephardt over $14 million, and Clark and Lieberman each over $13 million. Significant media attention accompanied this early fund-raising, most notably focused on Dean and to a lesser extent his closest fund-raising competitors—especially Kerry and Edwards—following the pattern that the candidates who achieve early fund-raising success are the focus of early and increasing media coverage as well.

Dean's overwhelming lead in fund-raising and media coverage of his fund-raising success as the formal nomination process began certainly made him the media's pick as the early front-runner; and if the success of previous candidates with comparable fund-raising superiority was any guide, his prospects for winning the nomination appeared to be strong. As it turned out, however, Kerry scored upset victories in the early nomination contests, quickly upending Dean's apparent juggernaut. Yet Kerry's emergence as the new frontrunner should not have come as a surprise in view of the strength in fundraising which his campaign also exhibited and the fact that he was the only Democratic candidate other than Dean to decline federal matching funds and thus to avoid federal state-by-state and overall spending ceilings, distinctions which brought Kerry very positive media attention in December 2003 and January 2004. Indeed, coupled with the personal wealth which permitted his presidential campaign committee access to massive credit, Kerry's standing as the second strongest fund-raiser at the start of the formal nomination process ensured his campaign's viability and fueled his rapid emergence as the new front-runner. Especially in the context of the Dean campaign's excessive early spending and low total in cash-on-hand going into the opening nomination contests, and perhaps aided by Dean's emphasis on fund-raising via the Internet rather than through direct donor contact, Kerry's fund-raising strength and the resulting media attention positioned him to mount a very competitive, and ultimately successful, campaign for the Democratic nomination.

The early start to presidential campaign 2004 continued a pattern in post-reform era presidential nomination campaigns that dates to the 1980s. Indeed, a fundamental yet largely unanticipated consequence of the presidential nomination reforms after 1968 has been the rise of the early campaign as a vital part of the presidential nomination process. Now entering its third decade and in all likelihood constituting an irreversible trend, this early campaign merits careful study by students of the presidential nomination process. As this study documents, the pre-candidacy and early candidacy periods in advance of the 1988 and 2000 presidential elections—the two election years in which both major parties had open nomination contests—stand out among these early nomination campaigns. Examining the early campaigns for the presidential nomination in these two election cycles and the trends that systematic comparison yields, especially with respect to fund-raising and media coverage of fund-raising success, highlights the significance of the early campaign and in particular the money primary for presidential nomination politics and presidential selection.

The early presidential nomination campaign and the money primary that dominates it certainly proved to have a decisive impact on the 1988 and 2000 presidential nomination campaigns. Recognizing this new reality of presidential nomination politics is indispensable to an understanding of the early campaign for the 2004 presidential nomination and to the study of the presidential nomination process now and in the future.

Acknowledgments

THE ASSISTANCE AND SUPPORT of many individuals and organizations have helped to make this research possible. I owe each one my sincere gratitude.

Early in this research, as I explored research interests and possible topics in the areas of the presidential nomination process, campaign fund-raising, and campaign finance reform, I received helpful background and assistance from numerous public interest research organizations. Staff at the Campaign Finance Information Center, the Center for Responsive Politics, the Citizen's Research Council, and Common Cause were especially helpful when I made inquiries and sought background information.

Indispensable assistance during the research design and data gathering phases of this research was provided by the Federal Election Commission and its courteous and helpful staff. The generally high quality of the FEC's campaign finance report archives, both electronic (from 1993 to 2000) and on microfilm (from 1976 to 1992), were the foundation for this research. FEC staff who were especially helpful include Jason Bucelato, Steve Kania, and Kevin Salley, each of whom spent innumerable hours responding to requests for financial disclosure reports, hunting down missing reports, and guiding me through the microfilm archives of the FEC. I also am grateful to Robert Biersack of the FEC for his time in discussing my research ideas as I planned this project.

The intercoder reliability test utilized in this study's content analysis required the involvement of a second reviewer. I am grateful to Mark Kelly of Loyola College in Maryland for his involvement as this second reviewer. My executive assistant, Susan Nakashima, provided enormous assistance in the arduous task of typing the manuscript, and as always I am very grateful to have such capable, loyal, and tireless support.

Georgetown University's Department of Government where I conducted this research and prepared the original manuscript as a doctoral dissertation was a major part of my life for the period spanning the 1988 and 2000 presidential election cycles that are the focus of this study. I am especially grateful to Dr. James Lengle for his stimulating classes on presidential electoral politics, for the time and interest he devoted to guiding numerous early research projects, and for the insight, wise counsel, and unflagging encouragement, which he provided as my faculty advisor for the doctoral dissertation that was the original version of this manuscript. I also am sincerely grateful to Dr. Diana M. Owen and Dr. George W. Carey, members of the doctoral committee, for their many insights and suggestions.

Finally, and most important, I am grateful for the loyalty, support, and love of my daughter, Marie-Therese Goff, who grew up in a home where presidential politics and the presidential nomination process were part of each day's routine.

Introduction

THE NEW POLITICS OF THE EARLY PRESIDENTIAL NOMINATION PROCESS, including the pre-candidacy and early candidacy phases and especially "the money primary," is the focus of this study. This money primary is examined as a critical period in defining the field of viable candidates that emerges before the primary and caucus process begins. The early presidential nomination campaigns of 1988 and 2000—the two all non-incumbent elections of the post-reform era—are utilized as case studies. Data on campaign fund-raising available at the Federal Election Commission comprise an important part of this analysis. Data on media coverage of campaign fund-raising during the period leading up to the caucus and primary schedule provide a further dimension to the analysis.

This study confirms the pivotal importance of money in presidential candidate survival, viability, and success. The extent of a potential candidate's success in fund-raising at the pre-candidacy phase is found to be associated with the candidate moving from pre-candidacy to announced candidacy and from simply survival to viability. Fund-raising success during the early candidacy phase, and the extent to which a candidate develops momentum in fund-raising, also are found to be associated with candidate survival, viability, and success.

A second dimension to the money primary examined in this study is media coverage of campaign fund-raising. The extent to which a candidate receives coverage of successful fund-raising, whether the orientation of this coverage is positive or negative, and whether horse race coverage compares the candidate's fund-raising favorably or unfavorably with other candidates, all are found to be associated with candidate survival, viability, and success.

In sum, this study confirms the pivotal importance of the money primary in the early presidential nomination campaign. Both fund-raising success and media coverage of fund-raising success during the pre-candidacy and early candidacy phases are found to be associated with candidate survival, viability, and success once the formal nomination process begins. That fund-raising and the money and media attention that result are such critical resources suggest the advent of yet a new period in the ever evolving system of presidential selection, a period that in effect constitutes an "unreformed post-reform era" in the modern presidential nomination process.

1

"The Money Primary" in the Early Presidential Nomination Process

MONEY IS AN INDISPENSABLE RESOURCE FOR SEEKING THE PRESIDENCY, and the process of raising money early and with increasing momentum is a pivotal hurdle for presidential candidates and would-be candidates. Less visible but just as important is the process of building a campaign organization that is capable of generating significant financial support during both the pre-candidacy and early candidacy phases of a presidential nomination campaign. Moreover, while raising money to fund a planned or ongoing presidential nomination campaign is clearly the immediate objective of both pre-candidacy and early candidacy fund-raising, a further dimension to the early presidential nomination process is the media coverage which a candidate receives that is focused on campaign fund-raising. To be sure, fund-raising success is essential simply to fund an unfolding presidential nomination campaign, but what might be described as the echo of this success in terms of media coverage of campaign fund-raising is critical as well. The necessity of campaign fund-raising and media coverage of campaign fund-raising for candidate survival, viability, and success during the pre-candidacy and early candidacy phases has created the new politics of the early presidential nomination process that today dominates presidential selection.

The pivotal importance of money in early presidential nomination politics is due in large part to the fact that it is a resource that can be used to purchase other campaign resources, namely professional staffing, campaign organization, and access to the media through advertising, all of which also are essential for a successful presidential bid. Candidates and would-be candidates generally make the raising of money their first and highest priority even as they ponder a presidential candidacy and certainly after they launch it. Funds raised at the start of a campaign obviously serve to pay for candidate travel, campaign events, and direct mail, which in turn help to establish and strengthen candidate name recognition and to raise the key campaign issues upon which a candidacy can be built. Such funds also provide the means to engage professional consultants who are increasingly essential and to build an ongoing campaign staff and organization. Even more important, early campaign funds are vital in order to provide the means to develop an ongoing and long-term fund-raising organization and operation, the only way to ensure the continuing supply of money that an emerging candidate needs both to launch a campaign and to build momentum for a viable and ultimately successful candidacy.

But money and the raising of money now also have become an end in and of themselves, constituting an early and in many instances a decisive step in the winnowing of presidential contenders. Media coverage of campaign fund-raising has elevated this always vital dimension to advancing a presidential candidacy to perhaps the first decisive test of candidate strength and potential. While party leaders, other candidates, and more recently political and organizational professionals once were the only ones who were attentive to a candidate's success in fund-raising, now the whole electorate and especially attentive voters and party loyalists all are aware of a candidate's fund-raising success or failure. Moreover, because media coverage of campaign fund-raising begins in the early and even pre-candidacy phases of the presidential pre-nomination campaign, news about campaign fund-raising may well be among the earliest images of a candidate which the voters see and hear. A wide array of other resources which are needed for early presidential candidate success, such as staff recruitment, endorsements, standing in presidential preference polls, media attention in general, and even ongoing fund-raising, therefore all can be profoundly affected by a candidate's fund-raising and media coverage of that fund-raising. Thus, beyond the practical necessity of fund-raising success as the means to secure funding and in turn an array of purchasable campaign resources, fund-raising success and media coverage of fund-raising success may well be the first crucial and ultimately decisive test for presidential candidates in the early presidential nomination process.

The phase of the presidential nomination process during which candidates seek the funds needed for a competitive nomination campaign, the organization to raise funds on an ongoing basis, and the credibility and standing that comes with this fund-raising capability constitutes "the money primary." The term "the money primary" actually has a journalistic origin, dating to 1987 when it was used in an article on presidential campaign fund-raising in *The Los Angeles Times*.[1] A year later the term found its way into the political science lexicon when it was used to describe a crucial early phase in political fund-raising in a campaign finance study on corporate campaign contributions.[2] The term has since gained general usage in the campaign finance and presidential nomination literature because it so aptly describes both a phase in nomination campaigns and the winnowing impact of money or the lack of money on early candidacy. The usefulness of this term in describing the period of early campaign fund-raising is evident from Bruce Ackerman and Ian Ayres' comment in *Voting with Dollars* in which they assert:

> A decade ago, nobody had heard of "the money primary." But it is now the name of the game in American politics. Long before the first primary voter casts her ballot, there is a mad effort by candidates to make this vote meaningless by scaring contenders out of the race.[3]

The money primary, understood as this crucial early phase in presidential nominee selection, is the focus of this study of how candidates position themselves for the nomination campaign with intensive early fund-raising as well as efforts to attract media coverage of their fund-raising success.

The role of money during the pre-candidacy and early candidacy phases of the presidential nomination campaign is inextricably linked with the trend toward an earlier beginning to nomination campaigns. As a consequence of the presidential nominating process reforms following the 1968 election, the point at which presidential nomination decision making occurs shifted from the nominating convention itself to the primaries and caucuses. As more states introduced primaries in response to the reforms, moreover, the states with the earliest caucuses and primaries—beginning with Iowa in January and New Hampshire in January or early February, and continuing through Super Tuesday in early March—assumed enormously increased importance. In recent years, this trend toward an earlier start to the nomination campaign has extended into the year prior to the nomination and election year and, as will be argued in this study, even earlier. An array of specific factors have contributed to this earlier and earlier presidential nomination campaign, including increased front-loading of the primary and caucus schedule, the role of the media in covering early campaign events and milestones, and the necessity for an early start in order to ensure that the essential funds and fund-raising apparatus are in place before the start of the pre-nomination campaign period. The fact that fund-raising success is one of the few empirical measures of candidate strength for the media to track during the increasingly extended early nomination campaign only makes the level of fund-raising success during that period all the more critical. The increasing importance of money for a viable and successful presidential nomination campaign and the trend toward ever earlier starts to presidential campaigns thus are mutually reinforcing: the importance of money and an established fund-raising capability necessitates an early start to individual candidates' campaigns; and ever earlier starts to presidential campaigns create longer pre-candidacy and early candidacy phases during which fund-raising success is one of the few ways to demonstrate a candidate's credibility and standing.

Money's central place in presidential nomination politics is related to two other vital elements of early nomination campaign politics that comprise what has been described as "the invisible primary"[4]: media attention and candidate rankings in presidential preference polls. The relationship among money, media attention, and poll rankings appears to be mutually reinforcing, just as is the case with the relationship between money's growing importance in the nomination process and the trend toward an ever earlier nomination campaign start. Achieving media attention and the name recognition which results clearly has an impact on preference poll rankings; yet at the same time, higher preference poll rankings give a candidate the legitimacy that attracts even more media attention. Both of these factors, moreover, in all likelihood affect campaign fund-raising. As candidates receive more media attention and climb in their rankings in presidential preference polls, fund-raising likewise generally improves and higher money totals are achieved. Equally important, the achievement of higher money totals and the development of an organization capable of additional fund-raising are vital campaign resources that may have a major impact on both the level of media attention and rankings in presidential preference polls. Money therefore is a campaign resource that is a central part of a complex dynamic that unfolds during the long pre-candidacy and early candidacy phases of the pre-nomination campaign, extending not only through the early primaries and caucuses and the immediate pre-nomination campaign period but through the pre-nomination campaign year and even before.

The pivotal role of fund-raising during the pre-candidacy and early candidacy phases of the presidential nomination process, especially the necessity for a broad-based fund-raising apparatus, is closely related to the framework for campaign finance enacted as part of the Federal Election Campaign Act (FECA) of 1971.[5] This campaign finance reform legislation, which was amended and strengthened during the post-Watergate reform era, was designed to limit the influence of money in elections for federal office. The FECA as amended included a wide array of reforms, including contribution limits, disclosure requirements, spending ceilings, federal matching funding for qualifying candidates seeking the presidential nomination, and full federal funding for qualifying party nominees in the presidential general election. Especially significant for the presidential nomination process was the provision for public funding of candidates seeking the presidential nomination who had achieved the basic threshold of $5,000 in contributions in each of twenty states. Under FECA, starting in 1976, qualifying presidential candidates were eligible for federal matching funds, a major innovation in that for the first time public funding was possible for presidential candidates in the primaries and caucuses, with these matching dollars being allocated to match the first $250 in individual contributions, leaving unmatched contributions beyond $250 up to the overall individual contribution ceiling of $1,000. Accepting federal matching funds also brought spending restrictions for candidates, both for the overall nomination campaign and state-by-state.[6]

But it was FECA's contribution limits, the only FECA provision not indexed to inflation, that would prove to have the greatest long-term impact on the presidential nomination process.[7] Set at $1,000 per candidate per federal election, this contribution limit remained unchanged from 1976 to 2002, a period of over twenty-five years that has seen seven presidential elections come and go.[8] While intended to circumscribe the importance of money in federal elections, it can be argued that this contribution ceiling in actuality has elevated the importance of campaign fund-raising. Because only the overall spending ceiling and the federal matching funds program were indexed to inflation, the overall total in campaign spending allowed during the presidential nomination process increased steadily after 1976 when these FECA provisions first took effect while the $1,000 ceiling on individual contributions to candidates remained fixed. With the overall total in legally permissible spending steadily increasing but the ceiling on individual contributions remaining at $1,000, candidates seeking the presidential nomination have had no choice but to exert ever greater efforts to raise more contributions, including more and more contributions at the maximum level of $1,000. Moreover, with wealthy candidates free to utilize their personal resources without limit following the U.S. Supreme Court's decision in *Buckley v. Valeo*,[9] other candidates are forced to consider declining federal matching funding (as George W. Bush did in 2000) in order to spend without limit in competing with self-financed nomination contenders. In short, contrary to the intentions of the reformers who enacted FECA, the impact of campaign finance reform has been to make fund-raising an even more prominent part of early nomination campaign presidential politics.

This study of money in the presidential nomination process examines the relationship between this resource and the survival, viability, and success of candidates and would-be candidates seeking the presidential nomination of the two major political parties. The analysis focuses on the pre-candidacy and early candidacy phases of the early nomination campaign period which are viewed as critical to a candidate's prospects in the presidential nomination process. It is hypothesized that the extent of advance campaign activity, in particular pre-candidacy fund-raising success followed by continued early candidacy fund-raising success, are critical to a candidate's prospects for survival, viability, and success. The thesis is that reaching a basic threshold in pre-candidacy fund-raising, achieving fund-raising success by raising a significant total in early campaign contributions, developing the capability for ongoing fund-raising success as the campaign proceeds, developing an ongoing fund-raising effort that gathers increasing momentum, and attracting the media attention that results, are all critical to a candidate's prospects for survival, viability, and success in the early presidential nomination process. Pre-candidacy and early candidacy activities that are given particular attention include the formation of some type of pre-candidacy committee, generally a political action committee (PAC), the conduct of an extended period of advance campaign activity and preparation, and the infusion of significant money and campaign assets into the formal campaign organization at the time that a presidential campaign committee is formed. Fund-raising success—defined as reaching basic thresholds in pre-candidacy fund-raising, achieving ongoing fund-raising success in terms of the total in dollars raised during the early candidacy campaign, and building fund-raising momentum—is hypothesized to be predictive of candidate survival, viability, and success defined both in terms of remaining active as a candidate as well as in terms of achieving a competitive share of the vote totals in the opening contests of the formal nomination process. Media coverage of early candidacy fund-raising success—in effect an echo of campaign fund-raising success itself—also is hypothesized to be predictive of candidate survival, viability, and success in the early nomination process. Thus the central position of fund-raising success in a mutually reinforcing dynamic that includes money and media attention is examined, with the objective of establishing the significance of the money primary as a decisive new phase in the early campaign. The position of money relative to other factors, any causal relationship between money and media attention, and other factors that may affect the early presidential selection process, however, are beyond the scope of this work. The result of this study is both a fuller understanding of money as a resource in early presidential nomination politics and of money's ascendancy as a factor during the pre-candidacy and early candidacy phases to the point that there now exists what in effect is a money primary" in which candidates must succeed if they are to become viable candidates and ultimately win the presidential nomination.

An array of questions underlie this study of money in the presidential nomination process and in particular the long early nomination campaign quest for dollars and fund-raising capability that has characterized campaigns for the presidential nomination in recent years. What level of initial resources in terms of funding and other campaign assets do the ultimately successful candidates bring to their early presidential nomination campaigns? Which organizational structures, whether leadership PACs, exploratory committees, special foundations, or state-based entities, are most commonly employed by candidates to amass and expend pre-candidacy and early candidacy resources? Are there basic thresholds in fund-raising that candidates must achieve, and points in the early campaign by which they must achieve these thresholds, if their candidacies are to remain viable? Is ongoing fund-raising success absolutely essential for candidate survival, viability, and success? And is the total in dollars raised the only significant indicator of fund-raising success? Or are there other key indicators of fund-raising success, such as the timing of fund-raising results, the momentum of the fund-raising effort, the amount in cash-on-hand available at specific junctures, and the extent of federal matching funding? And has the trend toward front-loading the presidential primary and caucus schedule in recent presidential election years made pre-candidacy and early candidacy fund-raising and organizational preparation even more important? To what extent does media coverage during the long early nomination campaign period focus on fund-raising as a measure of candidate credibility and standing? And are media evaluations of a candidate's fund-raising success also associated with candidate survival, viability, and success? Finally, what relationship, if any, is there between a candidate's total dollars raised during the pre-candidacy and early candidacy campaigns and media coverage of that candidate's fund-raising success, on the one hand, and whether a candidate remains active as a candidate through the opening nomination contests, achieves viability by reaching or surpassing a critical threshold in the opening nomination contests, or is successful in ultimately winning the opening nomination contests, on the other hand?

As this study seeks to answer these and other questions regarding the place of money in pre-candidacy and early candidacy presidential nomination campaigns, it presents both descriptive findings and analytical generalizations and conclusions that offer new insight into the evolution of the money primary in early presidential nomination politics. At the descriptive level, the examination of money in presidential nomination politics that is presented serves to document the increased level of fund-raising in support of presidential nomination candidacies, the substantially lengthened duration of the presidential pre-candidacy and early candidacy campaign periods, and the central position of fund-raising and media coverage of fund-raising in pre-candidacy and early candidacy activity. More specific descriptive findings also are produced regarding the ever earlier launch of pre-candidacy campaigns, the variety of organizational entities being used to support presidential pre-candidacy campaigns, and the transfer of funds and campaign assets to formal presidential campaign committees. Analysis of the relationship between money in presidential nomination campaigns during the pre-candidacy and early candidacy phases through the opening of the formal nomination campaign itself and candidate survival, viability, and success in the early nomination contests is an especially important objective. The analysis formally examines the relationship between pre-candidacy fund-raising success, early candidacy fund-raising success, the timing and momentum of fund-raising, and the achievement of competitive cash-on-hand and federal matching funding totals, on the one hand, and candidate survival, viability, and success in the early nomination process, on the other hand. Also formally examined is the relationship between media coverage of early candidacy fund-raising and media evaluations comparing candidates' early fund-raising, and candidates' survival, viability, and success in the early nomination process. The result is a fuller understanding of the impact of the money primary in presidential nomination politics and its significance in either winnowing out or bolstering presidential candidates based on their capacity for attracting dollars and donors to their early campaigns.

This study of presidential pre-candidacy and early candidacy campaign activity as distinct phases in the early presidential nomination process focuses on two key independent variables—pre-candidacy and early candidacy fund-raising, and media coverage of early candidacy fund-raising—with hypotheses relating to each of these aspects of the early presidential selection process being examined. The analysis includes two post-reform era presidential nomination campaigns as case studies—1988 and 2000—the only two election years of the post-reform era in which the nomination contests of both major political parties lacked incumbent Presidents as contenders.

The first hypothesis is critical to this study's thesis regarding the emergence of a money primary because it is concerned with the significance of early and ongoing fund-raising success as a predictor of candidate survival, viability, and success in the early presidential nomination process. It seeks to examine a candidate's early candidacy fund-raising success in terms of the achievement of basic dollar thresholds and the total dollar amounts raised as well as the extent to which a candidate's fund-raising effort develops momentum, ensures an adequate total in cash-on-hand, and qualifies for substantial federal matching funding. For the purposes of this analysis, candidate survival is defined as remaining in the nomination race as an active, announced candidate; candidate viability is defined in terms of the share of the vote received by the candidate in the Iowa caucuses and the New Hampshire primary; and candidate success is defined as winning in the early nomination contests. The first hypothesis, central to this study and focusing on the significance of early candidacy fund-raising success, is as follows:

Hypothesis I: Successful early and ongoing fund-raising during the early candidacy period, including the achievement of a basic threshold in dollars raised, the overall total in dollars raised, and the momentum of this fund-raising effort, as well as the achievement of competitive totals in cash-on-hand and federal matching funding, is a predictor of candidate survival, viability, and success in the early presidential nomination process.

An additional aspect of this study is the initial phase in the mounting of a presidential candidacy, in particular pre-candidacy activity utilizing leadership PACs, exploratory committees, non-profit organizations and foundations, and state-based entities. The second hypothesis therefore focuses on the impact and significance of pre-candidacy activity and in particular pre-candidacy fund-raising and organizational preparation through pre-candidacy committees on candidate survival, viability, and success in the opening presidential nomination contests. This second hypothesis, extending this analysis of campaign fund-raising to include the pre-candidacy phase of the campaign by examining the use of pre-candidacy organizational entities to enlist early financial support, is as follows:

Hypothesis II: The more extensive the level of a presidential candidate's pre-candidacy fund-raising activity and organizational preparation through pre-candidacy committees, the greater the prospect for early nomination campaign fund-raising success, and in turn the greater the prospect for candidate survival, viability, and success in the early presidential nomination process.

The third and final hypothesis of this study seeks to link the media's horse race coverage comparing candidates' fund-raising as well as candidate focused coverage examining individual candidates' fund-raising with candidate survival, viability, and success in the early presidential nomination process. This hypothesis not only endeavors to establish that fund-raising success is covered by the media as an indicator of candidate credibility and standing but also seeks to establish a relationship between media horse race coverage comparing candidates' success in fund-raising as well as media coverage of individual candidates' success in fund-raising with candidate survival, viability, and success in the early nomination process. This third hypothesis examining media coverage of campaign fund-raising is as follows:

Hypothesis III: Media coverage of early presidential campaign fund-raising during the early campaign period of the pre-election year through January of the election year is a significant dimension of presidential nomination campaign media coverage, and the extent of positive media evaluations of a candidate's success in fund-raising relative to other candidates as well as the level of media attention to an individual candidate's success in fund-raising are predictors of candidate survival, viability, and success in the early presidential nomination process.

This study of the money primary in the early presidential nomination process is organized into seven chapters that each address a distinct aspect of the overall presentation and analysis. After establishing the context of this study, identifying the research problems to be addressed, and raising some of the questions to be answered, this opening chapter has articulated three specific hypotheses that the analysis to follow examines. The second chapter places this research in perspective in the political science literature, tracing two major streams of literature related to this research: the literature on the post-reform era presidential nomination process; and the literature on campaign fund-raising and campaign finance reform. The limited recent literature relating to the early campaign, early campaign fund-raising, and the money primary also is presented, with the ways in which this work is different in focus or approach from this study being highlighted. The third chapter sets forth the research plan and methodology, defines the independent and dependent variables, and describes the sources of data utilized in the analysis. The main body of this study is presented in chapters 4, 5, and 6, which examine the early campaign from three distinct perspectives. Chapter 4 provides an overview of the early campaigns leading up to the 1988 and 2000 presidential nomination campaigns, the two presidential election years examined as case studies, directing particular attention to the development of the candidate field in each nomination race and the timing of these campaigns from the pre-candidacy and early candidacy phases through the opening of the formal nomination process. This fourth chapter not only summarizes the four major party nomination races included in the study but perhaps even more importantly identifies the major developments and trends in the presidential nomination process and the early campaign characteristic of the second and third decades of the post-reform era. Major separate chapters then are devoted to the two dimensions of the money primary that are the focus of this study. Chapter 5 addresses fund-raising during the early campaign, including both the early candidacy and pre-candidacy phases, examining the first and second hypotheses concerning the relationship between early candidacy and pre-candidacy fund-raising success and candidate survival, viability, and success in the early nomination process. Chapter 6 turns to media coverage of campaign fund-raising success, viewed as an echo of fund-raising success itself, examining the third hypothesis concerning the relationship between media coverage of campaign fund-raising and candidate survival, viability, and success in the early nomination process. A seventh chapter summarizes the findings of the data analysis, presents generalizations and conclusions regarding the three hypotheses, and discusses the implications of this research for the early presidential nomination process and the democratic character of presidential selection. Completing the study is an Afterword which lays out an agenda of approaches to presidential nomination process reform in general and campaign finance reform in particular.

The study which follows examines the impact of fund-raising and media coverage of fund-raising on candidate survival, viability, and success in the early presidential nomination process, focusing on the winnowing out of non-competitive candidates, the survival of selected candidates through the early campaign leading up to the formal nomination process, and the emergence of genuinely viable candidates competing for the nomination. Both the pre-candidacy and early candidacy phases of the presidential nomination campaign are examined, beginning with the pre-campaign period when potential candidates consider their prospects and explore a possible campaign, including the lengthy pre-candidacy phase when leadership PACs and other organizational entities such as foundations and state-based political committees are utilized by potential candidates preparing for campaigns, and finally extending through the early candidacy phase during the pre-presidential election year and the early nomination campaign period. Campaign fund-raising during the pre-candidacy and early candidacy phases of the nomination campaign is analyzed to determine the extent to which fund-raising success is associated with candidate survival, viability, and success. The extent to which leadership PACs, pre-candidacy political committees, foundations, and other organizational entities are utilized to facilitate pre-candidacy and early candidacy political activity also is given attention. Media coverage of campaign fund-raising, including horse race coverage comparing candidates' success in fund-raising and candidate-focused coverage examining individual candidates' fund-raising, also is studied to determine the extent to which fund-raising success is essential not only to provide campaign financial resources but also to ensure media visibility and, ultimately, credibility and standing. In short, this study focuses on the early presidential nomination campaign, presenting this crucial phase as a period when candidates and would-be candidates launch fund-raising efforts and build ongoing fund-raising organizations and also as a period when the media evaluates candidates based on their fund-raising success—all as part of the money primary that increasingly dominates the modern presidential nomination process.

Notes

1. Ronald Brownstein, "The Money Machine," *The Los Angeles Times*, 15 November 1987, 14.

2. Dan Clawson, Alan Neustadtl, and Mark Weller, *Dollars and Votes: How Business Campaign Contributions Subvert Democracy* (Philadelphia: Temple University Press, 1998), 1.

3. Bruce Ackerman and Ian Ayres, *Voting with Dollars: A New Paradigm for Campaign Finance* (New Haven, Conn., and London: Yale University Press, 2002), 162.

4. Arthur T. Hadley, *The Invisible Primary* (Englewood Cliffs, N.J.: Prentice-Hall, 1976), 1.

5. Federal Election Commission, *Federal Election Campaign Laws* (Washington, D.C.: U.S. Government Printing Office, 1997).

6. Anthony Corrado, *Paying for Presidents: Public Financing in National Elections* (New York: The Twentieth Century Fund Press, 1993), 37–45.

7. Trevor Potter, "The Current State of Campaign Finance Law," in *Campaign Finance Reform: A Sourcebook*, ed. Anthony Corrado, Thomas E. Mann, Daniel R. Ortiz, Trevor Potter, and Frank Sorauf (Washington, D.C.: Brookings Institution Press, 1997), 5–6.

8. New campaign finance reform legislation passed by Congress and signed by President George W. Bush in March 2002 adjusted contribution ceilings for the first time since 1976, including an increase in the ceiling for individual contributions from $1,000 to $2,000 per candidate per federal election. While the full impact of this adjustment as well as other elements of the new campaign finance reform legislation remain to be seen, it is likely that the higher individual contribution ceilings will increase the importance of pre-candidacy and early candidacy fund-raising and strategies such as fund-raising networks in what is termed "the money primary."

9. *Buckley v. Valeo*, 424 U.S. 1 (1976).

2

The Early Presidential Nomination Campaign and Presidential Campaign Finance in the Political Science Literature

THE NOMINATION PHASE OF THE PRESIDENTIAL SELECTION PROCESS is the subject of a significant body of political science research. The preponderance of the literature, however, focuses on the reforms that radically altered this nominating system beginning with the 1972 presidential election and continuing to the present. This nominating reform literature has examined the rise of direct primaries, the ensuing decline of the major political parties, electoral dealignment, the rise of candidate-centered election campaigns, the representativeness of primary electorates, and the new role of the media as intermediaries between candidates and the electorate. The time frame for much of this work has been the formal nomination period as well as the general election campaign itself.

The year before the presidential election year has received less attention among students of the presidential nomination process, and the period prior to that—from the day after the preceding presidential election through the beginning of the pre-election year—has received even less attention. Yet the early phase of the presidential nomination campaign, in particular the year or two or even three before the commencement of the election year itself, is very significant, both as a time when candidates emerge, prepare, and endeavor to attract volunteer, professional and financial support, and as a period when untold would-be candidates decide to abandon their presidential aspirations. The trend toward front-loading of the presidential nomination process, the ever advancing date for the start of active presidential campaigning, and what one distinguished scholar of the presidency recently described as the "non-stop, permanent campaign"[1] certainly suggests that systematic study of this crucial early period in presidential selection is warranted.

While the body of literature focused on the early nomination campaign is limited, an abundance of terms exist to describe this period of presidential nomination politics. Arthur Hadley uses the label "the invisible primary" to refer to the lengthy interval between the last election of a President and the next cycle of presidential primaries, and his book by that title offers a journalistic account of this period "when as many candidacies are aborted as brought to term."[2] A more formal analysis of the never-ending process of presidential selection is offered by Rhodes Cook who refers to the "exhibition season" to describe the period "from the day after a general election to the start of primary and caucus action more than three years later."[3] Cook asserts that the exhibition season is "a time for potential candidates to test the political waters, raise money, and begin to organize their campaigns around the country, wooing important individuals and interest groups and honing their basic campaign themes."[4] The political communications literature brings an important perspective to the early nomination campaign period, and Judith Trent's term "the surfacing period" is useful both to describe the early nomination campaign period itself and what she asserts is a "series of predictable and specifically timed rhetorical transaction . . . during the pre-primary phase of the campaign" which constitute candidate surfacing behavior.[5] Other scholars of the presidential nomination process have preferred simpler terminology to describe this period, for instance John Kessel who refers simply to "the early days" when he analyzes candidates' early nomination campaigns.[6]

The trend in recent presidential election cycles for political fund-raising to begin early, well in advance of any formal announcements of candidacy, and to be increasingly visible and competitive, also has received a variety of descriptive labels. Termed "the wealth primary" in a 1994 study by the Center for Responsive Politics, this period of early and increasingly publicized fund-raising activity by would-be candidates has become a distinct part of the nomination phase of electoral politics. The crucial importance of this financial phase is clear from this study's conclusion that at least in Congressional elections "the person who collects the most money—the 'winner' of the wealth primary— almost always captures his or her party's nomination. . . ."[7] A 1998 study, *Dollars and Votes*, refers to "the money primary" as a crucial phase in presidential selection, asserting that it is "the first, and in many instances, the most important round of the contest."[8] This study's conclusion, in fact, not only highlighted the money primary but asserted that corporate political spending used "money and power to subvert the political process."[9] Moreover, a wide array of journalistic coverage in the late 1990s, especially in *The New York Times* and *The Washington Post*, has given wide public circulation to the term the money primary as a distinct phase in the presidential selection process.[10] And on the eve of the 2000 presidential nomination process, a study by the Republican National Committee gave official credence to the anticipated centrality of money in the selection of presidential nominees, concluding:

> With so many primaries and caucuses jammed together, the only kind of candidate who can run effectively—who can campaign in five or ten states every week, who can field effective organizations in each of those states, who can simply fill full delegate slates—is someone who is already well-known and well financed.[11]

In short, both the early nomination campaign as a general phase and the money primary as the critical dimension of this early campaign are well established, not only as analytical terms for important aspects of the presidential selection process but now also as popularly understood periods in the quadrennial presidential horse race.

A major dimension of the primary reform literature has sought to examine the impact of the presidential pre-primary and primary campaigns in providing a window for certain candidates to emerge and gather strength and other candidates to be winnowed out. In fact, it is this winnowing process that gives this phase of the presidential selection process special significance and suggests the importance of additional study. Yet most of the literature on this candidate winnowing process is addressed to the primary and caucus phase of the campaign, not the pre-candidacy and early candidacy phases that are the focus of the planned study. Gary Orren and Nelson Polsby's study, *Media and Momentum*, draws attention to this winnowing process and emphasizes the key concept of momentum which is defined as a bandwagon effect whereby "a candidate portrayed in the media as viable and improving begins to attract more support."[12] But Orren and Polsby's focus is squarely on the early phase of the formal nomination process, in particular the New Hampshire primary. Larry Bartels' *Presidential Primaries and the Dynamics of Public Choice* offers a comprehensive study of the anatomy of momentum in presidential campaigns, but he also focuses on the early primaries and in particular the impact of media coverage of "the horse race."[13] John Aldrich likewise focuses on the primary period itself, describing the "winnowing effect" of the "serialization of presidential primaries."[14] He asserts that presidential primaries create a dynamic in which a wide field of candidates is rapidly narrowed by factors such as a decreasing likelihood of winning the nomination, a failure to meet performance expectations, and dwindling financial resources.

More recent primary reform literature has shifted the focus to the early campaign period, most notably John Haskell's *Fundamentally Flawed: Understanding and Reforming Presidential Primaries*, which endeavors to build on Hadley's descriptive account by citing three essential ingredients for success in the earliest stages of a presidential campaign: single-mindedness, money, and staff and strategy.[15] Particularly relevant to this study is Haskell's conclusion that "since 1980 the candidate with the most money in the bank going into the Iowa caucuses—that is, before a single delegate has been selected, has been the nominee of his party every time. . . ."[16] James Davis' study of the presidential primaries also addresses the early campaign winnowing process, although his focus is the pivotal role of the media in creating "front-runners," "second echelon candidates," and "long-shots," media characterizations that he contends persist throughout the early campaign period in the absence of any new information that would suggest a readjustment.[17] Davis concludes his 1997 study by noting that "this process of separating the serious contenders from the marginal candidates—sometimes termed the 'screening process'—has not been given the attention it deserves."[18]

The effect of the primary and pre-primary winnowing process on the composition of the candidate field is an especially interesting topic of study in this post-reform era nomination process literature. August Busch's *Outsiders and Openness in the Presidential Nominating System* is a recent and provocative analysis that focuses on the growing number of "unconnected outsiders"— defined as "political mavericks whose identity is personalized and not related to a larger organized movement"—in the candidate fields during the presidential nominating process.[19] Busch presents the thesis that the nominating reforms missed their objective to open the parties to movements such as the new politics and instead provided ready access to unconnected outsiders with personal political organizations who rely primarily on personal, content-free, and sometimes divisive appeal.[20] The post-reform era's new accessibility to unconnected outsiders, Busch argues, has turned the mixed system which existed through the 1960s on its head, with unconnected, personalized candidacies and weak movements being advantaged, and more establishment candidates and stronger movements being impaired.[21] Moreover, according to Busch, this trend favoring unconnected outsiders exploded in the 1990s, with the elections of 1992 and 1996 attracting "an unusually large number of 'outsiders,' most of whom were 'unconnected' to some degree,"[22] and with indications pointing to a continuation of this trend for the foreseeable future.[23] Busch concludes that this level of openness is not what the proponents of the presidential nominating reforms were seeking in the 1970s and that from a normative standpoint "the cause of stability is damaged by so clearly reducing the barriers to personalistic candidates without attaining compensating benefits for either movements or parties."[24]

Other recent additions to the literature evaluating the impact of the presidential nominating reforms present alternate analytical frameworks that are consistent with Busch's emphasis on the rise of candidate-centered politics but do not agree that there has been a concomitant rise in outsiderism. Steven Schier's *By Invitation Only* moves beyond the weak movement vs. strong movement framework to reassert the fundamental distinction between campaign strategies that are activation based vs. motivation based.[25] Schier links an activation campaign strategy with the candidate-centered campaigns that characterize the post-reform era and argues that this targeted approach to campaigns has supplanted the broader, more inclusive mobilization campaign strategy that characterized the political party era.[26] Yet while agreeing with Busch's conclusion that the result for presidential nomination politics is candidate-centered campaigns that are increasingly more personalized and factionalized, and correspondingly less party-driven and consensus based, Schier does not see the ascendancy of outsiders as the newly advantaged actors in the political process. Instead Schier sees candidates relying less on political parties and their old-style mobilization strategies that were directed to the mass electorate and substituting a new candidate-centered approach utilizing activation strategies to attract targeted groups of voters. And where Busch sees negative consequences for political stability due to the rise of outsiderism, Schier predicts that the even more important value of popular control of government will suffer as increasingly personalized and factionalized politics results.[27]

The fact that Busch's thesis of ascendent outsiderism in the post-reform era is not universally accepted also is evident from William Mayer's analysis of the 2000 presidential nominating process.[28] Noteworthy in terms of this study's focus on the pre-candidacy and early candidacy phases of nomination campaigns is Mayer's emphasis on the recently heightened importance of front-loading of the primary-caucus calendar and the necessity of fund-raising success for ongoing viability. Moreover, Mayer concludes that in the 2000 presidential nomination process it was precisely these two factors that effectively structured out all but the most established candidates.[29] Contrary to Busch's conclusion that outsiders are the newly advantaged candidates of post-reform era nomination politics, Mayer asserts that "thirty years after a series of reforms that were supposed to 'open up the parties' and 'level the playing field,' the American presidential nomination process has become, if anything, even more hostile toward outsiders and insurgents than the system that preceded it."[30]

The extensive literature on campaign finance that has developed over the past two decades provides a further backdrop to this study's focus on money as a variable in presidential nomination politics. Yet as with the literature on the presidential nominating reforms, most of the campaign finance literature examines the role of money in the formal nomination period or during the general election campaign itself. Making the case that candidate fund-raising and spending indeed have an impact on a candidate's prospects for success in presidential primaries and caucuses is a study by Audrey Haynes *et al.*[31] In addition to confirming that money does have an impact on success, this analysis is especially interesting in finding that this impact varies depending on the size of the competitive field.[32] But while establishing the impact of money as a nominating campaign resource, this work focuses on spending during the primaries and caucuses themselves, not on fund-raising during the much longer pre-candidacy and early candidacy phases prior to the presidential nomination and election year. Another study by David Damore has examined fund-raising in the presidential nomination process, concluding that electoral success and media coverage have a strong impact on subsequent fund-raising by long-shot candidates.[33] But while this research addresses fund-raising, like most studies it is focused on the period during which the primaries and caucuses unfold, once again leaving unexamined the pre-candidacy and early candidacy phases that are the focus of this work.

The pre-candidacy period of presidential nomination politics began receiving more rigorous attention in the literature in part due to the explosion of interest in political action committees (PACs) and their impact on electoral politics. Frank Sorauf's *Money in American Elections*, while primarily an overview of the role of money in Congressional and presidential election campaigns, introduces the newly heightened importance of money in the early presidential nomination campaign period by pointing to the development of "personal PACs" as a candidate strategy to support political activity during presidential pre-candidacy campaigns.[34] Michael Robinson, Clyde Wilcox, and Paul Marshall built on this observation a year later in their article "The Presidency: Not for Sale."[35] While their title suggests that money may be less than a crucial factor in electoral success, in actuality their findings are pertinent to the focus of this study in that they highlight the importance of money during the pre-candidacy and early candidacy phases. According to Robinson *et al.*, fund-raising success and spending are important factors during the period prior to the formal nomination process, with money having its greatest impact when candidates are relatively unknown to the electorate, when news coverage of individual candidates is sporadic or non-existent, and when paid advertising is the surest way to achieve name recognition and visibility.[36]

The 1988 presidential election, which is the first of two elections selected as case studies in this analysis, may well have crossed a threshold in terms of the importance of money in the early nomination campaign. Strong indications of the significance of money early in the 1988 presidential selection process are provided in post-election interviews with campaign managers and strategists published in the quadrennial report *Campaign for President: The Managers Look at '88.*[37] As Larry Eichel noted in a summation of this post-election discussion:

> By reason of sheer magnitude alone, money was a major factor in determining the outcome of the 1988 campaign. In the presidential saga, as in most political races, those candidates who did not pass a certain financial threshold never won the right to be taken seriously or decided not to run at all.[38]

Moreover, in the 1988 presidential election the focus on money began long before the opening of the election year itself. According to Eichel, "in 1987, the year before the voting, each candidate's ability to raise money became a key measure of his credibility and viability."[39] This early fund-raising, combined with a structural environment lacking early tests such as straw polls at state party conventions, "led many politicians and commentators alike to treat the candidates' financial reports to the Federal Election Commission as the single best indicator of candidate support."[40] The campaign managers' discussion of the role of money was not without some disagreement, with Gore manager Frederick Martin insisting that "money is a resource that makes the candidate" while Dukakis manager John Corrigan argued that "money is a result of a candidate's calibre."[41] The managers were all but unanimous, however, in agreeing with Bush manager Edward Rollins' assertion that success in fund-raising required an early start. As Rollins argued during this post-campaign discussion, "George Bush started ten years ago, 1978, putting his organization together. Anybody who doesn't start four years before the gun goes off is not going to be able to raise the money."[42]

As is the case with so much of the literature on the presidential nominating reforms, the literature on campaign finance is far from unanimous in assigning a pivotal role to money in assuring either pre-candidacy or early candidacy success. In fact, Barbara Norrander's analysis of the Republican presidential nomination contests between 1976 and 1988 produces the counter-intuitive conclusion that the biggest spenders sometimes are the biggest losers.[43] She cites the cases of Robert Dole and the Rev. Pat Robertson, both leading spenders and early losers in the 1988 Republican nomination contest, as two cases in point, adding that the Republican candidates for the presidential nomination who did win during this period were successful irrespective of how much money they raised or spent.[44] Stephen Wayne, presenting the view of most students of early presidential campaign fund-raising, argues that the overall pattern does not fit with Norrander's findings. According to Wayne, "having a solid financial base at the outset of the nomination process provides a significant strategic advantage . . . It is no coincidence that those candidates who raise and spend the most money tend to do best."[45] Wayne explains Norrander's contrary finding for Republican candidates in nomination contests between 1976 and 1988 as a case of "prospective losers (who) tried to compensate for their secondary status by spending more, and it did not work."[46] Thus, while the impact of money during the pre-candidacy and early candidacy phases of presidential selection appears to vary among candidates and from election to election and therefore must continue to be studied and debated, Wayne expresses the conventional wisdom in his summary of the discussion to date:

> Theoretically, campaign spending should have a greater impact on the nomination process than the general election and at the beginning of the process rather

than at the end. As the nomination process progresses, as candidates become more easily recognized by the public, the expenditure of funds is not as critical to electoral success.[47]

Beyond this theoretical foundation, and preliminary findings showing the necessity of achieving basic fund-raising thresholds, however, a firm consensus has yet to form on the impact of campaign fund-raising and spending during the early presidential nomination process.

In addition to analyzing the impact of fund-raising success on electoral results, a growing body of campaign finance literature also has examined how would-be presidential candidates are funding their pre-candidacy and early candidacy political activities. Building on Sorauf's early identification of personal PACs as important vehicles for funding pre-candidacy presidential campaigns, Anthony Corrado—perhaps the foremost authority on campaign finance—made a major contribution to understanding what are known as "leadership PACs" in his book *Creative Campaigning: PACs and the Presidential Selection Process.*[48] Corrado points to a significant rise in the number of presidential pre-candidacy PACs, noting that the FEC's permissiveness in only regulating announced candidates and not potential or likely candidates has opened the way to this growth.[49] Citing a pattern of PAC registration dates early in presidential election cycles, brief periods of intense operation, and the association of some very visible candidates with some of the most successful PACs, Corrado concludes that would-be presidential candidates "are primarily using these committees to conduct political activities in the earliest stages of the nomination process, well before they declare a candidacy.[50] In effect, Corrado concludes, these leadership PACs are really pre-candidacy committees that are actually "front organizations for presidential campaigns."[51] The "veritable explosion" in the use of these pre-candidacy leadership PACs in 1988 and thereafter is clearly a deliberate effort by unannounced presidential candidates to circumvent FEC enforcement of federal restrictions which limit fund-raising and spending by announced presidential contenders.[52]

Corrado develops his thesis that the growth in pre-candidacy leadership PACs in effect has eviscerated presidential campaign finance regulations in a subsequent book, *Paying for Presidents.*[53] This work traces the growth of pre-candidacy PACs, beginning with Ronald Reagan's establishment of Citizens for a Republic in 1977 as a means to utilize surplus funds from his unsuccessful 1976 nomination campaign. By 1980, three other contenders for the Republican nomination had followed suit by establishing pre-candidacy PACs, and by 1988 a total of ten out of thirteen announced candidates had utilized similar pre-candidacy PACs prior to formally declaring their candidacies.[54] Corrado concludes that there is a preponderance of evidence that pre-candidacy PACs are really "shadow campaign committees," and he predicts continued growth in their use as increased front-loading of the primary and caucus schedule and public funding of presidential nomination races prompt even earlier presidential campaign fund-raising.[55]

The campaign finance literature also documents other organizational vehicles, in addition to pre-candidacy leadership PACs, that are utilized by presidential aspirants as shadow campaign committees. Foundations, which are tax-exempt, non-profit organizations and hence public charities, have been shown to be a particularly popular means to build a presidential candidacy. A 1987 study by the Center for Responsive Politics entitled *Public Policy and Foundations: The Role of Politicians in Public Charities* documented the extent of this practice.[56] According to this CRP study, "many public charities in this study began to conduct policy activities a year or two before the politicians affiliated with their organizations declared for public office. This has occurred most often with charities founded by presidential aspirants."[57] The study identifies a variety of activities being conducted by these public charities, ranging from policy research and advocacy, to mailing list development and donor identification, to actual visibility activities for the would-be candidate. It also cites critics of such operations, most notably former IRS Commissioner Sheldon Cohen who asserted that "the new public charities are nothing but a way of spending deductible money for what the politician would be doing anyway."[58] The study concludes that "whether intentionally or accidentally, public charities may become another avenue used by presidential aspirants for providing policy research and staff support prior to a campaign."[59] The practice of utilizing not only leadership PACs but now also tax-exempt foundations to advance the fund-raising efforts of potential and likely presidential candidates are identified as long-term campaign fund-raising strategies in *US Elections Today*.[60] As Philip Davies notes in summarizing these fund-raising strategies, "candidates with a long-term strategy have also found that forming their own leadership PACs and tax-exempt foundations can provide a tool for the promotion of their policies, as well as an opportunity to increase name recognition."[61]

As the duration of the presidential campaign period has continued to lengthen, the literature has extended the time frame being studied to direct more systematic and rigorous attention to the early campaign and in particular early campaign fund-raising. Indicative of the campaign finance literature's new interest in early presidential campaign fund-raising is Clyde Wilcox's studies of fund-raising in presidential nomination campaigns. After analyzing fund-raising for the 1988 pre-nomination campaign, Wilcox concludes that "although the conventional wisdom among political scientists has been that campaign spending does not bring success, the two candidates who won their party's nominations in 1988 raised the largest sums early and had the most cash available throughout the campaign."[62] Interestingly, Wilcox goes on to suggest that perhaps "campaign spending matters most when little-known candidates contest the nomination, and it matters considerably less when the candidates are well known or when free media provide voters with sufficient information to make up their minds."[63] Clifford Brown, Lynda Powell, and Clyde Wilcox's book, *Serious Money*, presents a more comprehensive study of money in presidential nomination campaigns, but this research focuses on candidate fund-raising methods, the importance of personal solicitation networks, and the characteristics of individual campaign contributors.[64] While this study documents the scope and characteristics of fund-raising programs in support of candidates seeking the presidential nomination, it leaves unanswered such vital questions as the comparative performance of different candidates' fund-raising efforts and the implications of alternate levels of fund-raising effectiveness for the viability and success of presidential nomination contenders.

A recent stream of literature on the presidential nomination process beginning in the mid-1990s has focused on the period prior to the formal nominating process and has given more careful consideration to variables previously examined in only general terms by either the nominating reform literature or the campaign finance reform literature. The continuing evolution of the presidential nomination process may well explain this shift in attention because there can be no doubt that the early phase of this process is more important now than ever before. The rise of candidate-centered campaigns, and the high cost of achieving name recognition in a candidate-centered process, is a reality of American politics dating back at least to the 1970s that has fundamentally altered presidential politics. And the even more recent trend toward front-loading the presidential primary and caucus schedule, which began in the 1980s and accelerated rapidly through the 1990s, has affected the presidential nomination process to a degree that is still to be determined. Front-loading not only has pushed key primary and caucus dates earlier and earlier, but as a consequence has forced multi-state competition rather than the serial process that existed in the 1980s and before. The continuing trend toward greater media scrutiny of candidates, and especially the intensive media interest in the candidates' horse race, is a further dimension of this new nomination dynamic. The result, in short, is a contemporary presidential nomination process in which presidential nomination contenders must be at full strength as the formal process begins, a dynamic leaving little room for late-starters or dark horses. The attention now being focused on the early presidential nomination campaign unquestionably results from this new dynamic and the redefined presidential nomination process that it has produced.

A major contribution to this new literature on the early presidential nomination process is William Mayer's article, "Forecasting Presidential Nominations," which endeavors to identify the key early factors in a successful nomination quest.[65] Mayer builds on earlier studies of the significance of money in presidential politics by examining the impact of early fund-raising success during the pre-candidacy phase of presidential nomination campaigns. Arguing that forecasting models are applicable not only to presidential general elections but to the nomination process as well, Mayer identifies both fund-raising success and standing in national polls as the key predictive variables. Mayer presents data for 1980 through 1992 to support his conclusion that strength in fund-raising and standing in national polls during the year prior to the election year are predictors of success in the presidential nomination process. But while Mayer's analysis considers the impact of money during the early campaign period, it is limited to fund-raising through announced presidential campaign committees which are required to submit FEC reports and extends only through the 1992 presidential nomination campaign, stopping short of an examination of the long pre-candidacy phase which is a focus of this study.

Also representing a significant contribution to the recent literature on the early presidential nomination process is Wayne Steger's "Do Primary Voters Draw from a Stacked Deck?"[66] Steger cites the increased openness of the presidential nomination process, with the long-term trend since the early 1970s in the direction of more rather than fewer candidates. Yet he also presents data indicating that there are a declining number of effective or viable candidates.[67] Steger's thesis is that "the contemporary nomination system contains a paradox in which primary voters select among a larger number of candidates, yet which candidates have a realistic chance of winning the nomination is largely determined during the pre-primary season."[68] In an analysis that is directly applicable to this study, Steger argues that "party elites, campaign contributors, interest groups, and the media all play crucial mediating roles in the post-reform presidential nominating process by conferring or denying the resources candidates need to compete for primary voters' support."[69] Steger concludes that "presidential nominations are more mediated than is commonly recognized,"[70] with the reforms of the early 1970s having shifted the nominating power from party elites but not directly to primary and caucus voters; instead, the candidates, their organizations, campaign contributors, and the media now all have important roles in winnowing out weaker candidates and elevating a few selected contenders to contest the formal nomination process.[71]

Taking the examination of fund-raising in the early nomination process another step is very recent research on what factors influence the success of early presidential fund-raising. Randall Adkins and Andrew Dowdle's "The Money Primary: What Influences the Outcome of Pre-Primary Presidential Nomination Fundraising?"[72] puts aside the issue of fund-raising's impact on candidate viability and success and instead addresses which factors, including candidate viability, affect fund-raising success itself. According to Adkins and Dowdle's study, candidate performance and campaign organization are two major factors that since 1980 account for much of the variation in candidate fund-raising during the pre-nomination period. Their work uses national poll results, change in candidate viability, and length of candidacy as measures of candidate performance, and money spent on fund-raising, size of the candidate's electoral constituency, and whether the candidate self-financed his campaign as measures of campaign organization. Adkins and Dowdle's research is particularly applicable to the focus of this study in that it establishes a link between candidate viability and success on the one hand and fund-raising success on the other, a relationship running the opposite direction from the one hypothesized in this study, and it also establishes the relationship between campaign spending on fund-raising on the one hand and fund-raising success on the other. Also particularly applicable to the focus of this study is Adkins and Dowdle's interest in variables such as candidate viability, length of candidacy, and fund-raising success, each of which is included in this study as well. The fundamental conclusion of this recent article is very consistent with this study's thesis that pre-nomination phase fund-raising is critical to presidential nomination politics and, in fact, that the importance of even ballots and voters may be eclipsed by the factors which influence who wins the money primary.

A final part of the recent literature on the presidential nominating reforms and campaign finance focuses on the media and the crucial role it has assumed during the long pre-candidacy and early candidacy phases of the nomination process. Emmett Buell examined media coverage during the exhibition season, a study which found that most of this early presidential campaign coverage is in newspapers.[73] According to Buell, the largest portion of this coverage is of the horse race, with issue and theme coverage representing the second largest share, and scandal or flap coverage coming in last. Moreover, with no formal steps to cover during this long exhibition season, an obvious topic to cover from the outset is campaign fund-raising. Buell concludes that in general newspapers do a better job than is commonly recognized in informing the public during this long exhibition season.[74] A recent but journalistic examination of media coverage of presidential elections is Martin Plissner's *The Control Room: How Television Calls the Shots in Presidential Elections*, a study that focuses on television news rather than the print media.[75] Plissner asserts that the 2000 presidential race already was far along even in mid-1999. Television's power, according to Plissner, is as a mediating vehicle, framing the campaign and identifying which candidates are viable and which are not. Plissner argues that:

> Like the party leaders who used to make all the choices but the final one in November, television news will have the most far-reaching voice on who is plausible and who is not as contenders in the race. It will decide which of the fifty-seven primary and caucus contests are meaningful and which are not and what constitutes victory or defeat in each.[76]

These studies of the media, whether the print media or television, highlight the enormous power the media wields during the long pre-candidacy and early candidacy phases of the presidential nomination process. As both of these studies support, the devolution of power from parties and party leaders to other actors in the political process is perhaps nowhere as pronounced as in the power of the media today to identify particular candidates as viable or even front-running and, conversely, as unelectable or long shots.

A continuing source of data and analysis on the presidential nominating reforms and campaign finance in general and on presidential nomination campaign finance in particular are various public interest research centers such as Common Cause, the Campaign Finance Information Center, the Center for Responsive Politics, and the Citizen's Research Foundation. Common Cause's long record of challenging FEC enforcement decisions is a valuable source of information on the actual operation of federal campaign finance regulations and especially the lacunae which presidential candidates can utilize in their early fund-raising. The Campaign Finance Information Center, a national project seeking to assist journalists in their coverage of campaign finance issues, also is an invaluable source of information, especially on current topics and new developments in campaign fund-raising. Especially valuable for the purposes of this study, the Center for Responsive Politics in Washington, D.C., devotes considerable attention to reviewing and analyzing campaign finance reports submitted to the Federal Election Commission. While the focus of much of this research is Congressional campaign fund-raising, most notably an extensive study of fund-raising in Congressional primary campaigns entitled *The Wealth Primary*,[77] this research is nonetheless invaluable as background for the study of presidential nomination campaign fund-raising. Studies by the Center for Responsive Politics covering broader candidate fund-raising strategies, for instance a study of candidate reliance on individually established private foundations to support quasi-political activities, also serve to suggest the extent to which special not-for-profit entities can support would-be presidential candidates in their early campaign activities. Finally, the Citizen's Research Foundation, located at the University of California at Berkeley, is a source of ongoing research and publications on campaign finance and electoral reform.

While not part of the formal literature on the role of money in presidential nomination politics, journalistic coverage of presidential campaign fund-raising has reached an unprecedented level, providing an enormous amount of information and analysis on candidates' fund-raising activity and perform-ance. *The Washington Post* has made coverage of presidential nomination campaign fund-raising a priority during 1999 and early 2000, with literally dozens of major articles and almost daily news coverage. *Washington Post* headlines such as "Huge Money Chase Marks 2000 Race"[78] and "Bush's Fund-Raising Opens Huge Disparity: Unprecedented Edge May Limit Rivals"[79] have announced major pieces of journalistic analysis of the phenomenon of in-creasingly early fund-raising by presidential candidates. *The New York Times* also has made coverage of presidential nomination campaign fund-raising well ahead of the primary campaign a priority. A report with the headline "Early Rush of Contributions Opened the Floodgates for Bush" capped a year of stories chronicling George W. Bush's record fund-raising success.[80] Weekly news magazines also have given prominent attention to the significance of early fund-raising by candidates seeking the presidential nomination. A *Time* feature in 1995 entitled "The Money Chase" documented early presidential campaign fund-raising for the 1996 presidential election,[81] and another *Time* feature in February 2000 with the headline "Big Money and Politics" presented a special report on early presidential nomination campaign fund-raising for the unfolding 2000 presidential election.[82] This journalistic reporting and analysis certainly is a valuable source of information and insight concerning early nomination campaign fund-raising in the 2000 presidential election campaign. But more significantly, the record level of media coverage of presi-dential campaign fund-raising during the period leading up to the 2000 cam-paign is indicative of the impact which early fund-raising by presidential can-didates has in attracting media attention and in providing reporters with concrete data with which to support their early candidate evaluations and rankings. The extent of this coverage in 2000 points to the need for systematic examination of the impact of pre-candidacy and early candidacy fund-raising on the presidential nomination process.

This study addresses a gap in the literature on the early campaign leading up to the formal presidential nomination process by examining the pre-candidacy and early candidacy phases of the pre-nomination campaign. While increasing attention has been directed to the pre-nomination campaign in re-cent years, the pre-candidacy phase is seldom examined as a distinct phase in the early presidential nomination campaign. Moreover, studies of the early candidacy phase are limited and overly generalized in analyzing the crucial pre-election year. Early candidacy fund-raising success is examined in terms of fund-raising totals, momentum in fund-raising, and the achievement of competitive cash-on-hand and federal matching funding totals. Pre-candidacy fund-raising success is examined in terms of the variety of pre-candidacy committees and other organizational entities utilized by aspiring candidates and the pre-candidacy fund-raising totals achieved as a result. The dynamic between fund-raising success and media coverage of fund-raising success as in effect an echo of fund-raising success itself also is given much needed attention. The result is a greater understanding of pre-candidacy and early candidacy activity, advance campaign fund-raising, and media coverage of campaign fund-raising and their decisive impact on candidate survival, viability, and success in the early presidential nomination process.

Notes

1. Charles O. Jones, "Nonstop! The Campaigning Presidency and the 2000 Presidential Campaign," *Brookings Review* 18, no. 1 (Winter 2000): 12–15.

2. Arthur T. Hadley, *The Invisible Primary* (Englewood Cliffs, N.J.: Prentice-Hall, 1976).

3. Rhodes Cook, "The Nominating Process," in *The Elections of 1988*, ed. Michael Nelson (Washington, D.C.: Congressional Quarterly Press, 1989), 31.

4. Ibid., 31.

5. Judith S. Trent, "Presidential Surfacing: The Ritualistic and Crucial First Act," *Communication Monographs* 45 (November 1978): 282.

6. John Kessel, *Presidential Campaign Politics*, 4th ed. (Pacific Grove, Calif.: Brooks/Cole, 1992).

7. Center for Responsive Politics, *The Wealth Primary* (Washington, D.C.: Center for Responsive Politics, 1994).

8. Dan Clawson, Alan Neustadtl, and Mark Weller, *Dollars and Votes: How Business Campaign Contributions Subvert Democracy* (Philadelphia: Temple University Press, 1998), 1.

9. Ibid., 13.

10. Indicative of the extensive newspaper coverage of pre-candidacy and early candidacy presidential campaign fund-raising were such articles as "Huge Money Chase Marks 2000 Race" (*The Washington Post*, 28 February 1999, sec. A, pp. 1, 6, 7), "Presidential Hopefuls' First Race Is a Test of Fund-Raising Waters" (*The New York Times*, 31 March 1999, sec. A, pp. 1, 19), "The Race Before the Race—It's a Money Thing" (*The Christian Science Monitor*, 23 April 1999, sec. USA, p. 2), and "The Money Chase" (*Time*, 13 March 1995, 93).

11. Advisory Committee on the Presidential Nomination Process, "Perspectives on the Current Presidential Selection Process," in *Nominating Future Presidents* (Washington, D.C.: Republican National Committee, 1999).

12. Gary R. Orren and Nelson W. Polsby, eds., *Media and Momentum: The New Hampshire Primary and Nomination Politics* (Chatham, N.J.: Chatham House Publishers, 1987), 6.

13. Larry M. Bartels, *Presidential Primaries and the Dynamics of Public Choice* (Princeton, N.J.: Princeton University Press, 1988).

14. John H. Aldrich, "A Dynamic Model of Presidential Nomination Campaigns," *American Political Science Review* 74 (1980): 651–69.

15. John Haskell, *Fundamentally Flawed: Understanding and Reforming Presidential Primaries* (Lanham, Md.: Rowman & Littlefield Publishers, Inc., 1996).

16. Ibid., 45.

17. James W. Davis, *U.S. Presidential Primaries and the Caucus-Convention System: A Sourcebook* (Westport, Conn.: Greenwood Press, 1997).

18. Ibid., 140.

19. Andrew E. Busch, *Outsiders and Openness in the Presidential Nominating System* (Pittsburgh, Pa.: University of Pittsburgh Press, 1997).

20. Ibid., 151.

21. Ibid., 27.

22. Ibid., 152.

23. Ibid., 167.

24. Ibid., 51.

25. Steven E. Schier, *By Invitation Only: The Rise of Exclusive Politics in the United States* (Pittsburgh, Pa.: The University of Pittsburgh Press, 2000), 90.

26. Ibid., 80–81.

27. Ibid., 81.

28. William G. Mayer, "The Presidential Nominations," in *The Election of 2000*, ed. Gerald M. Pomper (New York: Chatham House Publishers, 2001).

29. Ibid., 44.

30. Ibid., 12.

31. Audrey A. Haynes, Paul-Henri Gurian, and Stephen M. Nichols, "The Role of Candidate Spending in Presidential Nomination Campaigns," *The Journal of Politics* 59, no. 1 (February 1997): 213–25.

32. Ibid., 223.

33. David F. Damore, "A Dynamic Model of Candidate Fundraising: The Case of Presidential Nomination Campaigns," *Political Research Quarterly* 50, no. 2 (June 1997): 343–64.

34. Frank J. Sorauf, *Money in American Elections* (Glenview, Ill.: Scott, Foresman and Company, 1988), 175.

35. Michael Robinson, Clyde Wilcox, and Paul Marshall, "The Presidency: Not for Sale," *Public Opinion* 2 (March/April 1989): 49–53.

36. Ibid., 51.

37. David R. Runkel, *Campaign for President: The Managers Look at '88* (Dover, Mass.: Auburn House Publishing Company, 1989).

38. Ibid., 169.

39. Ibid., 170.

40. Ibid., 171.

41. Ibid., 180–81.

42. Ibid., 194.

43. Barbara Norrander, "Nomination Choices: Caucus and Primary Outcomes, 1976–1988," *American Journal of Political Science* 37 (May 1993): 361.

44. Ibid., 361.

45. Stephen J. Wayne, *The Road to the White House, 2000: The Politics of Presidential Elections, Post-election Edition* (Boston: Bedford/St Martin's, 2001), 122.

46. Ibid., 155.

47. Ibid., 53.

48. Anthony Corrado, *Creative Campaigning: PACs and the Presidential Selection Process* (Boulder, Colo.: Westview Press, Inc., 1992).

49. Ibid., 106.

50. Ibid., 72.

51. Ibid., 85.

52. Ibid., 72.

53. Anthony Corrado, *Paying for Presidents: Public Financing in National Elections* (New York: The Twentieth Century Fund Press, 1993).

54. Ibid., 116.

55. Ibid., 71.

56. Center for Responsive Politics, *Public Policy and Foundations: The Role of Politicians in Public Charities* (Washington, D.C.: Center for Responsive Politics, 1987).

57. Ibid., 35.

58. Ibid., 43.

59. Ibid., 35.

60. Philip John Davies, *US Elections Today* (New York: St. Martin's Press, Inc., 1999).

61. Ibid., 196.

62. Clyde Wilcox, "Financing the 1988 Prenomination Campaign," in *Nominating the President*, ed. Emmett H. Buell, Jr. and Lee Sigelman (Knoxville: The University of Tennessee Press, 1991), 91.

63. Ibid., 92.

64. Clifford W. Brown, Jr., Lynda W. Powell, and Clyde Wilcox, *Serious Money: Fundraising and Contributing in Presidential Nomination Campaigns* (New York: Cambridge University Press, 1995).

65. William G. Mayer, "Forecasting Presidential Nominations," in *In Pursuit of The White House: How We Choose Our Presidential Nominees*, ed. William G. Mayer (Chatham, N.J.: Chatham House Publishers, Inc., 1996), 44–71.

66. Wayne Steger, "Do Primary Voters Draw from a Stacked Deck? Presidential Nominations in an Era of Candidate-Centered Campaigns," *Presidential Studies Quarterly* 30, no. 4 (December 2000): 727–53.

67. Ibid., 735.

68. Ibid., 727.

69. Ibid., 728.

70. Ibid., 728.

71. Ibid., 748–49.

72. Randall E. Adkins and Andrew J. Dowdle, "The Money Primary: What Influences the Outcome of Pre-Primary Presidential Nomination Fundraising?," *Presidential Studies Quarterly* 32, no. 2 (June 2002): 256–75.

73. Emmett H. Buell, Jr., "Meeting Expectations? Major Newspaper Coverage of Candidates During the 1988 Exhibition Season," in *Nominating the President*, ed. Emmett H. Buell, Jr., and Lee Sigelman (Knoxville: The University of Tennessee Press, 1991).

74. Ibid., 181–86.

75. Martin Plissner, *The Control Room: How Television Calls the Shots in Presidential Elections* (New York: The Free Press, 1999).

76. Ibid., 5.

77. Center for Responsive Politics, *The Wealth Primary.*

78. Ceci Connolly, "Huge Money Chase Marks 2000 Race," *The Washington Post*, 28 February 1999, sec. A, pp. 1, 6, 7.

79. Dan Balz, "Bush's Fund-Raising Opens Huge Disparity: Unprecedented Edge May Limit Rivals," *The Washington Post*, 1 July 1999, sec. A, pp. 1, 9.

80. Don Van Natta, Jr., "Early Rush of Contributions Opened the Floodgates for Bush," *The New York Times*, 30 January 2000, 20.

81. Michael Duffy, "The Money Chase," *Time*, 13 March 1995, 93.

82. Donald L. Barlett and James B. Steele, "Big Money and Politics: Who Gets Hurt? How the Little Guy Gets Crunched," *Time*, 7 February 2000, 38–41.

3

Research Plan and Methodology
for Examining "The Money Primary"

THIS STUDY EXAMINES "THE MONEY PRIMARY," a phase in the early presidential nomination process when candidates and would-be candidates seek the funds, and even more important the means to generate the funds, that permit a viable and successful presidential campaign. The focus is on individual candidates' presidential nomination campaigns as the unit of analysis. The two post-reform era presidential elections in which the nomination contests of both major political parties lacked incumbent contenders—the elections of 1988 and 2000—are the case studies for this analysis, thereby permitting a large number of individual candidate campaigns in election years with generally comparable political contexts. The time frame under study encompasses the crucial early nomination campaign period, the pre-nomination campaign months, and the entire year prior to the presidential election year, and also includes the early candidacy and pre-candidacy campaign phases extending back two, three, and even four years prior to the formal nomination campaign. For the purposes of this study, the early candidacy phase is defined as extending from the formal announcement of a presidential candidacy (which triggers the FEC requirement of a presidential campaign committee and regular financial disclosure reports) through the opening of the formal nomination process with the first caucus in Iowa and the first primary in New Hampshire. The pre-candidacy phase is more open-ended, extending back several years or more, encompassing what is often termed the "exploratory phase" and also including the preparatory phase during which the organizational infrastructure of a nascent campaign is put into place.

The three hypotheses that frame this study focus on the significance of early candidacy fund-raising success, the impact of pre-candidacy fund-raising success, and the echo of a candidate's early candidacy fund-raising success in terms of media coverage of that fund-raising success. The independent variables to be analyzed in this study are conceptualized in terms of early candidacy fund-raising activity and success, pre-candidacy fund-raising activity and success, and media coverage of fund-raising activity and success. Early candidacy fund-raising activity and success are operationalized in terms of a candidate's achievement of basic thresholds in fund-raising, overall fund-raising totals, the momentum of fund-raising, total cash-on-hand at the start of the formal nomination process, and the level of federal matching funding received at the start of the formal nomination process. Pre-candidacy fund-raising activity and success is operationalized in terms of a candidate's utilization of pre-candidacy fund-raising and organizational entities, the initial infusion of campaign assets and funding at the start of a pre-candidacy campaign, and pre-candidacy fund-raising totals. Media coverage of campaign fund-raising is operationalized in terms of the level of media attention to particular candidates measured in terms of the number, length, and positive, negative, or neutral spin of this media coverage, with media coverage of campaign fund-raising being categorized into horse race fund-raising coverage, candidate focused fund-raising coverage, and general campaign fund-raising coverage. The dependent variable of candidate viability is conceptualized in terms of each candidate's standing in the early nomination campaign results. This dependent variable is operationalized in terms of the share of the vote total achieved by each candidate for the presidential nomination in the Iowa caucuses and the New Hampshire primary, the two opening contests of the early presidential nomination campaign.

The independent variables to be analyzed in this study correspond with the three hypothesized relationships that comprise the money primary. These independent variables relate to early candidacy fund-raising activity and success, pre-candidacy fund-raising activity and success, and media coverage of campaign fund-raising. The term for each independent variable used in this study along with the corresponding definition appear in Box 3.1.

The dependent variables in this analysis are more straightforward and concern alternate categories into which candidates for the presidential nomination can be grouped in terms of their viability, active candidacy, and survival as candidates. The term for each dependent variable used in this study along with the corresponding definition appear in Box 3.2.

Data for this analysis of presidential pre-candidacy and early candidacy fund-raising and media coverage of early candidacy fund-raising as predictors of candidate survival, viability, and success in the early presidential nomination process is drawn from varied sources. The independent variables concerning

BOX 3.1
The Independent Variables

Term	Definition
Dollars Raised	The total in dollars raised by an individual seeking the presidential nomination over a particular period of time.
Dollars Raised Through an Early Fund-Raising Entity	The total in dollars raised by a possible presidential candidate utilizing an early fund-raising entity, such as a tax-exempt foundation or a state-based PAC, operating during the pre-candidacy phase.
Dollars Raised Through a Leadership PAC	The total in dollars raised by a possible presidential candidate utilizing a leadership PAC operating during the pre-candidacy phase, taken from line 11d of FEC Form 3X for total dollars raised.
Dollars Raised Through a Presidential Campaign Committee	The total in dollars raised by an announced presidential candidate utilizing an FEC registered presidential campaign committee, taken from line 17e of FEC Form 3P for total dollars raised.
Fund-Raising Momentum	A ratio that measures progress in fund-raising by comparing the total in funds raised over a period of time (a month, quarter, half-year, or year) as compared with the immediately preceding period.
Cash-on-Hand	The amount of cash-on-hand held by a presidential campaign committee at particular junctures in the early nomination campaign, taken from line 6 of FEC Form 3P for presidential campaign committees.
Federal Matching Funding	The amount of federal matching funding received by a candidate for a presidential campaign committee at particular junctures in the early nomination campaign, taken from line 16 of FEC Form 3P for presidential campaign committees.
Early Fund-Raising Entity	Any organization formed by an announced or prospective presidential candidate during the period prior to the year preceding the presidential election year. While these early fund-raising entities may include political action committees, they frequently also are 501 (c) (3) foundations, 501 (c) (4) lobbying organizations, and state-based political committees.
Media Coverage of Candidate and Campaign Fund-Raising	Media coverage of candidate and campaign fund-raising in the early presidential nomination campaign in *The New York Times, The Washington Post,* and *The Wall Street Journal* over particular periods of time, including the month and year, the number of articles, and their length in word count.

(continued)

Box 3.1 (continued)

Term	Definition
Horse Race Coverage of Campaign Fund-Raising	Media coverage comparing presidential candidates' and potential candidates' success in presidential campaign fund-raising, including the month and year, the number of articles, and their length in word count.
Candidate Focused Coverage of Individual Candidate Fund-Raising	Media coverage reporting on and sometimes evaluating individual presidential candidates' and potential candidates' success in presidential campaign fund-raising, including the month and year, the number of articles, and their length in word count.
General Coverage of Campaign Fund-Raising and Campaign Finance	Media coverage of campaign fund-raising for the presidential nomination and general election campaign, political parties, PACs, or federal campaign finance reform, including the month and year, the number of articles, and their length in word count.
Candidate Comparison/ Candidate Reference	Media coverage comparing a candidate relative to another candidate or the candidate field in a newspaper article categorized as horse race coverage of campaign fund-raising. A single newspaper article can have one or more candidate comparisons/candidate references.
Candidate Focused Article	Media coverage focusing on an individual candidate in a newspaper article categorized as candidate focused coverage of individual candidate fund-raising. A candidate focused article generally concerns a single candidate but in some instances can present candidate focused coverage of more than one candidate.
Positive Media Coverage	Media coverage in a particular newspaper article that is generally a positive statement regarding an individual presidential candidate.
Negative Media Coverage	Media coverage in a particular newspaper article that is generally a negative statement regarding an individual presidential candidate.
Neutral Media Coverage	Media coverage in a particular newspaper article that is generally neither a positive nor negative statement regarding an individual presidential candidate.

BOX 3.2
The Dependent Variables

Term	Definition
Viable Candidate/Viable Through Early Nomination Process:	A candidate who achieves a vote total of 10 percent or more in both the Iowa caucuses and the New Hampshire primary or, alternatively, who achieves a vote total of 20 percent or more in either one or the other of these early nomination contests.
Active Candidate/Active Through Early Nomination Process:	A candidate who remains an announced and active canddate even while not achieving either of the alternate vote total thresholds needed to be classified as a viable candidate in the early nomination contests.
Withdrawing Candidate/ Withdrawing Before Early Nomination Process:	A candidate who withdraws from the nomination contest after declaring candidacy but before the start of the caucus and primary schedule.
Withdrawing Non-Candidate/ Withdrawing Before Announcement of Candidacy:	An individual who withdraws from the nomination contest before an announcement of candidacy.
Other Potential Candidate:	An individual who is among "the mentioned" as a possible candidate but who never commences an active candidacy or pre-candidacy nomination campaign.
Successful Candidate:	A candidate who wins one or both of the opening nomination contests.

---

campaign fund-raising draw upon data available in candidate financial disclosure reports filed with the Federal Election Commission, including reports from 1993 forward which are available online at http://fec.gov and earlier reports back to 1976 which are only available at the FEC itself. These candidate financial disclosure reports each range in length anywhere from two pages to 3,500 pages, with the typical candidate submitting four quarterly reports and dozens of amended reports during the year prior to the presidential election year and monthly reports during the election year itself. Data on pre-candidacy fund-raising is generally available for leadership PACs which also are required to file financial disclosure reports with the FEC but is not always available for other fund-raising entities such as foundations which file non-public IRS reports and state-based entities which in most cases file specialized state reports. Data for the independent variables concerning media coverage of candidate and campaign fund-raising is gathered by means of a review and content analysis of campaign coverage in *The New York Times*, *The Washington Post*, and *The Wall Street Journal* for the early campaigns of both the 1988 and 2000 presidential elections, a period extending from January of the pre-presidential election year through January of the presidential election year that leads into the nomination campaign period. Data for the dependent variables concerning candidate survival, viability, and success in the early presidential nomination campaign is gathered from presidential caucus and primary results available in Congressional Quarterly's publication *Presidential Elections Since 1789* as well as from news articles in *The New York Times* and *The Washington Post*.

A major aspect of this study is the analysis of media coverage of campaign fund-raising which is presented as a second dimension of the money primary and in effect an echo of campaign fund-raising success. The research design for this study utilizes content analysis of this media coverage of campaign fund-raising to collect data on this important dimension of the money primary. Media coverage of campaign fund-raising in the three major newspapers included in the study is analyzed both to collect objective data and to classify the coverage based upon its overall or dominant content. Objective data includes the number of articles published, their respective dates of publication, and their length as measured by total word count—all of which can be determined with objectivity by a single researcher. Data collected based upon a content analysis of the news articles themselves, however, requires individual interpretation and judgment. This content analysis first classifies the media coverage of campaign fund-raising into three categories: horse race coverage, which involves comparisons among or between candidates; candidate focused coverage, which concerns a specific candidate; and general campaign coverage, which concerns campaign fund-raising or campaign finance reform in general. The content analysis then classifies the media coverage that is horse race coverage or candidate focused coverage in terms of its overall orientation toward the candidate: positive coverage; negative coverage; and generally neutral coverage.

An important methodological aspect of the research design for this study is the means by which intercoder reliability is ensured in the extensive review of news articles that comprise a major part of the media coverage analysis. The content analysis of media coverage that goes beyond objective data and includes interpretation and judgment regarding news articles entails the potential for individual bias to be introduced in the study. Yet ensuring an acceptable level of intercoder reliability clearly is essential in this research, both to preclude individual bias in the content analysis and classification and to ensure the reproducibility of the study's results. Intercoder reliability of the content analysis in this research's review of media coverage therefore is tested by selecting a sampling of the total collection of newspaper articles reviewed for the study and utilizing the methodology of a second reviewer whose categorizations and classifications are compared with the principal reviewer's work.[1]

TABLE 3.1
Summary of Intercoder Reliability Test
for Content Analysis of Media Coverage

	Total in Category	Test Group	Agreement Between Coders	Disagreement Between Coders
Three-Part Categorization of Media Coverage:				
Horse Race Coverage:	47	10	9	1
Candidate Coverage:	216	30	27	3
General Coverage:	228	20	20	0
Three-Part Classification of Media Orientation:				
Positive:	167	20	19	1
Negative:	125	15	14	1
Neutral:	20	5	5	0
Level of Interagreement:		94/100 or 94%		

This sampling included the articles judged to be the most difficult to classify by the principal reviewer, thereby providing an even greater test of the level of intercoder reliability. The second reviewer then is utilized to classify these news articles based upon the same classification definitions and methods utilized by the principal reviewer. The results of this intercoder reliability test, both in terms of the categorization of this media coverage and the classification of its orientation or spin, are summarized in Table 3.1.

As this analysis of intercoder reliability shows, the level of interagreement between the principal reviewer and the second reviewer—94 percent—is extraordinary for the sampling of newspaper articles examined. This high level of intercoder reliability certainly is reassuring in terms of the clarity with which the independent variable of media coverage of campaign fund-raising is conceptualized and operationalized and, most importantly, in terms of the reliability and reproducibility of this study's findings with respect to media coverage of campaign fund-raising and presidential selection.

Note

1. The method for testing intercoder reliability for this study utilizes an approach employed by Michael J. Robinson and Margaret A. Sheehan in *Over the Wire and on TV: CBS and UPI in Campaign '80* (New York: Russell Sage Foundation, 1980), 21–22. The same approach was followed by C. Richard Hofstetter in *Bias in The News* (Columbus: Ohio State University Press, 1976), 26.

4

The Cases of 1988 and 2000: The Two All Non-Incumbent Presidential Nomination Races of the Post-Reform Era

THE PRESIDENTIAL NOMINATION RACES of 1988 and 2000 stand apart among the nomination races of the post-reform era through 2000 as ideal case studies in this examination of pre-candidacy and early candidacy fund-raising and media coverage of campaign fund-raising. Among the eight presidential election years since the nomination reforms following 1968 and the seven election years since the campaign finance reforms of 1971 which took full effect in 1976, the elections of 1988 and 2000 are the only two in which neither political party had an incumbent President seeking re-nomination. In fact, 1988 was the first presidential election since 1960 in which a sitting President was in his second term and therefore constitutionally ineligible to run as a new presidential election approached, and the presidential election of 2000 was only the second all non-incumbent contest during this four decade span. Moreover, and in large part because there was no incumbent President in these races, the nomination contests of both 1988 and 2000 had wide candidate fields, at least in the early stages of the process, and were fairly competitively contended. In 1988, the overall field of announced candidates numbered fourteen, with eight candidates seeking the Democratic nomination and six candidates seeking the Republican nomination.[1] In 2000, the candidate field was even larger, numbering nineteen, with seven candidates seeking the Democratic nomination—although five withdrew before their official announcement—and twelve announced candidates seeking the Republican nomination.[2] Among all of the presidential nomination contests of the post-reform era, in fact, the elections of 1988 and 2000 had the broadest candidate fields and therefore afford an unusually large number of discrete presidential candidacies for study.

The presidential nomination contests of 1988 and 2000 are even more valuable as case study elections in that they present such a rich combination of characteristics as well as new and continuing trends. The nomination contests in both major parties and in both election years certainly exhibited many similarities, and in fact trends that were evident in 1988 can be seen to have advanced even further by 2000. Quite significantly, both of these election years can be seen as actual milestones in the post-reform era, with the impact of the consequences of the reforms continuing to advance in 1988 and advancing even further in 2000. Yet both of these election years also exhibit real differences that are the result of the unique political situations of the particular year and the individual candidates. These two elections therefore present a degree of variety that also is useful and that makes the overarching trends all the more significant. Finally, and especially important, the elections of 1988 and 2000 each exhibited significant new characteristics and innovations, offering new developments and trends that may prove to have long-term importance.

Even the superficial similarities between the nomination contests of 1988 and 2000 are striking. Both major party nomination races resulted in an incumbent Vice President as the nominee of one party and a Governor as the nominee of the other party. Yet while in 1988 the sitting Vice President ultimately was elected President, in 2000 it was the sitting Governor who ultimately—although narrowly—prevailed. Both nomination contests also included candidates with visible links to religious organizations, either as clergymen themselves or as individuals at the forefront of religiously based organizations. This relatively new phenomenon in presidential politics was most evident in 1988, with the Rev. Jesse Jackson seeking the Democratic nomination and the Rev. Pat Robertson seeking the Republican nomination.[3] In 2000, while not as clear, there likewise were candidates with strong religious ties, with the Rev. Jesse Jackson initially pursuing—and then abandoning—a Democratic presidential bid and with Gary Bauer of the Family Research Council seeking the Republican nomination.[4] In 1988 and 2000, moreover, popular sitting Presidents continued to have a significant influence on presidential politics, in both cases endeavoring to assist loyal Vice Presidents who were seeking to continue their administrations' legacies. While President Ronald Reagan at first was tentative in his support for George H. Bush, he soon offered strong support for his bid for the Republican nomination and ultimately provided invaluable assistance in his victory. President Bill Clinton was unstinting in his early and continuing support for Al Gore, and while Gore was cautious due to Clinton's damaging personal scandals, he too ultimately benefited enormously as a result. Finally, and perhaps most significant, the presidential nomination races of 1988 and 2000 both produced as the major party standard bearers the candidate who was the front-runner well before the formal nomination process began. While in some instances these victories were achieved only after overcoming intense early challenges, in each of the major party nomination contests in both 1988 and 2000 it was the early front-runner who ultimately prevailed in securing the presidential nomination. The fact that the nomination contests in both major parties in both 1988[5] and 2000[6] had early campaign front-runners who in the end were the presidential nominees not only is a significant similarity between these two election years but indeed sets them apart from many of the other non-incumbent nomination contests of the post-reform era.

Most significant as a common denominator between the 1988 and 2000 presidential nomination races is the amazing degree to which the continuing trends of the post-reform era were exhibited throughout these interesting and competitive campaigns. The trend toward front-loading in the primary and caucus schedule was evident in 1988 and advanced even further by 2000.[7] Super Tuesday on March 8, 1988, had seventeen state contests, bringing to twenty-one the total number of early primaries and caucuses that had occurred as of that date.[8] This trend continued through 2000, with Super Tuesday on March 7, 2000, featuring seventeen Democratic and thirteen Republican state contests, including for the first time critical major primaries in California and New York, bringing to nineteen and twenty-nine respectively the number of early Democratic and Republican primaries and caucuses as of that date.[9] The point in the formal nomination process in each of these years when the competitive contest actually was resolved and a successful nominee was ensured also moved steadily earlier. While in 1988 this decision point was reached in early June for the Democrats (with Michael Dukakis) and late April for the Republicans (with George H. Bush), by 2000 the decision point had shifted to March 14 for the Democrats (with Al Gore) as well as the Republicans (with George W. Bush).[10] Related to both the increased front-loading of the primary and caucus schedule and the ever earlier decision point in the nomination process is the trend toward longer pre-nomination campaigns that now encompass long early candidacy campaigns and ever longer and more important pre-candidacy campaigns. The increasing importance of fund-raising for ultimate success also is a common trend in 1988 and 2000, with the individual contribution limit of $1,000 and the eroding value of even this amount forcing broader and more organized campaign fund-raising efforts and, as this study will argue, with the longer pre-candidacy and early candidacy phases making the success of this fund-raising more important than ever as one of the only indicators of candidate success during the long early campaign period.[11]

The presidential nomination campaigns of 1988 and 2000 also exhibited significant developments in the crucial area of campaign finance that are common to both election years but that actually began with the 1988 presidential election cycle and reached fruition during the 2000 presidential election cycle. While the campaign finance reforms enacted in the Federal Election Campaign Act of 1971 and strengthened in a series of FECA amendments through the mid-1970s radically altered presidential campaign fund-raising, forcing candidates to look beyond a limited circle of major donors to broad-based fund-raising campaigns, by the nomination race of 1988 the process of circumventing these regulations was in full throttle. In fact, the election of 1988, seventeen years after the enactment of campaign finance reform, was a watershed year in the erosion of these reforms. Most notably, as Anthony Corrado notes in *Creative Campaigning*, his study of political action committees, 1988 saw "a virtual explosion in the number of candidate-sponsored PACs," with nine of the fourteen major candidates utilizing a PAC as part of their pre-nomination campaign strategy.[12] By utilizing this organizational device, candidates were able to begin campaign activity much earlier, including the all-important process of building a campaign fund-raising organization, while also evading federal ceilings on campaign spending and contribution limits by means of such "shadow campaign committees."[13] The year 1988 also saw the introduction of an entirely new organizational strategy, namely the use of candidate-affiliated tax-exempt foundations, as a further avenue for funding presidential pre-candidacy activity beyond the reach of FEC limitations.[14] Four candidates out of the fourteen major candidates in 1988 established such foundations, including Gary Hart who was the first candidate to employ this approach when he founded the Center for a New Democracy, and three others—Bruce Babbitt, Jack Kemp, and Pat Robertson—all of whom also utilized PACs as part of their campaigns. Three other candidates—Pierre du Pont, Gary Hart, and Jesse Jackson—utilized "some other type of organization to avoid federal limits."[15] Only two of the fourteen major candidates in 1988 had no special organizational vehicle at the federal level, whether a PAC, a tax-exempt foundation, or some other type of organizational entity, namely Michael Dukakis and Al Gore, but even Dukakis had the benefit of a state level political committee established as the Dukakis Gubernatorial Committee.[16]

By election year 2000, the use—or misuse—of various creative organizational entities, including PACs and foundations, had become the norm, with virtually every candidate except the few who relied instead on state level entities, utilizing one or more of these organizational devices.[17] Beginning in 2000, moreover, the erosion and even collapse of the campaign finance reforms as an effective framework for campaign fund-raising and spending reached a new high water mark as candidates began employing more sweeping means of evading campaign finance reform limitations, namely the declining of federal matching funds (as George W. Bush did with such success) and the self-funding of presidential nomination campaigns (as was the case with Steve Forbes). The effect in both instances was to permit unlimited spending by both candidates, the spending ceilings on the rest of the candidate field notwithstanding.[18] In short, the presidential nomination races of 1988 and 2000 were pivotal years in the long-term trend toward the dismantlement of effective campaign finance reform, with the 1988 campaign exhibiting important new strategies aimed at circumventing specific reforms and with the 2000 campaign bringing this erosion to such levels that the future efficacy of the overall framework of campaign finance reform is now in question.[19]

Notwithstanding the many similarities and significant long-term trends that the 1988 and 2000 presidential nomination campaigns share in common, there also are unique features that distinguish these nomination campaigns from one another. Most notable among these distinguishing features is the position of front-runners and their aura as the pre-ordained major party nominees. While the nomination races in both major parties indeed had front-runners as the early nomination contests in both 1988 and 2000 approached, in 1988 these front-runners were regarded as being at least somewhat vulnerable to challengers rather than as inevitable nominees,[20] while in 2000 the front-runners in both parties were commonly viewed as the all but inevitable party nominees.[21] In spite of these differing perceptions, however, the party nomination races in both 1988[22] and 2000[23] proved to be genuinely competitive, at least in their opening weeks, with all of the front-runners exhibiting vulnerability and with one or more of their challengers proving to be viable. Also distinguishing the 1988 and 2000 nomination contests was the new phenomenon of early candidate withdrawals that emerged in 2000. The pattern of candidates withdrawing before their formal announcement of candidacy existed in 1988 and continued in 2000, including at least nine Democrats and seven Republicans in 1988[24] and five Democrats and five Republicans in 2000.[25] But the 2000 race exhibited a significant new pattern, namely the early withdrawal of announced candidates,[26] with a record one Democrat and five Republicans withdrawing after their announcement but before the formal opening of the primary and caucus schedule.[27] Finally, and consistent with this study's focus on the significance of campaign finance issues, while fund-raising and spending were a central issue in both the 1988 and 2000 nomination races, it was only in 2000 that the structure of the campaign finance reforms had eroded to the point that every candidate was to some degree functioning well beyond the original reform framework and some candidates—such as Bush who did not accept federal matching funding and Forbes who self-funded his nomination campaign—were functioning almost totally beyond the regulations.[28] Thus, even while reflecting common characteristics and trends, the 1988 and 2000 nomination contests also exhibited distinctive features, providing two case studies with a multitude of candidates and campaigns that in their totality enrich this analysis.

In sum, the two presidential election cycles and in particular their nomination campaigns that are utilized in this analysis present exceptionally strong case studies of the post-reform era presidential nomination process. As the fifth and eighth presidential election cycles of the post-reform era that dates to the 1972 presidential election, the 1988 and 2000 campaigns fall well into the post-reform era and thus reflect not only the reforms and their impact but also the reaction to the reforms in terms of the adjustments and innovations of candidates and campaigns responding to them. As already noted, these two election cycles stand apart from the others of the post-reform era as the only nomination campaigns without an incumbent President seeking re-nomination. They also stand apart as bookends to what can be viewed as a new phase in the post-reform era of presidential nomination politics, a phase which appropriately might be termed "the unreformed post-reform era." This new phase of the post-reform era is especially important in that it exhibits the impact of the reforms themselves, especially campaign finance reform, in terms of candidate and campaign strategies that seek to counteract and even undermine the reforms. It is during this phase, beginning in 1988, that candidates for the presidential nomination are utilizing pre-candidacy committees such as leadership PACs and other organizational entities as vehicles to conduct longer and more intensive campaigns and as the means to develop broader and more organized fund-raising operations.[29] And it is at the other end of this new era in 2000 that candidates for the presidential nomination have in effect overwhelmed the campaign finance framework, whether by utilizing pre-candidacy committees over extended periods of time and to unprecedented degrees, by declining federal matching funds in order to raise unlimited funds, or by self-funding their campaign in its entirety—all with the effect of evading campaign spending limitations and in some instances contribution limits and disclosure requirements.[30] The selection of 1988 and 2000 as case study elections for this analysis therefore provides a rich source of data on the characteristics and trends in funding presidential nomination campaigns, providing new perspective on the impact of campaign finance reform on the presidential nomination process in the new "unreformed post-reform era" in which candidates and campaigns are moving aggressively to undermine and evade any regulatory framework that limits fund-raising and spending in their pursuit of the presidential nomination.

The 1988 Early Nomination Campaign

The early nomination campaign in 1988 is an excellent case study of fund-raising and media coverage of fund-raising as factors in presidential nominee selection in modern presidential nomination politics. While the period that is known as the post-reform era of presidential nomination politics began with the presidential election of 1972, it took the passing of sixteen more years and four presidential elections before not only the reforms themselves but the full impact of the reforms in terms of significantly adjusted strategic behavior took full effect. By the presidential election of 1988, the full impact of the presidential nominating reforms in terms of adjustments to candidate behavior and campaign strategy had taken hold, and with it a significant level of altered behavior as candidates and campaigns endeavored to take advantage of, circumvent, and in some instances even subvert the nominating system reforms. An examination of post-reform era presidential elections focusing on the pre-candidacy and early candidacy phases therefore is well served by a case study of the 1988 early nomination campaign.

The 1988 presidential nomination process was first and foremost a year of the extraordinary, of unanticipated developments and turnabouts, and most significantly of path-breaking innovation and change. Perhaps most bizarre in this generally extraordinary year was the figure of Gary Hart, who after his strong challenge to Walter Mondale in 1984 was the early favorite for the Democratic nomination in 1988. But when scandal dogged his early campaign, most notably the charge of "womanizing," he endeavored to bolster his denials by challenging the media to trail him if they did not accept his word on face value. Within weeks the media did just that, exposing the front-runner's marital infidelity and precipitating a media frenzy of scandal coverage that ultimately forced Hart from the race in May 1987, nine months before the start of the caucus and primary schedule. Even more strange, however, Hart later doubled-back on his withdrawal, deciding in December 1987 to reenter the nomination contest, an effort that ultimately proved unsuccessful, with the candidate finally withdrawing once and for all in March 1988.[31] And Hart was not the only candidate whose campaign fell to scandal and the resulting media feeding frenzy. Senator Joseph Biden faced a very different scandal in September 1987 when he was confronted by media charges that one of his speeches had been plagiarized from the work of a British politician. The charges were a reminder of earlier ethical issues dating from Biden's law school years, and the intense negative media attention soon forced him from the race as well.[32]

Besides being an extraordinary year in terms of forced candidate withdrawals, the 1988 nomination contest also was a year of the non-candidate, namely the refusal by very popular presidential prospects to even enter the early nomination campaign. Three enormously popular Democrats who were among the most frequently mentioned candidates for the presidential nomination in 1988—Governor Mario Cuomo and Senators Edward Kennedy and Sam Nunn—all steadfastly resisted efforts to draw them into the early campaign.

While at first they each declined to put speculation about their possible candidacies definitively to rest, each one ultimately decided not to run and withdrew from any active campaigning and even speculation about possible future campaigns.[33] In short, in some respects the early nomination campaign for the 1988 presidential election was more about who ended up not running than about who actually ran, and certainly it was during the pre-candidacy and early campaign phases of the early nomination campaign that unexpected candidate withdrawals were forced and highly anticipated candidacies were foreclosed.

A variety of other developments distinguish the early presidential nomination contest in 1988 from any previous election of the post-reform era. Religiously affiliated candidates, in fact ordained clergymen, made their presidential candidacy debut as strong and viable presidential candidates for the first time in 1988, with the Rev. Jesse Jackson seeking the Democratic nomination and the Rev. Pat Robertson seeking the Republican nomination. Both of these clergyman proved to be competitive candidates, in fact appearing to be possible victors early in the caucus-primary schedule, with Jackson ultimately winning 29 percent of the Democratic primary vote, including seven primaries and another seven caucuses,[34] and with Robertson performing even better than expected by coming in second in the Iowa caucuses with 25 percent of the vote.[35] While both of these candidates ultimately withdrew from the nomination contest, both had proven to be viable contenders, and the strength of their religiously based campaigns introduced a whole new dimension to presidential nomination politics. The year 1988 also was a year of early caucus and primary upsets and certainly not the year to be a complacent early front-runner. Hart's early front-runner status certainly did not last long, both in his first campaign and when he announced a resuscitated second bid, and even Michael Dukakis who soon took his leading position faced serious early challenges that threatened his ultimate victory.[36] On the Republican side, George H. Bush's early front-runner status received a serious jolt in the Iowa caucuses where his 19 percent showing ranked third behind Bob Dole who received 37 percent and Pat Robertson who garnered 25 percent.[37] The overall nomination contest ultimately proved to be a roller-coaster ride, with the nomination contests for both major party nominations offering weekly surprises and taking many unexpected turns as candidates see-sawed back and forth in vote shares, delegate counts, and the media attention which inevitably results.

The candidate field in the 1988 presidential nomination race was one of the largest, and indeed one of the most volatile, of the post-reform era. In both major political parties there were an unusually large number of contenders, including numerous potential candidates who considered running but then took themselves out of the race before a formal announcement, and a broad field of announced contenders for each party nomination. Candidates for the nomination in both parties entered the race at varying points during the pre-election year, altering the candidate field significantly as the respective party campaigns progressed and making both party contests unusually dynamic. Adding even further to the excitement of the 1988 campaign were some un-expected withdrawals, most notably Gary Hart and Joseph Biden. Most of the candidate withdrawals in the 1988 nomination races, however, were after the formal nomination process had begun, spanning the whole period from shortly after the opening of the nomination process all the way to the eve of the nominating conventions. In short, the presidential nomination in both parties in 1988 was pursued by a wide field of candidates running in compet-itive races in the early phase of the process, and in the case of the Democrats this contest extended well into the formal nominating period, making for an overall nomination campaign that ranked as one of the most competitive and interesting of the post-reform era.

The 1988 Democratic Early Nomination Campaign

The nomination campaign on the Democratic side in 1988 certainly was the most widely contested and perhaps the most protracted of any nomina-tion campaign of the post-reform era to that date. As Table 4.1 indicates, at least nine Democrats considered presidential runs during the year or two be-fore the nomination process but then decided not to run, including Demo-cratic Party stalwarts such as Mario Cuomo, Edward Kennedy, and Sam Nunn.

TABLE 4.1
Comparison of Withdrawing Vs. Remaining Candidates
Prior to Start of Formal Nomination Process
1988 Presidential Election Cycle
Democrats

Candidates Withdrawing Before Formal Announcement and Other Potential Candidates	Announced Candidates Withdrawing Prior to December 31, 1987	Candidates Remaining Through January 1988
Bill Bradley	Joseph Biden	Bruce Babbitt
Dale Bumpers		Michael Dukakis
Bill Clinton		Richard Gephardt
Mario Cuomo		Al Gore
John Glenn		Gary Hart
Edward Kennedy		Rev. Jesse Jackson
Sam Nunn		Paul Simon
Charles Robb		
Patricia Schroeder		

The fact that all three of these leading Democratic presidential possibilities ultimately refused to enter the nomination race certainly left a vacuum in the overall field of prospective contenders.[38] This gap was expanded even further when Gary Hart—the presumed 1988 front-runner ever since 1984 when he gave the previous Democratic nominee a scare through most of the primary season—was pressured from the race by media attention focusing on his questionable personal life.[39] Six other frequently mentioned prospective Democratic candidates ultimately also demurred on possible nomination runs, even before any formal announcement of candidacy, setting the stage for a nomination contest in which those who did not run would have a greater impact on the race than those who actually did run.[40] The net effect of these withdrawals, both the ones that were candidate driven and the ones that were forced, was a substantially reduced field of announced Democratic contenders that consisted of a Governor (Michael Dukakis), a former Governor (Bruce Babbitt), a Congressman (Richard Gephardt), three Senators (Joseph Biden, Al Gore, and Paul Simon), and the Rev. Jesse Jackson. Not counting Gary Hart, because his withdrawal in May was not reversed until his later re-entry in December, this decimated field was aptly described as "the seven dwarfs."[41] Joseph Biden's withdrawal early in the fall, under media pressure just weeks after his formal announcement, decimated the field of possible Democratic contenders further still.[42]

The significant number of candidate withdrawals from the Democratic nomination race by candidates who had never formally announced their candidacy was notable not only because of the number of non-candidate withdrawals but also because this phenomenon was to be repeated in subsequent nomination races. As Table 4.2 indicates, these withdrawals by unannounced candidates not only involved a substantial group of at least nine candidates but took place over a two year period from December 1985 when Edward Kennedy withdrew through November 1987 when Charles Robb announced his decision not to run. In terms of the period of time prior to the New Hampshire primary in which these withdrawals occurred, they spanned a time frame ranging from 789 days in the case of Edward Kennedy to just 97 days in the case of Charles Robb. Unannounced candidates withdrawing from the nomination process in the 1988 Democratic nomination contest did so on average a total of 312 days prior to the New Hampshire primary, an indication of just how long the pre-candidacy and early candidacy phases were even in the 1988 presidential election cycle.

The original candidate field of announced contenders for the Democratic nomination in 1988 actually included a total of eight candidates. As Table 4.3 details, all eight of these contenders made their formal announcement during 1987, the year immediately preceding the presidential election year. These for-

TABLE 4.2
**Analysis of Candidates Withdrawing Before Formal Announcement
and Other Potential Candidates
1988 Presidential Election Cycle
Democrats**

Candidate	Date of Withdrawal	Days (Before) After New Hampshire Primary
Edward Kennedy	December 19, 1985	(789)
Mario Cuomo	February 19, 1987	(362)
Sam Nunn	February 20, 1987	(361)
Dale Bumpers	March 20, 1987	(333)
Bill Clinton	July 14, 1987	(217)
Bill Bradley	August 2, 1987 (approx.)	(198)
Patricia Schroeder	September 28, 1987	(141)
John Glenn	—	—
Charles Robb	November 11, 1987	(97)
	Average Number of Days (Before) After New Hampshire Primary:	(312)

Source: Dates of withdrawal compiled from news reports in *The New York Times* and *The Washington Post.*

mal announcements actually occurred throughout the pre-election year, beginning with Richard Gephardt in February 1987 and continuing through the Rev. Jesse Jackson in October 1987. Relative to the New Hampshire primary, the opening primary of the nomination process, these formal announcements of candidacy ranged from the earliest announcement which fell 358 days prior to New Hampshire to the last public announcement which fell just 129 days prior to New Hampshire. Thus the development of the Democratic field of contenders for the 1988 nomination was concentrated in the immediately preceding year, 1987, with the average date of public announcement of candidacy coming 274 days prior to the New Hampshire primary. Dating candidacy from the date of a candidate's initial FEC filing of organization or candidacy, the starting dates were even earlier although likewise all in 1987, ranging from January 1987 which was 405 days prior to the New Hampshire primary to September 1987 which was just 147 days prior to the New Hampshire primary. In terms of their average date of initial FEC filing of organization or candidacy, the 1988 Democratic field began to take shape even earlier in the pre-campaign period than the dates of public announcement suggest, with the average date of initial FEC filing coming 312 days prior to the New Hampshire primary. While the formal nomination process from the first caucus through the last primary in 1988 extended for four and a half months or about 128 days, 1988's all-important early campaign period extended for most of 1987, including individual candidates' early campaigns that on average extended for 312 days.

TABLE 4.3

Analysis of Candidate Field by Date of Public Announcement of Candidacy and Initial FEC Filing
1988 Presidential Election Cycle
Democrats

Candidate	Date of Public Announcement of Candidacy	Days (Before) New Hampshire Primary	Date of Initial FEC Filing of Organization or Candidacy	Days (Before) New Hampshire Primary
Richard Gephardt	February 23, 1987	(358)	February 24, 1987	(357)
Bruce Babbitt	March 10, 1987	(343)	January 7, 1987	(405)
Gary Hart	April 13, 1987	(309)	April 15, 1987	(307)
Michael Dukakis	April 29, 1987	(293)	March 25, 1987	(328)
Paul Simon	May 18, 1987	(273)	April 16, 1987	(306)
Joseph Biden	June 9, 1987	(252)	March 3, 1987	(350)
Al Gore	June 29, 1987	(232)	April 27, 1987	(295)
Rev. Jesse Jackson	October 10, 1987	(129)	September 22, 1987	(147)
Average Number of Days Before New Hampshire Primary:		(274)		(312)

Sources: Dates of public announcement of candidacy compiled from news reports in *The New York Times* and *The Washington Post.* Dates of initial FEC filing of organization or candidacy compiled from Federal Election Commission, Statements of Organization, FEC Form 1, or Statements of Candidacy, FEC Form 2, filed by candidates.

The formal nomination process for the Democrats in 1988 began with the Iowa caucuses on February 8 and the New Hampshire primary on February 16, taking the process of winnowing the candidate field to a new level of intensity and finality.[43] While the results of the Iowa caucuses did not bring any immediate changes to the Democratic candidate field, the New Hampshire primary a week later began the actual thinning of the field of announced Democratic contenders, with Bruce Babbitt being the first to go on February 18.[44] Additional Democratic candidates withdrew every couple of weeks for the remainder of the formal nomination calendar, with Super Tuesday's results on March 8 driving Gary Hart from the race for the second time,[45] and with Gephardt, Gore, and Simon all withdrawing by the end of April. Aside from the ultimate nominee, Michael Dukakis, only Jesse Jackson persevered through the entire formal nominating period,[46] holding his withdrawal announcement until July 19, 1988, probably in large part in an effort to exercise greater leverage at the national convention.[47] As Table 4.4 presents, the length of individual Democratic candidates' formal nomination campaigns measured by the number of days after the New Hampshire primary that they remained as candidates ranged from Babbitt's campaign which was aborted just two days after New Hampshire all of the way to Jackson's marathon candidacy which persisted for 154 days after New Hampshire. In sharp contrast to the lengthy period between these Democratic contenders' formal announcements of candidacy and the New Hampshire primary, which on average was 274

TABLE 4.4
Analysis of Candidate Field by Date of Withdrawal from Race
1988 Presidential Election Cycle
Democrats

Candidate	Date of Withdrawal	Days (Before) After New Hampshire Primary
Joseph Biden	September 24, 1987 (approx)	(145)[a]
Bruce Babbitt	February 18, 1988	2
Gary Hart	May 8, 1987	
	March 11, 1988	24
Richard Gephardt	March 28, 1988	41
Paul Simon	April 7, 1988	51
Al Gore	April 21, 1988	65
Rev. Jesse Jackson	July 19, 1988	154
Michael Dukakis	—	—
	Average Number of Days (Before) After New Hampshire Primary:	56

Source: Dates of withdrawal compiled from news reports in *The New York Times* and *The Washington Post.*
[a] *Note:* Joseph Biden's unannounced candidacy is excluded from this calculation because it is the only pre-New Hampshire primary withdrawal and was 145 days prior to the New Hampshire primary.

days, the average period of time during which the Democratic contenders continued their campaigns after New Hampshire was just 56 days.

The results of the early Democratic caucus and primary schedule were strikingly clear, as Table 4.5 summarizes. The Iowa caucuses on February 8 gave Richard Gephardt first place with 31 percent followed by Paul Simon with 27 percent and Michael Dukakis with 22 percent.[48] The rest of the candidate field trailed far behind, beginning with Jackson at 9 percent and going all of the way to Al Gore and Gary Hart with just 0.5 percent each. The New Hampshire primary a week later on February 16 likewise was clear in its results, with the same three candidates leading the field, although in reshuffled order, namely Dukakis in first place at 36 percent, Gephardt coming in second at 20 percent, and Simon running third at 17 percent. Four other candidates divided the balance of the vote in these early contests, continuing their campaigns for anywhere from a couple more weeks all of the way through mid-summer.[49] Using this study's definition of candidate viability, which regards as viable for continuing primary competition any candidate who receives 10 percent of the vote in both the Iowa caucuses and the New Hampshire primary or, alternatively, 20 percent of the vote in either of these early contests, the opening phase of the nomination process produced three viable Democratic contenders, namely Dukakis, Gephardt, and Simon. Thus, while the pre-candidacy and early candidacy phases of the early campaign over the course of more than two years reduced the Democratic field from an original total of 17 or more candidates to the seven contenders at the start of the formal nomination process, the opening week of this formal process in effect identified fewer than half of this field as viable candidates. This permitted the remain-

TABLE 4.5
Candidate Vote Totals in the Two Opening Nomination Contests
1988 Presidential Election Cycle
Democrats

Candidates	Iowa	New Hampshire
Bruce Babbitt	6%	5%
Michael Dukakis	22%	36%
Richard Gephardt	31%	20%
Al Gore	.5%	7%
Gary Hart	.5%	4%
Rev. Jesse Jackson	9%	8%
Paul Simon	27%	17%
Uncommitted and Other	4%	3%

Sources: E. J. Dionne, Jr., "Dole Wins in Iowa, With Robertson Next," *The New York Times*, 9 February 1988, p. 1.; and E. J. Dionne, Jr., "Bush Overcomes Dole's Bid and Dukakis Is Easy Winner in New Hampshire Primaries," *The New York Times*, 17 February 1988, p. 1.

der of the formal process to focus on these three candidates as well as one other—Jackson—whose candidacy was to pick up steam late in the process and end up continuing almost to the very end.

The early nomination process to select the Democrats' 1988 presidential nominee certainly was a competitive and dynamic race but clearly also was a year in which significant new developments and future trends came to the fore. The extent of the Democrats' 1988 candidate field, both in terms of unannounced candidates who declined to be contenders and announced candidates who pursued active campaigns, eclipses most of the nomination campaigns of the post-reform era. Even more striking, the length of the early Democratic campaign, extending virtually for the entire pre-presidential election year and for some candidates for the year before as well, also was impressive. Making this nomination contest both exciting and memorable, moreover, was the unusual volatility of the candidate field, including the significant impact of candidates deciding not to enter the race or withdrawing once in it. Especially memorable, of course, were the sensational aspects of the campaign, including Gary Hart's withdrawal in the face of personal scandal and then his dramatic re-entry for what proved to be a futile second bid for support, and Joseph Biden's sudden withdrawal in the face of accusations of plagiarism. The 1988 Democratic campaign also was a year of firsts, with Jackson's candidacy representing both the first time a religiously affiliated candidate mounted a serious campaign for the Democratic nomination and, even more significantly, the first time a truly competitive African American candidate sought a major party's presidential nomination.[50] Most notably, however, the 1988 Democratic presidential nomination process was a campaign in which what happened in the early campaign—early withdrawals, early announcements, an ongoing winnowing process, and the gradual emergence of a front-runner—was extraordinarily significant in defining the field of candidates and the range of viable candidate choices for the far briefer formal presidential nomination process which was to follow.

The 1988 Republican Early Nomination Campaign

The Republican presidential nomination process in 1988 to an amazing degree reflected many of the same developments and trends that characterized the Democratic campaign. As Table 4.6 presents, at least seven Republicans considered candidacies during the year before the nominating process began but then decided not to run. Among those declining to seek the 1988 Republican nomination were such prominent Republicans as Howard Baker, Jeane Kirkpatrick, and Paul Laxalt. But in general the list of Republican non-candidates was unimpressive at best, including generally lesser known individuals such as William

TABLE 4.6
Comparison of Withdrawing Vs. Remaining Candidates
Prior to Start of Formal Nomination Process
1988 Presidential Election Cycle
Republicans

Candidates Withdrawing Before Formal Announcement and Other Potential Candidates	Announced Candidates Withdrawing Prior to December 31, 1987	Candidates Remaining Through January 1988
William Armstrong		George H. Bush
Howard Baker		Robert Dole
Patrick Buchanan		Pierre du Pont
Jeane Kirkpatrick		Alexander Haig
Paul Laxalt		Jack Kemp
Donald Rumsfeld		Pat Robertson
James Thompson		

Armstrong, Patrick Buchanan, and James Thompson. More than any single factor, of course, the influence hanging over the pre-candidacy phase of the campaign when potential candidates either demurred on a possible nomination race or announced their candidacy was the presence of an incumbent Vice President in the Republican race, namely George H. Bush.[51] While Ronald Reagan at first was tentative in his support for his Vice President, as the pre-election year progressed the still popular sitting President's support for his Vice President moved from tepid to genuinely enthusiastic.[52] The number of early withdrawals by still unannounced prospective candidates surely was in part a result of President Reagan's clear and enthusiastic support for Bush as the heir to his political legacy.

As was the case on the Democratic side of the 1988 nomination contest, the number of candidate withdrawals from the Republican nomination race by candidates who had never formally launched their candidacies was significant both in terms of the number of such potential candidate withdrawals and the possible new pattern in the development of presidential candidate fields that it represented. As Table 4.7 details, these withdrawals by unannounced candidates mostly occurred in the early part of the pre-election year, with three of the four withdrawals—namely Howard Baker, Patrick Buchanan, and Donald Rumsfeld—occurring between January and April 1987. In terms of the period of time prior to the New Hampshire primary in which these withdrawals occurred, they spanned a time frame ranging from 392 days in the case of Patrick Buchanan who withdrew in January 1987 to 174 days in the case of Paul Laxalt who withdrew in August 1987, still five months before the first voting. The other withdrawals, moreover, were by candidates whose pre-candidacy activity was so ambiguous that their withdrawals were not marked

TABLE 4.7
Analysis of Candidates Withdrawing Before Formal Announcement
and Other Potential Candidates
1988 Presidential Election Cycle
Republicans

Candidate	Date of Withdrawal	Days (Before) After New Hampshire Primary
Patrick Buchanan	January 20, 1987	(392)
Howard Baker	February 27, 1987	(354)
Donald Rumsfeld	April 2, 1987	(320)
Paul Laxalt	August 26, 1987	(174)
William Armstrong	—	—
Jeane Kirkpatrick	—	—
James Thompson	—	—
Average Number of Days (Before) After New Hampshire Primary:		(310)

Source: Dates of withdrawal compiled from news reports in *The New York Times* and *The Washington Post*.

by any public announcement, namely William Armstrong, Jeane Kirkpatrick, and James Thompson. Only one of the early non-candidate withdrawals, Paul Laxalt, persisted with pre-campaign activity until midway through the pre-election year, finally withdrawing in August 1987 when it was clear that both his failed fund-raising and his languishing position in public opinion polls made him an unrealistic contender. Unannounced candidates who withdrew from the nomination process for the 1988 Republican nomination with a specific public statement did so on average a total of 310 days prior to the New Hampshire primary, a time frame almost exactly the same as was the case on the Democratic side and again a period in advance of the start of the formal nomination process that is indicative of the length of the pre-candidacy and early candidacy phases in the 1988 presidential election cycle.

The candidate field of announced contenders for the Republican nomination in 1988 began with six contenders, an amazing candidate field for a race in which an incumbent Vice President who served under a very popular sitting President was seeking his party's nomination. As Table 4.8 presents, the first of these contenders to formally enter the race was Pierre du Pont who made a public announcement of candidacy in September 1986—518 days before the New Hampshire primary—and actually made an even earlier formal statement of candidacy with an FEC filing in June 1986—a record-setting 623 days before the New Hampshire primary. The other five contenders for the 1988 Republican presidential nomination all made the formal announcement of their candidacy during 1987, the pre-election year. These other formal announcements actually were spaced throughout the pre-election year, with du

TABLE 4.8

Analysis of Candidate Field by Date of Public Announcement of Candidacy and Initial FEC Filing
1988 Presidential Election Cycle
Republicans

Candidate	Date of Public Announcement of Candidacy	Days (Before) New Hampshire Primary	Date of Initial FEC Filing of Organization or Candidacy	Days (Before) New Hampshire Primary
Pierre du Pont	September 16, 1986	(518)	June 3, 1986	(623)[a]
Alexander Haig	March 24, 1987	(329)	April 2, 1987	(320)
Jack Kemp	April 6, 1987	(316)	April 6, 1987	(316)
Pat Robertson	October 1, 1987	(138)	October 15, 1987	(124)
George H. Bush	October 12, 1987	(127)	February 19, 1987	(362)
Robert Dole	November 9, 1987	(99)	March 3, 1987	(350)
Average Number of Days Before New Hampshire Primary:		(255)		(349) (including du Pont)
				(294) (excluding du Pont)

Sources: Dates of public announcement of candidacy compiled from news reports in *The New York Times* and *The Washington Post*. Dates of initial FEC filing of organization or candidacy compiled from Federal Election Commission, Statements of Organization, FEC Form 1, or Statements of Candidacy, FEC Form 2, filed by candidates.

[a] *Note*: The Statement of Candidacy for Pete du Pont filed on June 3, 1986, was actually in the 1986 election cycle and therefore it may not be appropriate to count the ensuing 20-month interval as being related to the subsequent 1988 presidential election cycle.

Pont's very early announcement being followed by Alexander Haig in March 1987, Jack Kemp in April 1987, and Pat Robertson and George H. Bush in October 1987. Bob Dole, who ultimately would prove to be the strongest challenger to Bush, formally announced his candidacy in November 1987, the last candidate to join the Republican field. Relative to the New Hampshire primary on February 16, 1988, these formal announcements of candidacy ranged from the earliest announcement which fell 518 days prior to New Hampshire to the last public announcement by Dole which fell just 99 days prior to New Hampshire. In short, the development of the Republican candidate field of contenders for the 1988 nomination took shape only gradually during the pre-election year, with candidates not only taking themselves out of consideration but also formally joining the race throughout 1987, and with the average date of public announcement of candidacy coming 255 days prior to the New Hampshire primary. Dating candidacy from the date of the candidate's initial FEC filing of organization or candidacy, the starting date was even earlier, ranging from June 1986 which was 623 days prior to the New Hampshire primary to October 1987 which was just 124 days prior to the New Hampshire primary. In terms of their average date of initial FEC filing of organization or candidacy, the 1988 Republican field began to take shape even earlier in the pre-campaign period than the dates of public announcement suggest, with the average date of initial FEC filing coming 349 days prior to the New Hampshire primary if du Pont's 1986 filing is included and 294 days prior to the New Hampshire primary when du Pont's unusually early 1986 election cycle activity is excluded. Compared to the formal nomination process from the first caucus through the last primary in 1988 which spanned four-and-a-half months or about 128 days,[53] the Republican early campaign period preceding the 1988 nomination process extended for all of 1987 and for some candidates even part of 1986, a period including the individual candidates' early campaigns that began from 623 days to just 124 days prior to New Hampshire, a lengthy early pre-nomination campaign.

The formal nomination process for the Republicans in 1988 generally mirrored the Democratic contest and like the Democrats began with the Iowa caucuses and the New Hampshire primary. The formal process, as was the case on the Democratic side, took the process of winnowing the candidate field even further than the pre-campaign process had done, doing so with the finality that only actual voting can achieve. Beginning with the Iowa caucuses on February 8, 1988, the Republican field began to thin, with Haig dropping out of the race just four days later, even before the New Hampshire primary. And the New Hampshire voting on February 16, 1988, led to the withdrawal of du Pont, the second Republican to leave the race due to a poor early showing with the voters. Additional Republican candidates withdrew only gradually as the formal nomination calendar progressed, with Super Tuesday on March 8 prompting Kemp to withdraw two days later. Dole—the only Republican contender to actually threaten Bush's early front-runner status with victories in three of the four opening contests, namely Iowa, South Dakota, and Minnesota—finally withdrew on March 29. The final hold-out among the field of Republicans challenging Bush was Robertson who ultimately announced the abandonment of his campaign on April 6. As Table 4.9 summarizes, the length of individual Republican candidates' formal nomination campaigns measured by the number of days after the New Hampshire primary that they remained as candidates ranged from Haig's campaign which was aborted four days before the New Hampshire primary and du Pont who withdrew just two days after, to Robertson's candidacy which outlasted the other contenders by persisting for 50 days after New Hampshire. As was the case with the Democratic field, there was a sharp contrast between the lengthy period that elapsed from these Republican contenders' formal announcements of candidacy to the New Hampshire primary, which averaged 255 days, and the average period of time during which the Republican contenders continued their campaigns after New Hampshire, which was just 23 days. This relative brevity of the formal 1988 Republican nomination campaigns on average also stands in marked contrast with the formal 1988 Democratic nomination campaigns on average, namely 23 days for the Republicans versus 56 days for the Democrats, perhaps not a surprising difference in view of the presence of an incumbent Vice President in the Republican field.

The results of the early Republican caucus and primary schedule included more surprises than were evident initially on the Democratic side, although

TABLE 4.9
Analysis of Candidate Field by Date of Withdrawal from Race
1988 Presidential Election Cycle
Republicans

Candidate	Date of Withdrawal	Days (Before) After New Hampshire Primary
Pat Robertson	April 6, 1988	50
Robert Dole	March 29, 1988	42
Jack Kemp	March 10, 1988	23
Pierre du Pont	February 18, 1988	2
Alexander Haig	February 12, 1988	(4)
George H. Bush	—	—
Average Number of Days (Before) After New Hampshire Primary:		23

Source: Dates of withdrawal compiled from news reports in *The New York Times* and *The Washington Post.*

the overall Republican campaign ultimately turned out much more one-sided in the ultimate victor's favor than was the case with the Democratic race. As Table 4.10 summarizes, the Iowa caucuses on February 8 were quite an upset, with Bush's total of 19 percent representing a third place finish behind Dole who had 37 percent and, to Bush's dismay, Robertson who had 25 percent.[54] Yet by the New Hampshire primary a week later, Bush re-established his front-runner position, coming in first with a convincing 38 percent, followed by Dole with 29 percent. Three other candidates divided the rest of the New Hampshire vote, including Kemp with 13 percent, du Pont with 10 percent, and Robertson with 9 percent.[55] Using once again this study's definition of candidate viability, which regards as viable for continuing competition any candidate who receives 10 percent of the vote in both the Iowa caucuses and the New Hampshire primary or, alternatively, 20 percent of the vote in either of these early contests, the opening phase of the 1988 nomination process can be regarded as having produced four viable Republican contenders, namely Bush, Dole, Kemp, and Robertson. Thus, reflecting a pattern similar to the one on the Democratic side, while the pre-candidacy and early candidacy phases over the course of more than two years reduced the Republican field from an original total of thirteen or more candidates to the six contenders at the start of the formal nomination process, the opening week of the formal process in effect identified four of the six candidates in this field as viable candidates and made the withdrawal of the other two candidates in the ensuing early weeks of the nomination process all but inevitable.

In sum, the early nomination process to select the Republican presidential nominee in 1988 certainly was comparable to the Democratic process in the vigor and competitiveness of its early campaign. But once the formal nomination

TABLE 4.10
Candidate Vote Totals in the Two Opening Nomination Contests
1988 Presidential Election Cycle
Republicans

Candidates	Iowa	New Hampshire
George H. Bush	19%	38%
Robert Dole	37%	29%
Pierre du Pont	7%	10%
Alexander Haig	0%	0%
Jack Kemp	11%	13%
Pat Robertson	25%	9%
Other	1%	1%

Sources: E. J. Dionne, Jr. "Dole Wins in Iowa, With Robertson Next," *The New York Times*, 9 February 1988, p. 1.; and E. J. Dionne, Jr., "Bush Overcomes Dole's Bid and Dukakis Is Easy Winner in New Hampshire Primaries," *The New York Times*, 17 February 1988, p. 1.

process began, and especially after the opening few primaries and caucuses, the one-sidedness and predictability of the Republican race bore little resemblance to the vigorous Democratic contest. As was the case on the Democratic side, the Republicans' 1988 candidate field was broad and active, including at least seven potential candidates who ultimately decided not to run and six candidates who pursued active campaigns, a Republican candidate field that like the Democratic candidate field eclipsed most of the nomination campaigns of the post-reform era. Also like the Democratic nomination campaign, the length of the early Republican campaign was exceptional, extending virtually for the entire pre-presidential election year and for some candidates for the year before as well. While George H. Bush as the recognized front-runner and Bob Dole as his main challenger did not publicly announce their candidacies until October and November 1987 respectively, the rest of the candidate field was far earlier in their timing, beginning with Pierre du Pont in September 1986, Alexander Haig in March 1987, and Jack Kemp in April 1987, followed later by Pat Robertson in October 1987. A first that occurred on the Democratic side in 1988 was the candidacy of the Rev. Jesse Jackson who was matched on the Republican side with the presence of another religiously affiliated candidate, the Rev. Pat Robertson. Combining religion, television, and politics, Robertson mounted a very effective candidacy built on the foundation of his television ministry, utilizing the Christian Broadcasting Network (CBN), his CBN—based fund-raising organization called the "700 Club," a non-profit foundation called the Freedom Council, and his strength among Christian conservatives.[56] The 1988 Republican nomination contest certainly stood apart from the Democratic contest because of incumbent Republican Vice President George H. Bush's dominant position from beginning to end, but even moreso because the Republican contest unfolded under the shadow of President Reagan who still was very popular even as his second term approached its close.

In the final analysis, however, the Republican nomination contest in 1988, unlike the Democratic race, was more about continuity than firsts, with the incumbent Vice President not only taking the traditional front-runner position but even more importantly with the campaign being centered around continuing the Reagan legacy. As was the case with the 1988 Democratic nomination process, the key period in the 1988 Republican nomination process was the early campaign, namely the early withdrawals, the early announcements, and the winnowing process to define the field of candidates who would compete in the ensuing formal nomination process. It was during this early campaign that Bush as the early front-runner established the foundation that permitted him to withstand the vigorous challenge which Dole mounted in the early part of the formal process, beating Bush not only in the opening contest in Iowa but in the South Dakota primary and the Minnesota caucuses two weeks later as well. Bush's emergence as the inevitable nominee, while at least partly due to his victory in New Hampshire the week in between, also was due in large part to the strong foundation his campaign had built during the long early campaign that for Republicans and Democrats alike proved to be the decisive phase of the 1988 presidential nomination process.

The 2000 Early Nomination Campaign

Election year 2000's early nomination campaign offers another excellent case study that provides a second set of early nomination races to complement the 1988 early nomination races in this study of campaign fund-raising and media coverage of campaign fund-raising as factors in presidential nominee selection. This presidential election once again illustrated the ever increasing length of presidential campaigns as potential candidates explore possible candidacies, new candidates seek to launch their campaigns, and even established candidates and front-runners endeavor to ward off challengers and achieve the aura of invincibility.[57] The new reality of lengthened presidential campaigns was a hallmark of the 2000 campaign, and inextricably linked with this lengthened campaign was the further reality of continually greater front-loading of the caucus and primary schedule which in turn made a successful early campaign increasingly critical.[58] The 2000 election's early campaign had a momentous impact on the outcome of that year's presidential selection process, and may well have been more important than the early campaign of any previous presidential nomination campaign of the post-reform era. During the 2000 election's early nomination campaign a notable number of potential candidates declined running, a record overall field of candidates ultimately announced presidential nomination bids, and most interesting of all, an unprecedented number of candidates actually withdrew from contention before the formal nomination process even began.[59] Most important of all, moreover, this 2000 election's early nomination campaign included a "money primary" that may well have had the greatest impact on the overall candidate field and ultimate candidate survival, viability, and success of any presidential nomination campaign of the post-reform era.[60]

Making election year 2000's early nomination campaign especially useful as a case study is that it marked a watershed in the erosion of the presidential nomination reforms, especially with respect to campaign finance reform.[61] By 2000 more than two-and-a-half decades and six presidential elections had elapsed since the enactment of campaign finance reform, and the intervening years had afforded candidates ample time to devise and refine strategies for evading the reforms to the point where their original intent had lost any real meaning or significance. Perhaps most widespread and effective as a device for evading the federal campaign finance system was the use of "leadership PACs" as well as other special and unregulated organizational entities as vehicles for pre-candidacy fund-raising and spending, a tactic originally utilized by Ronald Reagan after his 1976 nomination defeat and then copied by other candidates in 1984 and especially 1988.[62] The 2000 presidential nomination process stands as a high water mark in the proliferation of pre-candidacy or leadership PACs as the preferred means for funding and conducting presidential pre-candidacy campaigns, with this organizational device that was employed by many of the candidates in 1988 being utilized almost across the entire pre-candidate field by 2000,[63] the exceptions being candidates who utilized gubernatorial campaign committees or other state-based political action committees.[64]

The 2000 presidential nomination campaign also stands apart in the extent to which foundations, other not-for-profit organizations and what are called "section 527 committees" were utilized as vehicles for pre-candidacy campaign activity.[65] The net impact of such rampant use of organizational entities that are beyond the campaign finance reform framework and hence FEC regulation was the same: to evade campaign spending limits, and in some cases even contribution limits, and to permit candidates to begin building their fund-raising and organizational base earlier and earlier in the presidential election cycle.[66] Distinguishing the 2000 nomination campaign further still is an entirely new development of that year, namely the complete contravention of campaign finance limitations either by not accepting federal matching funds, as was George W. Bush's tactic, or by complete self-funding, as Steve Forbes was able to do.[67] All in all, in short, the 2000 nomination process surely set new records all around for candidates undermining and evading campaign finance regulations, for the first time rendering the post-reform contribution and spending limits nearly null and void at the pre-candidacy and early candidacy phases of the presidential nomination process.[68]

A dimension of the 2000 nomination contest that also was evident in the 1988 contest was the record-breaking candidate field. Both major political parties had large early candidate fields in 2000, including numerous potential candidates who considered running but then took themselves out of the race before a formal announcement, and a broad field of announced contenders for each party nomination, with the candidate field on the Republican side being truly extraordinary. While the Democratic race ended up with just two announced candidates vying in the actual primary and caucus process, a field of five other strong candidates had considered candidacies in the early campaign but then withdrew before any formal announcement. The Republican race drew a record-setting array of candidates numbering sixteen or more, including at least five who explored candidacies but then withdrew before a formal announcement and—in a remarkable new pattern—a record five other candidates who actually announced their candidacies but then withdrew even before the start of the formal nomination process. In short, like 1988, the 2000 nomination campaign set new records for the size of the candidate field as well as for the volatility of this field during both the pre-candidacy and early candidacy phases of the nomination campaign. But unlike 1988 during which the large number of candidate withdrawals were at the pre-candidacy phase, before any formal announcement of candidacy, 2000 brought the significant new pattern of early candidate withdrawals not only among unannounced candidates but among announced candidates as well—a development that may well prove to be yet another step in the ever increasing importance of the early campaign for candidate survival and viability.[69]

The 2000 Democratic Early Nomination Campaign

The nomination campaign on the Democratic side in 2000 began at its earliest phase in 1998 and 1999 with a strong group of contenders but very quickly thinned to a race between just two announced candidates—Al Gore, the incumbent Vice President, and former Senator Bill Bradley. As Table 4.11 indicates, at least five Democrats had considered running for President during the year or two before the nomination process but then decided not to run, including significant Democratic Party leaders such as Richard Gephardt, Bob Kerrey, John Kerry, the Rev. Jesse Jackson who had demonstrated such surprising strength in his previous 1988 campaign, and long-shot Paul Wellstone.[70] Perhaps not a complete surprise in a nomination race with an incumbent Vice President seeking the presidential nomination, all of these early possible candidates declined to launch formal campaigns, withdrawing even before making

TABLE 4.11
Comparison of Withdrawing Vs. Remaining Candidates
Prior to Start of Formal Nomination Process
2000 Presidential Election Cycle
Democrats

Candidates Withdrawing Before Formal Announcement and Other Potential Candidates	*Announced Candidates Withdrawing Prior to December 31, 1999*	*Candidates Remaining Through January 2000*
Richard Gephardt		Bill Bradley
Rev. Jesse Jackson		Al Gore
Bob Kerrey		
John Kerry		
Paul Wellstone		

a formal announcement of candidacy and leaving a candidate field of just two, Gore and Bradley, thereby making the 2000 Democratic nomination race a relatively rare one-on-one contest. This very early narrowing of the Democratic candidate field in the 2000 nomination contest stands in marked contrast to the 1988 Republican nomination contest, the last previous election in which an incumbent Vice President who served under a popular President was running for his party's nomination. While in 1988 the Republican field had five active challengers to incumbent Vice President Bush, the 2000 Democratic field of incumbent Vice President Gore and Bradley presented a striking difference indicative of the growing importance of the early campaign in prompting early candidate withdrawals and thereby narrowing the candidate field at earlier junctures in the campaign.[71] While Vice President Gore certainly was the long-standing favorite and front-runner for the Democratic nomination, Bradley's challenge proved to be surprisingly strong and for a brief period of the early campaign appeared to pose a genuine threat.[72] Yet in the end Gore not only prevailed but became the first major party nominee in decades to win literally every primary and caucus,[73] an amazing result in view of the strong challenge that Bradley had represented just weeks before.

The pattern of candidate withdrawals from the 2000 Democratic nomination race by candidates who had never formally announced their candidacy continued a trend that also was evident in both party contests in the 1988 election. As Table 4.12 summarizes, there were at least five candidates who withdrew from the 2000 Democratic race even before announcing their candidacy. Unlike 1988, however, when the candidate withdrawals were spaced over a long period extending from the early campaign into the pre-election year, in 2000 these withdrawals were concentrated in just a four month span during the early part of the pre-election year, and reduced the candidate field to just two contenders—the incumbent Vice President, Gore, and his lone challenger, Bradley. While a much wider Democratic candidate field had seemed likely as late as November 1998, the general political dynamic during the post-impeachment period included a resurgence in President Clinton's popularity which was reflected in the strong Democratic showing in the 1998 mid-term congressional elections.[74] This general dynamic worked in Gore's favor, with his standing likewise improving and with potential challengers becoming wary as a result. The fact that this resurgence in the incumbent administration's standing coincided with the new presidential election's early campaign undoubtably prompted most of the withdrawals, thereby winnowing the candidate field to just two candidates and certainly strengthening Bradley's candidacy as the only viable challenge to Gore's position as front-runner.

In terms of the period of time prior to the New Hampshire primary in which these potential candidate withdrawals occurred, they ranged from Bob

TABLE 4.12
Analysis of Candidates Withdrawing Before Formal
Announcement and Other Potential Candidates
2000 Presidential Election Cycle
Democrats

Candidate	Date of Withdrawal	Days (Before) After New Hampshire Primary
Bob Kerrey	December 13, 1998	(415)
Paul Wellstone	January 9, 1999	(388)
Richard Gephardt	February 3, 1999	(363)
John Kerry	February 26, 1999	(340)
Rev. Jesse Jackson	March 24, 1999	(314)
	Average Number of Days (Before) After New Hampshire Primary:	(364)

Source: Dates of withdrawal compiled from news reports in *The New York Times* and *The Washington Post.*

Kerrey who was the first to withdraw in December 1998, 415 days prior to New Hampshire, to the Rev. Jesse Jackson who was the last of the five early withdrawals, removing himself from contention in March 1999, a total of 314 days prior to New Hampshire. These unannounced candidates who withdrew early in the 2000 Democratic nomination process did so on average a total of 364 days prior to the New Hampshire primary, an average indicative of an even earlier early campaign in 2000 than in 1988 when the comparable average number of days prior to New Hampshire for early withdrawals by unannounced candidates was 312 days. This trend among potential presidential nomination candidates to remove themselves from possible candidacy at ever earlier junctures in the campaign is a significant new dimension to the increasing length of the presidential nomination process and is indicative of the shift to an ever earlier start to this campaign that now includes both precandidacy and early candidacy phases. Even more significantly, this trend is indicative of the increased importance of the early campaign in both winnowing the candidate field and structuring the choices available to voters in the overall presidential nomination process.

As Table 4.13 details, Gore and Bradley formally entered the 2000 nomination contest in mid-1999, well after the other potential candidates had withdrawn. Gore actually was the first to make a public announcement of candidacy, formally entering the race in June 1999, a total of 230 days before the New Hampshire primary, followed by Bradley in September 1999, a total of 146 days before the New Hampshire primary. As was also the case in 1988, therefore, the Democratic field of contenders for the 2000 nomination was finalized during the pre-election year, 1999, with the average date of public announcement of

TABLE 4.13

Analysis of Candidate Field by Date of Public Announcement of Candidacy and Initial FEC Filing 2000 Presidential Election Cycle

Democrats

Candidate	Date of Public Announcement of Candidacy	Days (Before) New Hampshire Primary	Date of Initial FEC Filing of Organization or Candidacy	Days (Before) New Hampshire Primary
Al Gore	June 16, 1999	(230)	January 1, 1999	(396)
Bill Bradley	September 8, 1999	(146)	December 4, 1998	(424)
Average Number of Days Before New Hampshire Primary:		(188)		(410)

Sources: Dates of public announcement of candidacy compiled from news reports in *The New York Times* and *The Washington Post.* Dates of initial FEC filing of organization or candidacy compiled from Federal Election Commission, Statements of Organization, FEC Form 1, or Statements of Candidacy, FEC Form 2, filed by candidates.

candidacy coming 188 days prior to the New Hampshire primary—timing that was notably later than the comparable average announcement date of 274 days prior to New Hampshire in 1988. But dating candidacy from the date of a candidate's initial FEC filing of organization or candidacy, the starting dates for the Gore and Bradley campaigns in 2000 were actually much earlier, namely January 1, 1999 for Gore and December 4, 1998 for Bradley. These much earlier official campaign starting dates were 396 days prior to New Hampshire in the case of Gore and 424 days prior to New Hampshire in the case of Bradley, with the average date of the initial FEC filing coming a record 410 days prior to New Hampshire—timing that likewise was much earlier than the comparable average FEC filing date of 312 days prior to New Hampshire in 1988. Thus the official pre-nomination campaign period for the two announced Democratic candidates in 2000 was over fourteen months long, significantly longer than the comparable period in 1988 and more than three times the length of the actual formal nomination period that would follow—lengthy pre-candidacy and early candidacy time periods that certainly reflect the growing length of the early campaign in the presidential nomination process.

Following the long early campaign in 2000 came the formal nomination process which also began early, with the Iowa caucuses on January 24 and the New Hampshire primary on February 1. Gore won decisively in Iowa, gaining 63 percent of the vote to Bradley's 35 percent,[75] and he also prevailed a week later in a closer contest in New Hampshire, winning 50 percent of the vote to Bradley's 46 percent.[76] Gore again won by decisive margins in the Delaware primary on February 5 where he received 57 percent of the vote to Bradley's 40 percent and in the Washington primary on February 29 where he received 68 percent of the vote to Bradley's 31 percent.[77] On March 7, Super Tuesday, Gore swept all eleven primaries, all by margins in the 10 percent range or greater. Having failed to win even a single caucus or primary, Bradley finally withdrew from the race on March 9.[78] As Table 4.14 summarizes, Bradley's withdrawal came thirty-seven days after the New Hampshire primary, a relatively short and unsuccessful formal nomination campaign that stands in sharp contrast to the lengthy and effective pre-candidacy and early candidacy campaign which Bradley conducted during the prior twelve month period.

Using this study's definition of viability, the categorization of candidates in the 2000 Democratic nomination campaign falls into two groupings at opposite ends of the candidacy viability continuum, with two candidates falling into the viable grouping and all of the rest being candidates who withdrew before a formal announcement of candidacy. Viable candidates in this study are those who received 10 percent of the vote in both the Iowa caucuses and the New Hampshire primary or, alternatively, 20 percent of the vote in either of these early contests. Because the Democratic nomination contest in 2000 had narrowed to

TABLE 4.14
Analysis of Candidate Field by Date of Withdrawal from Race
2000 Presidential Election Cycle
Democrats

Candidate	Date of Withdrawal	Days (Before) After New Hampshire Primary
Bill Bradley	March 9, 2000	37
Al Gore	—	—
	Average Number of Days (Before) After New Hampshire Primary:	37

Source: Dates of withdrawal compiled from news reports in *The New York Times* and *The Washington Post.*

become a two candidate race by the time the formal nomination process had begun, each candidate readily met the standard for viability under both alternatives, namely each exceeded the 10 percent threshold in both of the opening contests and each also exceeded the 20 percent threshold in at least one—and in fact both—of these opening contests. As Table 4.15 details, and as noted earlier, Gore captured 63 percent of the vote to Bradley's 35 percent in Iowa, an overwhelming opening victory for Gore. Preserving some hope for Bradley's candidacy, the New Hampshire primary proved to be much closer, with Gore receiving just 50 percent of the vote to Bradley's 46 percent. Even more than candidate viability, however, the results of these early nomination contests highlighted the fact that the 2000 Democratic nomination race had been a two candidate race since mid-1999 as a result of the early campaign that preceded the opening caucus and primary,[79] a reality that reflected the ever growing importance of the period before the formal nomination process opens.[80] While the result in New Hampshire confirmed both Gore and Bradley as viable candidates, Gore's narrow victory—especially coming after his overwhelming victory in Iowa the week before—spelled the beginning of the end for Bradley's challenge.[81]

TABLE 4.15
Candidate Vote Totals in the Two Opening Nomination Contests
2000 Presidential Election Cycle
Democrats

Candidates	Iowa	New Hampshire
Bill Bradley	35%	46%
Al Gore	63%	50%
Other	2%	4%

Sources: Richard Berke, "The 2000 Campaign: The Overview, Iowans Deliver Victory to Bush and Gore," *The New York Times,* 25 January 2000, p. 1.; Adam Clymer, "The 2000 Campaign: The Democrats; Tough Fight Ahead," *The New York Times,* 2 February 2000, p. 1; and William G. Mayer, "The Presidential Nominations," in *The Election of 2000,* ed. Gerald M. Pomper (New York: Chatham House Publishers, 2001), 31–32.

While the 2000 Democratic nomination process viewed a year or two in advance seemed on course to be a contentious and competitive race, in actuality it turned out to be a relatively straightforward and predictable campaign. Gore, as the sitting Vice President, obviously was the odds-on favorite, not only well in advance of the nomination process but throughout the early campaign and the formal nomination process as well. But at two junctures he faced credible threats to his front-runner standing, both early on when the candidate field was first developing and later in the pre-election year on the eve of the formal nomination process itself. The first crucial period came in late 1998 and early 1999 as potential candidates were confronting decisions about whether to join the candidate field for the 2000 Democratic nomination. The improved public standing which President Clinton enjoyed in the post-impeachment period and the Democrats' favorable showing in the 1998 mid-term elections combined to benefit Vice President Gore, significantly improving his prospects at this crucial early juncture when potential challengers were considering their own prospects. The result of this general political context, namely the withdrawal of several strong potential challengers, helped Gore significantly by averting the possibility of a fractious Democratic race but also helped Bradley by leaving him as the single remaining challenger. A second crucial period, namely the second half of the pre-election year campaign, proved to be an even greater challenge to Gore's front-runner status as Bradley's early campaign gained significant momentum and he began to outpace Gore in many of the indicators of early campaign strength such as fundraising, volunteer involvement, and organizational preparation. Gore also withstood this second challenge late in the pre-election year, confirming his front-runner status and his position as the inevitable nominee with his convincing wins early in the formal nomination period. But it is significant indeed that the truly critical junctures of the 2000 Democratic nomination race were during 1999, the pre-election year, as the candidate field narrowed to just a two candidate race and as the lone challenger's insurgent campaign crested and then ebbed. The Democrats' ensuing nomination process of primaries and caucuses in early 2000 thus ultimately served to confirm what the preceding early campaign during 1999 already had determined, namely that the incumbent Vice President and nomination front-runner, Al Gore, indeed would be the nominee of the Democrats in the 2000 presidential election.

The 2000 Republican Early Nomination Campaign

The Republican early nomination campaign in 2000, as was also the case twelve years earlier in 1988, reflected many of the trends and developments that characterized the Democratic early nomination campaign. Similar to the

Democratic early campaign in 2000, a wide field of potential Republican candidates pursued pre-candidacy activities and explored entering the formal nomination contest in 2000, with sixteen Republicans—almost three times the number of Democrats—taking at least this initial step toward seeking the nomination. Unlike the 2000 Democratic contest which ended up with just two announced candidates, however, the final candidate field for the Republican nomination included eleven announced candidates, suggesting that the formal caucus and primary process would be a fractious one. But as was also the case on the Democratic side, the Republicans' early campaign in 2000 was relentless in eliminating potential candidates as well as announced candidates, with the five early potential candidates who withdrew before making a public announcement of candidacy being joined by another five early announced candidate withdrawals.[82] Yet even with an early campaign that had this unprecedented level of activity, a broad field of six announced Republican candidates ultimately emerged as contenders by the time the formal nomination process approached.[83] Moreover, just as the Republican field of potential and announced candidates in 2000 was a record-breaking one, so too was the length and impact of the Republicans' early campaign, including both the pre-candidacy and early candidacy phases. Thus, as commentators on the 2000 presidential election generally agree, the number of potentially viable candidates who either explored or actually announced candidacies but then withdrew before even a single caucus or primary vote was cast was a striking feature of this historic election's early campaign.[84]

The structure of the 2000 Republican nomination contest also presented significant similarities as well as some important distinctions when compared with the Democratic contest of the same year. Like the Democratic nomination process, the Republican nomination process was highly front-loaded, continuing and in some respects even advancing the trend toward front-loading that started in the early 1980s and was so evident in 1988.[85] Yet distinguishing the Republican schedule from the Democratic schedule was the asymmetry that developed between the major parties' caucus and primary calendars beginning in 2000. While the front-loaded Democratic calendar had only four opening contests in January and early February, ending with the Washington caucuses on February 5 and not resuming until the Virginia primary on February 29, the Republican calendar continued all through the month of February, with primaries in Delaware on February 8, South Carolina on February 19, Arizona and Michigan on February 22, and finally Virginia and Washington on February 29.[86] This difference in the front-loaded calendars of the Democratic and Republican parties in 2000 was significant, making the early Democratic contests all the more important because an upset victory would give the winning candidate more time to capitalize on his newfound momentum, while on the Republican side candidates would have continuing opportunities to stay in the race and compete. For both Democrats and Republicans, however, the 2000 nomination process exhibited a continuing trend toward a very front-loaded schedule leading up to Super Tuesday on March 7 with its treasure trove of caucus and primary delegates, making the early campaign during 1999 and before more important than ever for Democratic and Republican candidates alike.[87] But the schedule of weekly Republican contests through the month of February, combined with the broad Republican candidate field, certainly made the early campaign—and early campaign activities such as fund-raising, volunteer recruitment, and organizational preparation—especially critical in determining the outcome of the 2000 Republican nomination process.

Money and its potential to have a decisive impact during the early campaign was evident in both major party nomination contests in 2000, especially in the early campaign for the Republican nomination. As destructive as PACs and other pre-candidacy organizational entities were to the FECA campaign finance reform framework in both major party early nomination races, two of the candidates in the Republican contest opted completely out of the campaign finance reform system in 2000, with Bush deciding to decline federal matching funds and Forbes choosing to self-fund his nomination campaign. As a result, these two Republican contenders were able to circumvent campaign spending limits that nonetheless would bind the rest of the Republican candidate field.[88] Bush's all-time record fund-raising success made him a towering presence in the early Republican candidate field, not only by lending enormous credibility to his candidacy but also by limiting other Republicans' fund-raising potential due to the sense of inevitability such fund-raising success created.[89] To be sure, the penultimate factor in the 2000 election's early nomination campaign on the Republican side may well have been money, with front-runner Bush's unparalleled fund-raising success in effect preventing many candidates from even getting started in the race for money, thereby driving a record number of potential and announced candidates from the race earlier than ever before in a nomination contest.[90]

The ascendancy which Bush enjoyed in the Republicans' early campaign in 2000, while certainly built on amazing fund-raising success and the plentiful flow of money it provided, also reflected political forces that were even more powerful. From its inception, Bush's early campaign enjoyed overwhelming support from the Republican Party's elite.[91] In the aftermath of the Republican Party's poor showing in the 1998 mid-term elections, Republican leaders nationally became convinced that their prospects for regaining the presidency in 2000 hinged upon unifying their party behind a candidate not identified with the Congressional party leadership, someone who had broad ideological appeal and who would provide new and unifying leadership.[92] Bush was singularly positioned to be the beneficiary of this powerful political force because of his record as a successful state Governor who embraced a future-oriented, consensus-based message, his broad appeal within his party as well as his reputation for inclusiveness, and perhaps most important the name recognition which he already enjoyed as the son of a former President.[93] Behind Bush's early ascendancy and even his astonishing fund-raising success during the early campaign, therefore, was an even more powerful force, namely the very real determination of the Republican Party's leadership to identify a unifying presidential nominee and through his candidacy to ensure a rapid resolution of the Republican nomination process.[94] From the inception of Bush's campaign, the full Republican Party establishment—elected officials, party leaders, professional fund-raisers, and major contributors—rallied behind his candidacy to a degree unprecedented in post-reform presidential politics. So overwhelming was this elite support, in fact, that some commentators even saw an echo of the past, namely a return to the pre-reform era when party leaders "attempted to identify a candidate who would unite the party and win the White House and helped him toward the nomination."[95] In short, Bush's fund-raising juggernaut certainly was the factor that more than anything propelled him from pre-candidacy and early candidacy to become the inevitable Republican presidential nominee. But the overwhelming support of Republican party leaders and elites, in the tradition of pre-reform presidential nomination politics, provided an invaluable national force that perhaps more than any single factor made this remarkable fund-raising success possible.

The field of potential and announced candidates for the Republican presidential nomination in 2000 was one of the largest of any post-reform era nomination campaign.[96] As Table 4.16 summarizes, a total of sixteen candidates either explored or actually undertook campaigns for the Republican nomination in 2000. As already noted, five of these candidates withdrew from the race even before they announced their candidacy, a pattern also evident on the Democratic side in 2000 in which five candidates also withdrew even before reaching the announcement of candidacy phase. But even more striking during the Republican early campaign was the number who actually announced their candidacies but then withdrew before the formal nomination process even began, a group including yet another five candidates. This group of candidates who announced their candidacies but then withdrew included Republican notables such as Lamar Alexander, Elizabeth Dole, and former Vice President Dan Quayle, making the inability of this group of announced candidates to survive even the early campaign all the more remarkable. Other announced candidates who withdrew during the pre-election year included Patrick Buchanan and Robert Smith, both of whom were regarded as long-

TABLE 4.16
Comparison of Withdrawing Vs. Remaining Candidates
Prior To Start of Formal Nomination Process
2000 Presidential Election Cycle
Republicans

Candidates Withdrawing Before Formal Announcement and Other Potential Candidates	Announced Candidates Withdrawing Prior to December 31, 1999	Candidates Remaining Through January 2000
John Ashcroft	Lamar Alexander	Gary Bauer
John Kasich	Patrick Buchanan	George W. Bush
Jack Kemp	Elizabeth Dole	Steve Forbes
Tommy Thompson	Dan Quayle	Orin Hatch
Pete Wilson	Robert Smith	(withdrew on 1/25/00)
		Alan Keyes
		John McCain

shot candidates. One by one, however, each of these announced candidates withdrew their candidacy, even though the first voting in Iowa and New Hampshire was still months away. The surviving candidate field in place in January 2000 as the early campaign gave way to the formal nomination process numbered six—a third of the original group of Republican presidential hopefuls just a year earlier.[97]

The pattern of candidate withdrawals from the 2000 Republican nomination race by candidates who had never formally announced their candidacies mirrored the pattern in the 2000 Democratic race. As Table 4.17 details, five unannounced potential candidates for the Republican nomination withdrew during the early campaign, and each of these withdrawals was during the early to mid-year part of the pre-election year. In terms of the period of time prior to the New Hampshire primary in which these potential candidate withdrawals occurred, they ranged from John Ashcroft who was the first to withdraw in January 1999, a total of 392 days prior to New Hampshire, to John Kasich who was the last of the unannounced candidates to demur, announcing his departure from the race in July 1999, just 202 days prior to New Hampshire. These unannounced potential candidates withdrawing early in the Republican nomination process did so on average a total of 389 days prior to the New Hampshire primary. While this average time frame for unannounced Republican candidate withdrawals, namely just over a year, is about the same as the comparable average for unannounced Democratic candidate withdrawals in 2000, comparison of these 2000 time frames with average time frames from the 1988 nomination campaign provides further indication of the advancing early campaign. Comparing the average date of withdrawal of unannounced Democratic candidates in 2000 with the comparable average in

TABLE 4.17
Analysis of Candidates Withdrawing Before Formal
Announcement and Other Potential Candidates
2000 Presidential Election Cycle
Republicans

Candidate	Date of Withdrawal	Days (Before) After New Hampshire Primary
John Ashcroft	January 5, 1999	(392)
Pete Wilson	February 22, 1999	(344)
Tommy Thompson	May 5, 1999	(272)
John Kasich	July 14, 1999	(202)
Jack Kemp		
	Average Number of Days (Before) After New Hampshire Primary:	(389)

Source: Dates of withdrawal compiled from news reports in *The New York Times* and *The Washington Post.*

1988 reveals that the average point of withdrawal shifted from 310 days prior to the New Hampshire primary in 1988 to 389 days prior to the New Hampshire primary in 2000. Thus, as was the case on the Democratic side in 2000, unannounced Republican candidates who withdrew from the nomination process did so on average about three months earlier in 2000 than in 1988, a shift that provides further indication of the developing early campaign and the advancing impact of its early winnowing effect on the presidential candidate field.[98]

The field of announced contenders for the Republican nomination in 2000 was very impressive indeed. In sharp contrast to the 2000 Democratic field, the 2000 Republican field originally included twelve announced candidates, with John Kasich being included even though he only announced an exploratory committee, an even broader array of Republican candidates than announced their candidacies in the 1988 race. As Table 4.18 summarizes, these candidates made their entrance into the presidential nomination race throughout the pre-election year. The first announced contender was Dan Quayle, who formed an exploratory committee on February 4, 1999, a total of 362 days before the New Hampshire primary, having made his initial FEC filing of organization or candidacy just seven days earlier. The Republican candidate field grew rapidly during the next few weeks, with two other candidates—John Kasich, who announced an exploratory committee, and Robert Smith—joining the race in February 1999, and four more candidates—Patrick Buchanan, Lamar Alexander, Elizabeth Dole, and Steve Forbes—announcing their candidacies in March 1999. Most of the remainder of the Republican candidate field announced their candidacies between April and June

TABLE 4.18

Analysis of Candidate Field by Date of Public Announcement of Candidacy and Initial FEC Filing

2000 Presidential Election Cycle

Republicans

Candidate	Date of Public Announcement of Candidacy	Days (Before) New Hampshire Primary	Date of Initial FEC Filing of Organization or Candidacy	Days (Before) New Hampshire Primary
Dan Quayle	February 4, 1999	(362)	January 28, 1999	(369)
John Kasich[a]	February 16, 1999 (exploratory committee)	(353)	February 1999	(365)
Robert Smith	February 18, 1999	(348)	January 4, 1999	(393)
Patrick Buchanan	March 2, 1999	(336)	March 1, 1999	(337)
Lamar Alexander	March 9, 1999	(329)	January 8, 1999	(389)
Elizabeth Dole	March 10, 1999 (exploratory committee)	(328)	March 10, 1999	(328)
Steve Forbes	March 16, 1999	(322)	March 16, 1999	(322)
Gary Bauer	April 22, 1999	(285)	February 3, 1999	(363)
George W. Bush	June 12, 1999	(234)	March 8, 1999	(330)
Orin Hatch	June 22, 1999	(224)	July 1, 1999	(215)
Alan Keyes	September 20, 1999	(134)	June 16, 1999	(230)
John McCain	September 27, 1999	(127)	December 30, 1998	(404)
Average Number of Days Before New Hampshire Primary:		(282)		(337)

Sources: Dates of public announcement of candidacy compiled from news reports in *The New York Times* and *The Washington Post.* Dates of initial FEC filing of organization or candidacy compiled from Federal Election Commission, Statements of Organization, FEC Form 1, or Statements of Candidacy, FEC Form 2, filed by candidates.

[a]John Kasich never made a formal announcement of candidacy; he announced an exploratory committee.

1999, although Alan Keyes held off his announcement until September 1999. Surprisingly, John McCain—who later emerged as Bush's strongest challenger—was the last to formally announce his candidacy, with his public announcement coming on September 27, 1999, just 127 days prior to the New Hampshire primary. But while McCain saved his official announcement until later in the pre-election year, he actually had made his initial FEC filing of organization or candidacy the previous year on December 30, 1998, a total of 404 days prior to the New Hampshire primary—making him the first Republican in the 2000 race to make this official filing.

The time frame during which the candidate field for the Republican nomination in 2000 came together continued the pattern evident in both parties in the 1988 election cycle as well as on the Democratic side in the 2000 election cycle, with the pre-election year being the general time period for candidates to publicly announce their candidacies. Yet also evident was the increasing prominence of the early campaign and the progressive shifting of candidate activity to ever earlier dates during the pre-election year and sometimes even before. As was the case in both major parties in 1988 as well as for the Democratic field in 2000, the field of publicly announced candidates for the Republican nomination came together gradually as the pre-election year of 1999 unfolded. The average date for the start of the 2000 Republican early candidacy period is particularly noteworthy in that it reflects a strong trend toward an earlier official start to early candidacy activity, a pattern also evident on the Democratic side in the 2000 election cycle. While the average date for public announcement of candidacy by Republican candidates in 1988 was 255 days prior to New Hampshire, by 2000 this average date had shifted to 282 days prior to New Hampshire, a shift to about a month earlier. Dating candidacy by the date of initial FEC filing, the average date for Republican candidates in 1988 was 294 days prior to New Hampshire (excluding du Pont who entered during the 1986 election cycle), and by 2000 this average date also had shifted to 337 days prior to New Hampshire, again a shift to about a month earlier. In short, for the 2000 Republican candidate field just as for the 2000 Democratic candidate field, there is a definite pattern toward an ever earlier start to the early candidacy phase, a trend indicative once again of the advance of the early campaign in early nomination politics.

The field of announced candidates for the 2000 Republican nomination that emerged from the early campaign numbered twelve, a group already narrowed from the original cohort of sixteen. Yet in an unprecedented development, this group was to be thinned further still in what may prove to be a new pattern in winnowing the pre-election year candidate field. As Table 4.19 summarizes, this field of announced candidates for the 2000 Republican nomination lost six of its twelve candidates before a single vote was cast in the

TABLE 4.19
Analysis of Candidate Field by Date of Withdrawal from Race
2000 Presidential Election Cycle
Republicans

Candidate	Date of Withdrawal	Days (Before) After New Hampshire Primary
Robert Smith	July 13, 1999	(203)
John Kasich[a]	July 14, 1999	(202)
Lamar Alexander	August 16, 1999	(168)
Dan Quayle	September 27, 1999	(127)
Elizabeth Dole	October 20, 1999	(104)
Patrick Buchanan	October 25, 1999 (to seek Reform Party nomination)	(99)
Orin Hatch	January 25, 2000	(7)
Gary Bauer	February 4, 2000	3
Steve Forbes	February 9, 2000	8
John McCain	March 9, 2000	37
Alan Keyes	July 25, 2000	175
George W. Bush	—	—
Average Number of Days (Before) After New Hampshire Primary:		(62)

Source: Dates of withdrawal compiled from news reports in *The New York Times* and *The Washington Post*.
[a]*Note:* John Kasich never made a formal announcement of candidacy; he announced an exploratory committee.

formal nomination process beginning in Iowa and New Hampshire.[99] This continued winnowing of the announced candidate field began with Robert Smith and John Kasich in July 1999, and continued with Lamar Alexander in August 1999, Dan Quayle in September 1999, and Elizabeth Dole and Patrick Buchanan (who actually withdrew to seek the Reform Party nomination) in October 1999. Making these early withdrawals even more remarkable was the fact that they included some significant Republican figures, names such as Alexander, Dole, and Quayle, each of whom was regarded as a potentially strong candidate in the early handicapping. Relative to the date of the New Hampshire primary, February 1, 2000, these early announced candidate withdrawals came an average of 62 days prior to the New Hampshire primary. This new pattern of withdrawals by announced candidates during the pre-election year represented a significant change in how the candidate field generally develops during the pre-election year. Almost without exception, moreover, these withdrawing candidates cited a lack of money as the single factor forcing them from the race, an acknowledgment made all the more striking by how early in the campaign they reached this conclusion.[100] In stark contrast to the withdrawals from the field of announced Republican candidates in 2000 which came an average of 62 days prior to New Hampshire, the 1988 announced candidate withdrawals on the Democratic side came an average of 56 days after New Hampshire and on the Republican side came an average of 23 days after New Hampshire. In the 2000 Democratic contest, just one candidate—Bill Bradley—reached the stage of publicly announcing his candidacy to formally challenge Vice President Gore, and his withdrawal after failing to win even a single caucus or primary came 37 days after the New Hampshire primary. The record-setting candidate field in the 2000 Republican nomination contest therefore emerged from the pre-election year of 1999 reduced by half as a result of a significant number of early pre-nomination campaign withdrawals. This unprecedented winnowing of even established party names so far in advance of the start of the formal nomination process marked yet another milestone in the advance of the early campaign in the pre-election year nomination process.

As the formal nomination process opened in January and February 2000, a field of six remaining candidates continued their pursuit of the Republican presidential nomination.[101] While George W. Bush maintained and even strengthened his standing as the overwhelming front-runner, John McCain emerged as a serious challenger.[102] In addition, other candidates such as Gary Bauer, Alan Keyes, and especially Steve Forbes made strides in gaining credibility and strength.[103] Unlike the Democratic side of the nomination process in 2000, moreover, the Republican contest soon provided some excitement and even a few surprises. As Table 4.20 summarizes, the Iowa caucuses on January 25 gave Bush his first victory, with 41 percent, an opening win that finally certified his long-standing claim as the front-runner.[104] But the Iowa caucuses also offered some surprises, with Steve Forbes placing second with 30 percent and Alan Keyes coming in third with 14 percent, runner-up victories that resulted in part from McCain's decision to sit out Iowa in order to focus on New Hampshire. A week later, however, the opening primary in New Hampshire was a major victory for McCain who received 48.5 percent to Bush's 30.4 percent.[105] To be sure, Bush's lackluster win in the Iowa caucuses and his lopsided loss to McCain in the New Hampshire primary appeared to alter the dynamics of the campaign completely. Bush's overwhelming strength in the early campaign notwithstanding, confident predictions of a quick Bush victory in the nomination contest seemed to be "turned upside down" in the space of a single eventful week.[106]

Even as the Republican campaign seemed to open up, however, Bush's overwhelming advantages in money, volunteers, and organization, all developed during his extraordinarily successful early campaign, remained the dominant force as the formal nomination process continued.[107] While the 2000 Demo-

TABLE 4.20
Candidate Vote Totals in the Two Opening Nomination Contests
2000 Presidential Election Cycle
Republicans

Candidates	Iowa	New Hampshire
Gary Bauer	9%	1%
George W. Bush	41%	30.4%
Steve Forbes	30%	13%
Orin Hatch	1%	0%
Alan Keyes	14%	6%
John McCain	5%	48.5%
Other	0%	1%

Sources: Richard Berke, "The 2000 Campaign: The Overview, Iowans Delivers Victory to Bush and Gore," *The New York Times*, 25 January 2000, p. 1.; Allison Mitchell with Frank Bruni, "The 2000 Campaign: The Republican Insurgent, McCain and Bush Revving Up Their Campaigns," *The New York Times*, 3 February 2000, p. 1.; and William G. Mayer, "The Presidential Nominations," in *The Election of 2000*, ed. Gerald M. Pomper (New York: Chatham House Publishers, 2001), 34–35.

cratic calendar for February included only two contests after New Hampshire, namely the Delaware primary on February 5 and the Washington primary more than three weeks later on February 29, the 2000 Republican calendar provided a full schedule of caucuses and primaries—an asymmetry in scheduling between the two major parties that was a new phenomenon in the formal nomination process.[108] After losing the Delaware primary to Bush just a week after New Hampshire, McCain's campaign targeted the South Carolina primary on February 19 as the next opportunity to derail Bush's "aura of inevitability." But Bush's enormous advantages, and the support of virtually the entire state Republican leadership, gave him a much-needed victory, with the final vote going 53 percent to Bush and 42 percent to McCain.[109] A week later on February 22, McCain rallied with victories over Bush in Arizona and Michigan, but these were to be "the last good moment for his campaign."[110] The following week Bush swamped McCain in the Virginia and Washington primaries as well as the North Dakota caucuses.

As the Republican nomination contest moved into high gear, the overwhelming advantages inherent in Bush's national organization came into play, with March 7's Super Tuesday schedule of eleven primaries necessitating the capacity to run a coast-to-coast campaign.[111] Super Tuesday indeed proved to be a decisive victory for Bush who won seven states, including California, New York, Ohio, Maryland, Missouri, Georgia, and Maine, winning all but New York and Maine by margins of 20 percent or more. While McCain took four of the Super Tuesday contests, his victories were confined to New England and, except for Massachusetts, were all small states. Bush's Super Tuesday triumph was even clearer in terms of the delegate totals won on a single day: Bush, 433; McCain 113.[112] Two days later, on March 9, McCain acknowledged that his challenge to Bush was over, and his withdrawal from the nomination contest removed Bush's last obstacle to the Republican presidential nomination.[113] To be sure, McCain's strength during the opening five weeks of the formal nomination process had shown the extent to which an effective national candidate with strong fund-raising could challenge even an early and overwhelming front-runner. Yet the failure of this challenge also left little doubt that Bush's tremendous success in the early campaign during 1999 and before, and the overwhelming advantages that he had as a result, ultimately were what carried the day for Bush once the formal nomination campaign hit full stride.

Classification of the overall candidate field for the Republican nomination in 2000 results in three groupings: two candidates who proved to be viable; four candidates who remained active through the opening nomination contests; and six candidates who withdrew after their public announcement but before the opening nomination contests. Using this study's definition of viability, namely receiving 10 percent of the vote in both the Iowa caucuses and New Hampshire primary or, alternatively, 20 percent of the vote in either of these early contests, only Bush and McCain are classified as viable. Four other candidates remained in the nomination race through the opening contests, including Orin Hatch (who actually withdrew on January 25 after the Iowa caucuses), and Gary Bauer and Steve Forbes who withdrew on February 4 and 9 respectively. The final active candidate, Alan Keyes, persisted in his campaign until the eve of the Republican national convention. The remaining six candidates, as already noted, all withdrew from the Republican nomination contest before the formal nomination process even began.

Summary

The presidential nomination races in both major parties in 1988 and 2000 first and foremost are a story of the front-runner's dominance in the post-reform presidential nomination process. The incredible requirements of running a nationwide presidential campaign, combined with the impact of front-loading on the primary and caucus schedule and the necessity of significant advance fund-raising, are realities of the modern presidential nomination campaign that leave little room for late or surprise candidates.[114] While the campaign finance reform framework in its early years leveled the field to some degree, even opening the door to the possibility of long-shot, dark horse candidates, the collapse of campaign finance reform in the face of increasingly creative and unregulated campaign fund-raising strategies has seriously diminished any possibility for "out-

siders" to capture either major party's presidential nomination.[115] Thus the reality of presidential nomination politics, confirmed in 1988 and underscored
again in 2000, is that the early campaign is pivotal in presidential nominee selection today.[116] To be sure, as both the 1988 and 2000 nomination campaigns indicate, it is during this early campaign that candidates undertake pre-candidacy
activities that build a successful fund-raising program as well as a volunteer and
organizational base, all in advance of publicly launching a presidential campaign.
It also is during this early campaign that the candidate field is significantly narrowed, with many unannounced and publicly announced candidates withdrawing as a significantly winnowed candidate field finally emerges to compete in the
formal nomination process itself. This early campaign, moreover, is becoming
more important with each passing presidential election, a reality which a comparison of the 1988 and 2000 nomination campaigns makes quite clear. The
demand for early success in all of the dimensions of the early campaign—
fund-raising success most notable among them—likewise is becoming greater
with each passing presidential election year. The challenge of this early campaign and the money primary certainly dominated the presidential nomination
process in 1988 and 2000 and promises to continue to dominate presidential
nominee selection in the "unreformed post-reform era" that is the new reality of
the presidential nomination process.

Notes

1. Rhodes Cook, "The Nominating Process," in *The Election of 1988*, ed. Michael
Nelson (Washington, D.C.: Congressional Quarterly Press, 1989), 39, 46.

2. William G. Mayer, "The Presidential Nominations," in *The Election of 2000*, ed.
Gerald M. Pomper (New York: Chatham House Publishers, 2001), 17, 19.

3. Kenneth D. Wald, "Ministering to the Nation: The Campaigns of Jesse Jackson
and Pat Robertson," in *Nominating the President*, ed. Emmett H. Buell, Jr. and Lee
Sigelman (Knoxville: The University of Tennessee Press, 1991), 119.

4. James W. Ceaser and Andrew E. Busch, *The Perfect Tie* (Lanham, Md.: Rowman
& Littlefield Publishers, Inc., 2001), 64.

5. Gerald M. Pomper, "The Presidential Nominations," in *The Election of 1988:
Reports and Interpretations*, ed. Gerald M. Pomper (Chatham, N.J.: Chatham House
Publishers, 1989), 33–34.

6. Larry J. Sabato and Joshua J. Scott, "The Long Road to a Cliffhanger: Primaries
and Conventions," in *Overtime: The Election 2000 Thriller*, ed. Larry J. Sabato (New
York: Pearson Education, 2002), 18, 23.

7. Mayer, "The Presidential Nominations," 13.

8. Cook, "The Nominating Process," 42–44, 48–50.

9. Mayer, "The Presidential Nominations," 32, 35.

10. Associated Press, "Heading Up the Ticket," *The New York Times*, 15 March 2000, sec. A, p. 18.

11. Stephen J. Wayne, *The Road to the White House: The Politics of Presidential Elections—Postelection Edition* (Boston: Bedford/St. Martin's, 2001), 45–48.

12. Anthony Corrado, *Creative Campaigning: PACs and the Presidential Selection Process* (Boulder, Colo.: Westview Press, Inc., 1992), 77.

13. Anthony Corrado, *Paying for Presidents: Public Financing in National Elections* (New York: The Twentieth Century Fund Press, 1993), 71.

14. Center for Responsive Politics, *Public Policy and Foundations: The Role of Politicians in Public Charities* (Washington, D.C.: Center for Responsive Politics, 1987), 35.

15. Corrado, *Creative Campaigning*, 77.

16. Ibid., 77, 83.

17. Anthony Corrado, "Financing the 2000 Elections," in *The Election of 2000*, ed. Gerald M. Pomper (New York: Chatham House Publishers, 2001), 94–95.

18. Ibid., 97–98.

19. Clyde Wilcox and Wesley Joe, "Dead Law: The Federal Election Finance Regulations, 1974–1996," *PS: Political Science and Politics* 30, no. 1 (March 1998): 14–17.

20. Cook, "The Nominating Process," 39-40, 45.

21. Mayer, "The Presidential Nominations," 16, 20.

22. Cook, "The Nominating Process," 40, 47.

23. Mayer, "The Presidential Nominations," 31, 34.

24. Cook, "The Nominating Process," 44–45.

25. Mayer, "The Presidential Nominations," 17, 19, and Table 2A at www.chatham house.com/pomper2000.

26. Mayer, "The Presidential Nominations," 27.

27. News reports in *The New York Times*, 1999, and Corrado, "Financing the 2000 Elections," 101.

28. Corrado, "Financing the 2000 Elections," 94.

29. Wilcox and Joe, "Dead Law."

30. Corrado, "Financing the 2000 Elections," 94–97.

31. Cook, "The Nominating Process," 45–46.

32. Ibid., 46.

33. Ibid., 26, 44–45.

34. Andrew E. Busch, *Outsiders and Openness in the Presidential Nominating System* (Pittsburgh: University of Pittsburgh Press, 1997), 111–12.

35. Cook, "The Nominating Process," 34.

36. Ibid., 47–51.

37. Ibid., 40–42.

38. Ibid., 44–45.

39. Ibid., 45–46.

40. Paul Taylor, "Candidates Turn Corner Toward '88: Democrats a Formless Field," *The Washington Post*, 8 September 1987, sec. A, p. 1.

41. Cook, "The Nominating Process," 46.

42. Ibid., 46.

43. "The Race Ahead: Campaign Calendar," *The New York Times*, 27 December 1987, sec. 4, p. 1.

44. Cook, "The Nominating Process," 48.

45. Ibid., 46,

46. Ibid., 50–55.

47. Ibid., 55–56.

48. Ibid., 47–48.

49. Ibid., 48, 54.

50. R. W. Apple, Jr., "Jackson Is Seen as Winning a Solid Place in History," *The New York Times*, 29 April 1988, sec. A, p. 16.

51. Cook, "The Nominating Process," 39.

52. Ibid., 40, 42.

53. Ibid., 40–41.

54. Ibid., 40.

55. Ibid., 41.

56. Charles R. Babcock, "Robertson Blending Charity and Politics: Tax-Exempt Television Ministry Was Foundation for Campaign," *The Washington Post*, 2 November 1987, sec. A, p. 1.

57. Michael G. Hagen and William G. Mayer, "The Modern Politics of Presidential Selection: How Changing the Rules Really Did Change the Game," in *In Pursuit of the White House: How We Choose Our Presidential Nominees*, ed. William G. Mayer (New York: Chatham House Publishers, 2000), 21, 26.

58. Ceaser and Busch, *The Perfect Tie*, 51.

59. Mayer, "The Presidential Nominations," 17, 27.

60. Ceci Connolly, "Huge Money Chase Marks 2000 Race," *The Washington Post*, 28 February 1999, sec. A, pp. 1, 6.

61. Corrado, "Financing the 2000 Elections," 93.

62. Corrado, *Creative Campaigning*, 73–76.

63. Anthony Corrado, *Campaign Finance Reform* (New York: The Century Foundation Press, 2000), 66.

64. Corrado, "Financing the 2000 Elections," 98–100.

65. Ruth Marcus, "Flood of Secret Money Erodes Limits," *The Washington Post*, 15 May 2000, sec. A, pp. 1, 6.

66. Corrado, *Campaign Finance Reform*, 65–66.

67. Corrado, "Financing the 2000 Elections," 97–98.

68. Ibid., 93–94.

69. Mayer, "The Presidential Nominations," 17, 27.

70. Ibid., 17.

71. Ceaser and Busch, 62.

72. Ibid., 72, 74.

73. Mayer, "The Presidential Nominations," 33.

74. Ceaser and Busch, 54–55.

75. Mayer, "The Presidential Nominations," 31.

76. Ibid., 32.

77. Ibid., 32.

78. Ibid., 33.

79. Richard Berke, "Nominees May Be Chosen Quickly in Rare Competitive Primary Season," *The New York Times*, 2 January 2000, 22.

80. William G. Mayer, "Perspectives on the Current Presidential Selection Process," statement presented to the Advisory Committee on the Presidential Nomination Process, Republican National Committee, November 22, 1999, in *Nominating Future Presidents* (Washington, D.C.: Republican National Committee, May 2000), 114.

81. Sabato and Scott, "The Long Road to a Cliffhanger," 26.

82. Mayer, "The Presidential Nominations," 27.

83. Ceaser and Busch, 63.

84. Ibid., 61.

85. Mayer, "The Presidential Nominations," 15–16.

86. Ceaser and Busch, 52–53.

87. Corrado, *Campaign Finance Reform*, 64, and Corrado, "Financing the 2000 Elections," 98.

88. Ceaser and Busch, 67–68.

89. Corrado, "Financing the 2000 Elections," 100–101.

90. Mayer, "The Presidential Nominations," 27.

91. Ibid., 22–23.

92. Ceaser and Busch, 56.

93. Mayer, "The Presidential Nominations," 20–22.

94. Ceaser and Busch, 56–57.

95. Dan Balz, "GOP Process Is Echo of the Past," *The Washington Post*, 8 August 1999, sec. A, p. 1.

96. Mayer, "The Presidential Nominations," 19.

97. Ibid., 27.

98. Ibid., 19–20.

99. Ibid., 19.

100. Ruth Marcus, "Dollars Dictate Field's Early Exits," *The Washington Post*, 21 October 1999, sec. A, p. 1.

101. Ceaser and Busch, 63.

102. Berke, "Nominees May Be Chosen Quickly in Rare Competitive Primary Season," 1–22.

103. Mayer, "The Presidential Nominations," 30–31.

104. Richard L. Berke, "Iowans Deliver Victory to Bush and Gore," *The New York Times*, 25 January 2000, sec. A, p. 1.

105. Ceaser and Busch, 19.

106. Mayer, "The Presidential Nominations," 34.

107. Ceaser and Busch, 67–68.

108. Ibid., 52.

109. Mayer, "The Presidential Nominations," 36.

110. Ibid., 37.

111. Ceaser and Busch, 99–100.

112. Mayer, "The Presidential Nominations," 37.

113. Ibid., 37.

114. Ceaser and Busch, 51.

115. Andrew E. Busch, *Outsiders and Openness in the Presidential Nominating System*.

116. Mayer, "The Presidential Nominations," 12, 15.

5

Early Campaign Fund-Raising Success and Candidate Viability

THE QUEST FOR THE PRESIDENCY BEGINS—and for most candidates ends—as a quest for money during the early campaign period appropriately called "the money primary." Candidates and would-be candidates preparing to seek their party's presidential nomination invariably begin with fund-raising, both because it is the main fungible resource in politics—readily converted into staffing, consulting expertise, campaign advertising, and so forth—and increasingly also because it has become a measure of candidate credibility and even electability. Whether a candidate is simply exploring the feasibility of a possible candidacy, laying the groundwork for a planned campaign, or seeking to achieve a threshold in support in order to establish early credibility, campaign fund-raising success has become the defining step not only of early candidacy but of pre-candidacy as well. The surest predictor of success in this quest for money, moreover, is a track record of previous success, whether from an earlier presidential campaign, a previous federal or state campaign, or significant pre-candidacy activity, and the organization and capability for significant fund-raising which such a track record entails. Candidates and would-be candidates for the presidential nomination therefore are quick to launch fund-raising efforts as they explore a possible presidential bid. To be sure, getting an early start to fund-raising and especially to building an organization capable of successful long-term fund-raising must be at the forefront for any candidate aspiring to conduct a viable and ultimately successful presidential nomination campaign.[1]

The pivotal role of money and fund-raising in the early presidential nomination process in large part is a consequence of the overall structure of this

process in the post-reform era. The extensive calendar of primaries and caucuses that developed following the post-1968 reform of the nomination
process necessitates that candidates conduct nationwide campaigns in their
pursuit of the presidential nomination.[2] Moreover, the front-loading of this
primary and caucus schedule since the 1980s has made the need for major advance fund-raising even more acute, with candidates having to amass significant funding not only to develop their campaign during the pre-election year
but to be prepared to move into high gear in the opening weeks of the formal
nomination process as well. The hard reality of this front-loaded nomination
calendar is that candidates must begin the primary and caucus schedule prepared to conduct a nationwide nomination campaign right from the start.
Even as the nomination contest begins gradually with the Iowa caucuses in
January and the New Hampshire primary in late January or early February, a
candidate who hopes to be successful must be prepared not only to proceed to
the ensuing schedule of primaries and caucuses in February but also to conduct literally a coast-to-coast campaign on Super Tuesday in early March.[3]
Only candidates who have a successful fund-raising program in place as the
formal nomination process begins in January are prepared to build on any
momentum generated in these opening contests or, alternatively, to recover
from any initial setbacks. Candidates instead relying upon their success in
these opening contests to generate additional support for the ensuing contests
inevitably will be disappointed as their campaigns are overwhelmed by competing candidates who have entered the formal nomination process finan-
cially prepared. In short, largely as a result of the structure of the post-reform
era nomination process, a candidate's success in raising money early and in
building an effective organization to raise money long-term certainly is essential to keep a candidacy alive and to build increased recognition and credibility. Yet even more importantly, a candidate's success in enlisting significant
early funding and in building a broad-based long-term fund-raising effort
also is essential in order to have the funding needed to conduct a nationwide
nomination campaign in a compressed time frame, the ultimate test facing
every prospective presidential nominee.

A further structural reality that significantly increases the role of money in
presidential nomination politics is the federal legislation and associated regulatory and judicial rulings that collectively comprise campaign finance reform. The campaign finance system originally was legislated in the landmark
Federal Election Campaign Act of 1971 (FECA), was substantially strengthened in 1974 in response to the Watergate scandal and other financial abuses
during the 1972 presidential election, and was updated and to an extent expanded with the passage of the Bipartisan Campaign Finance Reform Act of
2002. The campaign finance framework established by FECA limits contribu-

tion levels, requires public disclosure of contributions and financial transactions, provides federal matching funding to qualifying candidates, and when federal matching funds are accepted sets limits on overall and state-by-state spending. The original FECA individual contribution limit was $1,000 per candidate per election, a contribution limit that was not indexed to inflation and so remained at the same amount from 1976 through 2002, including the two presidential election cycles included in this study. FECA also limited an individual's overall total in contributions to all candidates in an election cycle to $25,000 and also limited political action committee (PAC) contributions to an individual candidate to $5,000. In addition, FECA also required public disclosure of all contributions and financial transactions.[4]

A further dimension of FECA with significant implications for the presidential nomination process was the public funding of presidential elections at both the nomination and general election stages, with matching funding being available at the nomination stage and with full funding being available at the general election stage. Federal matching funding at the nomination stage was dollar-for-dollar up to $250 for each individual contribution, with candidates being eligible upon achieving a threshold of contributions totaling at least $5,000 in twenty or more states. Because this matching support was indexed to inflation, the ceiling for federal matching funds for individual candidates in the nomination process was able to increase, going from the $10 million originally established in 1976 to $27,660,000 in 1988[5] and $45,600,000 in 2000.[6] FECA bound all candidates to the individual contribution limit of $1,000 per candidate per election, regardless of whether or not the candidate accepted matching funds, but additional restrictions that set an overall spending ceiling and state-by-state spending ceilings for the nomination contest applied only to candidates who accepted federal matching funds.[7] This landmark FECA campaign finance reform framework remains on the books three decades after its original enactment, with the ceiling on individual contributions recently raised from $1,000 to $2,000 and an array of new restrictions on political parties and "soft money" being added with passage of the Bipartisan Campaign Finance Reform Act of 2002.[8]

The impact of the campaign finance reform framework on the presidential nomination process has been enormous. Money has been a critical factor in presidential politics almost from the beginning, but reformers seeking to limit its impact in presidential selection implemented a system that has changed how money is raised and the part it plays in presidential nominations and elections. Since FECA was instituted, presidential candidates not only have needed to raise money in vast amounts—which was the case before as well—but now must do so by seeking relatively modest contributions of $1,000 or less (and starting with the 2004 election cycle, of $2,000 or less). Faced with this contribution limit, presidential candidates in the post-reform era have had no choice but to develop broad-based fund-raising programs as a key part of their presidential campaigns.[9] Candidates who have the personal and political networks to conduct such broad-based fund-raising efforts already in place, as well as those with related skills and experience, clearly are advantaged as they confront this fund-raising challenge. Also clearly advantaged are candidates whose ideological and issue positions appeal to groups with the capacity to make contributions.

But the FECA campaign finance framework has proven to have an even greater impact on campaign fund-raising and the presidential nomination process by what it does not control, whether because the legislation itself or subsequent regulatory or judicial rulings have exempted it or because of loopholes which candidates have identified in order to evade it. Candidates in the presidential nomination process who do not accept federal matching funds, for instance, while bound by the individual contribution limit, are not bound by the overall spending ceiling or the state-by-state spending ceilings, providing an enormous advantage to candidates with extraordinarily successful fund-raising—as George W. Bush proved in 2000—especially when the remainder of the candidate field is bound by these spending ceilings. Even more advantaged, of course, are totally self-funded candidates because they not only are exempt from spending ceilings but are not burdened with the need to raise funds in the first place.[10] The greatest impact of the original campaign finance legislation, however, confirmed and reinforced by the new 2002 reform legislation, is long-term as presidential candidates develop their campaign strategies and fund-raising programs not only to conform to federal requirements but to take advantage of loopholes as well. While FECA's most visible impact has been that every candidate in the presidential nomination process of necessity must develop a significant fund-raising program, its longer term impact has been to spur an explosion of alternate funding strategies, including the proliferation of advocacy groups or leadership PACs, which generally are active during the long pre-candidacy phase, and the increased use of other organizational entities such as tax-exempt foundations, other non-profit organizations, and state-based political committees as devices to evade federal regulation.[11] In fact, the proliferation of strategies for evading the campaign finance framework became so extensive by the 2000 nomination cycle that some observers viewed the system of campaign finance to be operating more like the pre-reform era than the post-reform era, with candidate fund-raising and spending by means of one or more of these organizational entities appearing to be out of control.[12]

Emerging as a long-term consequence of both the nominating reforms and campaign finance reform is the money primary which since the 1980s has become the first and perhaps most difficult challenge confronting presidential aspirants.[13] The money primary is part of a broader phase in pre-nomination presidential politics, referred to variously as the invisible primary or the shadow campaign, an early phase in the presidential nomination process during which candidates develop national name recognition and issue identification, build an organizational base, and develop the political network that all are essential to a successful presidential campaign. But foremost among these early campaign phases is the money primary, the phase during which every presidential aspirant must meet the critical challenge of developing a successful ongoing fund-raising program to support an unfolding presidential nomination campaign. At first this fund-raising challenge is simply to raise sufficient funding to conduct pre-candidacy activities and to launch a nascent presidential campaign. But soon the challenge of the money primary becomes even greater as would-be announced candidates seek to establish their credibility and standing as presidential aspirants. Ultimately, however, the challenge is to have in place an effective fund-raising organization that provides substantial funding, not only to meet immediate campaign needs but to position a candidate to meet the enormous funding requirements for a full-fledged presidential nomination campaign. The extensive calendar of primaries and caucuses that has developed in the post-reform era, and the trend toward front-loading of this calendar, means that candidates now must have significant funding available from the very beginning in order to compete in what almost from the start is a coast-to-coast nomination contest. Moreover, due to federal campaign finance reform legislation which limits individual contributions to $1,000 (and now $2,000), candidates have no alternative but to raise the substantial sums needed by means of broad-based fund-raising campaigns.[14] The emergence of the money primary as a pivotal phase in pre-candidacy and early candidacy presidential campaigns is indicative of the extent of this challenge and of the number of presidential aspirants who fail to meet it.

The money primary first and foremost is about fund-raising—both raising a significant total in early campaign funds, and building the organizational capability to raise significant campaign funds on an ongoing basis. This study seeks to explore the importance of early and ongoing fund-raising for candidate survival, viability, and success in the early presidential nomination process. The principal hypothesis examines whether successful early and ongoing fund-raising during the early candidacy phase is predictive of candidate survival, viability, and success in the early presidential nomination process. By comparing fund-raising totals across candidate fields, considering whether there are basic threshold and timing needs, and examining the impact of momentum in fund-raising, conclusions are developed concerning the significance of early candidacy fund-raising success for candidate survival, viability, and success. Comparisons also are made across candidate fields concerning cash-on-hand and federal matching funding as additional indicators of a candidate's fund-raising success, permitting further conclusions regarding the relationship between early candidacy fund-raising success and candidate viability and success. Looking earlier in the pre-nomination campaign of the presidential selection process to the pre-candidacy phase, a related hypothesis focuses upon prospective candidates' pre-candidacy fund-raising success. This second hypothesis, closely related to the first, examines whether a greater level of pre-candidacy fund-raising and organizational preparation through pre-candidacy committees is predictive of early candidacy fund-raising success and, in turn, candidate survival, viability, and success in the early presidential nomination process.

The data analysis which follows is organized in terms of two distinct phases of the presidential pre-nomination campaign, namely the pre-candidacy phase and the early candidacy and early nomination phases. While the starting date for the pre-candidacy phase is difficult to determine, it certainly includes the period immediately before the pre-election year and, for purposes of this study, any activity through registered PACs, state-based committees, or other organizational entities for the two years prior to the pre-election year. The pre-candidacy phase extends up to the point at which a candidate makes a public announcement of candidacy or makes an FEC filing of organization or candidacy, a step which ends any pre-candidacy or exploratory phase and classifies the individual as a presidential candidate. The early candidacy phase commences with the filing of an FEC statement of organization or candidacy, an official step that results in the creation of the candidate's presidential campaign committee. This early candidacy phase for purposes of this study extends from the establishment of the presidential campaign committee through the end of the pre-election year, with the opening two months of the election year itself constituting the early nomination phase. The analysis includes two presidential election cycles, 1988 and 2000, the two all non-incumbent presidential elections of the post-reform era and the two election years which delineate a significant period in the evolution and disintegration of the post-reform era presidential nomination process. This analysis studies the party nomination contests in each of these election years separately, with four distinct candidate fields being examined, namely the Democratic and Republican nomination contests for the 1988 as well as the 2000 presidential election cycles.

Campaign Fund-Raising in the 1988 Early Nomination Campaign

Fund-raising by candidates seeking their party's presidential nomination moved to a new level in the early campaign leading up to the 1988 presidential nomination process. As the fifth presidential election cycle of the post-reform era, and with campaign finance reform now almost a decade and a half old, the 1988 presidential election—and the pre-nomination campaigns leading up to it—represented a milestone in the evolution of the early presidential nomination campaign. It was beginning with the 1988 nomination campaign that the trend toward front-loading of the primary and caucus calendar began, introducing a major new structural reality that would make significant early fund-raising essential for success in the accelerated nomination process.[15] Perhaps even more significantly, it also was during the 1988 early nomination campaign that the undermining of FECA which began in the early 1980s accelerated and the framework of campaign finance reform began to disintegrate.[16] The proliferation of issue advocacy groups or leadership PACs as "shadow campaign committees" as well as other organizational entities to evade nomination campaign spending ceilings likewise dates to this 1988 pre-nomination campaign. In fact, the emergence of the money primary as an identifiable phase in the early presidential nomination campaign in many ways dates to this 1988 presidential election cycle during which both early campaign fund-raising and extensive media coverage of this early campaign fund-raising reached levels never seen previously. Making the 1988 presidential nomination campaign an especially interesting one is that the presidential nominees it produced, contrary to most post-reform era nomination campaigns, were the ones it originally had been expected to produce.[17] Yet in a year of such significant change in the structure of the nomination process itself, this unexpected result perhaps should not have been such a surprise after all.

Democratic Campaign Fund-Raising in 1988

The early campaign for the 1988 Democratic presidential nomination, the first pre-nomination campaign examined in this study, included a money primary that was more pronounced than any previous Democratic contest. A first indication of this distinct new phase in the early nomination campaign was the proliferation of leadership PACs and other organizational entities such as foundations, other tax-exempt organizations, and state-based political committees that operated beginning very early in the 1988 Democratic campaign. As Table 5.1 summarizes, of the sixteen active Democratic candidates in 1988, eleven utilized some form of pre-candidacy committee, and eight of these candidates utilized a leadership PAC. Moreover, of the seven Democratic candidates categorized as either viable or active through the early nomination process, all but one utilized a pre-candidacy committee, generally a leadership PAC. In fact, two of the three candidates categorized as viable through the

TABLE 5.1
Summary Analysis of Candidates Grouped by Viability
with Associated Number of Candidate Leadership PACs
and Other Early Fund-Raising Entities
1988 Presidential Election Cycle
Democrats

Candidates Grouped by Viability	Number of Candidates	Other Early Entities	Leadership PACs	Neither
Viable Through Early Nom. Process:	3	2	2	0
Active Through Early Nom. Process:	4	3	3	1
Withdrawing Before Early Nom. Process:	1	0	1	0
Withdrawing Before Formal Announcement:	8	3	2	4
Other Potential Candidates:	1	1	0	0

early nomination process and three of the four candidates categorized as active through the early nomination process utilized both a leadership PAC and another organizational entity during their early pre-nomination campaign. Finally, of the eight candidates who withdrew before making a formal announcement, four did not utilize any form of pre-candidacy committee. In short, a pre-candidacy committee, generally a leadership PAC, was part of the early campaign of every candidate who achieved viability through the early nomination process and all but one of the candidates who remained active through the early nomination process, a feature of the early 1988 Democratic campaign that is indicative of the emergence of early fund-raising as a significant dimension of the early campaign and of its indispensable importance for candidate survival, viability, and success.

The variety in the types of pre-candidacy committees and other organizational entities utilized for early candidacy fund-raising in the 1988 Democratic pre-nomination campaign and their level of early fund-raising activity also are impressive. An array of leadership PACs and other organizational entities was employed by the emerging Democratic candidate field, with many of them already active as early as 1985—three years before the formal nomination process itself. Two of the three candidates classified as viable through the early nomination process utilized PACs quite successfully, with Richard Gephardt's Effective Government Committee raising over $1 million and Paul Simon's Democracy Fund raising over $450,000 from 1985 to 1987. The third viable candidate, Michael Dukakis, did not utilize a PAC but instead relied on a very successful state level political committee, the Dukakis Gubernatorial

Committee, which raised over $2.2 million during 1986 alone. Three of the four Democratic candidates who were active through the early nomination process also utilized PACs. Gary Hart's Americans with Hart was especially successful in early fund-raising during 1985 and 1986, exceeding $500,000 in each of these years, support that was augmented by additional significant funding through his tax-exempt foundation, the Center for a New Democracy, which was a novelty in pre-candidacy activity and fund-raising when it was founded in May 1985. The Rev. Jesse Jackson maintained a whole group of political and fund-raising organizations which his campaign utilized extensively, most notably the Rainbow PAC, his PUSH Foundation, and the National Rainbow Coalition itself. Of the ten other candidates, whether they withdrew before or after announcing their candidacy or were never more than possible candidates, only three utilized PACs, including Joseph Biden's Fund for '86, Mario Cuomo's Empire Leadership Fund, and Edward Kennedy's Fund for a Democratic Majority, with only the Kennedy PAC truly achieving fund-raising success. Quite significantly, seven of these ten Democratic contenders who were not viable or active in 1988 did not utilize a PAC, although three of these seven did utilize tax-exempt foundations to fund aspects of their activities. The limited data publicly available on these foundations make it clear that they were very important to their candidates' campaigns, making the phenomenon of tax-exempt foundations having a presidential nomination and general election impact a documented trend beginning with the 1988 presidential election.

An overview of the level of early fund-raising beginning in 1985 and extending through 1987 leaves no doubt that the pre-candidacy phase of the early 1988 presidential nomination campaign was a very active and important period. As Table 5.2 summarizes, whether through the more commonplace vehicle of the leadership PAC or an alternate organizational entity, almost every would-be candidate engaged in early fund-raising during all or at least a major part of the three year period leading up to the presidential election year. All three of the candidates categorized as viable through the early nomination process—Michael Dukakis, Richard Gephardt, and Paul Simon—raised substantial dollars during their pre-candidacy campaigns. Dukakis' early fund-raising totals eclipsed his competitors, although unlike most of them he did not form a leadership PAC but instead relied upon his gubernatorial campaign committee, an entity which raised over $2.2 million in 1986 alone. Gephardt's early fund-raising totals also stand out, especially during 1986 when his total of $645,091 surpassed all of his active competitors except Dukakis, who ultimately secured the nomination, and two others—Hart and Kennedy—who ended up withdrawing for reasons unrelated to campaign fund-raising. Hart actually led the active field in early fund-raising but ultimately was forced to

TABLE 5.2
Summary Analysis of Candidates Grouped by Viability
with Associated Levels of Pre-Candidacy Fund-Raising Success
1988 Presidential Election Cycle
Democrats

Candidates Grouped by Viability	Early Fund-Raising		Leadership PAC		
	Pre-1986	1986	1985	1986	1987
Viable Through Early Nom. Process:					
Michael Dukakis	$1,387,584 (1984–1985)	$2,239,452			
Richard Gephardt			$361,547	$645,091	$83,840
Paul Simon			$161,678	$260,620	$29,910
Active Through Early Nom. Process:					
Bruce Babbitt	$81,000	$400,000	$52,050	$103,908	
Al Gore					
Gary Hart	$494,000	$360,000	$593,915	$700,018	$189,593
Rev. Jesse Jackson	$601,000				$1,989,310
Withdrawing Before Early Nom. Process:					
Joseph Biden				$130,755	0
Withdrawing Before Formal Announcement:					
Bill Bradley	$760,000	$237,000			
Dale Bumpers					
Bill Clinton					
Mario Cuomo					$108,570
Edward Kennedy	$150,000		$1,243,543	$1,395,850	$112,753
Sam Nunn					
Charles Robb		$500,000			
Patricia Schroeder					

withdraw due to character questions, and Edward Kennedy, who was far and away the strongest early fund-raiser but who nonetheless withdrew before any formal announcement, actually had a broader political and issue-focused agenda behind his PAC-run fund-raising effort. A distinct second tier of would-be candidates for the Democratic nomination is comprised of the four candidates who remained active through the early nomination process, with three of these four active candidates—Bruce Babbitt, Gary Hart, and the Rev. Jesse Jackson—conducting successful early fund-raising programs, and with just one of the four—Al Gore—deferring any early fund-raising through PACs or other entities. These three active candidates not only utilized leadership

PACs but also developed other organizational entities for primarily fund-raising purposes as part of their pre-candidacy campaigns. A third group of eight candidates who withdrew even before any formal announcement of candidacy generally either did not have any vehicle for pre-candidacy fund-raising—as was the case with four of them—or utilized a pre-candidacy entity for very limited fund-raising. The lone exception to this pattern was Edward Kennedy who far surpassed the entire Democratic field in the early campaign leading up to 1988 but who simply chose not to undertake a second presidential run. In short, not only were pre-candidacy entities and especially leadership PACs a major new dimension in the 1988 Democratic pre-nomination contest, but the candidates with more successful and longer term early fund-raising generally also proved to be the candidates who achieved viability through the early nomination process.

The use of leadership PACs by would-be candidates for the 1988 Democratic nomination clearly was an important part of their early efforts to mount nomination campaigns. In fact, simply the pattern in the level of activity by these leadership PACs supports the generalization that in most cases they were established to support pre-presidential candidacy activity and to engage in early campaign fund-raising. As Table 5.3 documents, eight possible candidates for the 1988 Democratic presidential nomination established leadership PACs in advance of the announced candidacy period, in most cases during 1985 but in one case during 1986 and in another case during 1987. Quite significantly, in six of these eight cases the height in terms of fund-raising activity was during 1986, the year before the pre-election year when formal presidential campaign committees generally begin operation. Total fund-raising activity among these leadership PACs during 1986 ranged from a low of just $103,908 in the case of Babbitt's PAC to a high of $1,395,850 in the case of Kennedy's PAC. The other candidate-affiliated PACs generally had 1986 fund-raising totals in the quarter to half million dollar range. Also quite significantly, as would be expected if these PACs indeed were functioning as pre-candidacy fund-raising entities, the fund-raising totals for six of the eight leadership PACs fell off substantially in 1987, the pre-election year when candidate fund-raising efforts could be expected to shift to the official presidential campaign committees. The only leadership PACs in the 1988 Democratic presidential election cycle not fitting this pattern were Cuomo's and Jackson's, with Cuomo's Empire Leadership Fund not even being formed until April 1987, and with the Jesse Jackson for President '88 Committee being established in 1987 and reaching a height in total fund-raising of $8,345,558 in 1988, a pattern indicating that Jackson had broader and longer-term intentions aside from the 1988 Democratic nomination contest when he established this leadership PAC. These exceptional cases aside, the overall pattern in leadership PAC fund-raising from 1985 through

TABLE 5.3
Comparison of Contributions to Presidential Candidate Leadership PACs
Prior to and During Presidential Election Years
1988 Presidential Election Cycle
Democrats

Candidate and Leadership PAC	1985	1986	1987	1988
Richard Gephardt— Gephardt Presidential Exploratory Committee/ Effective Government Committee (10/3/84)	$361,547	$645,091	$83,840	$122,900
Paul Simon— The Democracy Fund (12/3/84)	$161,678	$260,620 (amended later)	$29,910	— (Terminated 1/1/88)
Bruce Babbitt— Americans for the National Interest (9/9/85) (Terminated 4/25/86)	$52,050	$103,908 (Terminated 4/25/86)	—	—
Gary Hart— Americans with Hart, Inc.	$593,915	$700,018	$189,593	
Rev. Jesse Jackson— Jesse Jackson for President '88 Committee			$1,989,310	$8,345,558
Joseph Biden— Fund for '86 (4/25/86)	—	$130,755	— (Terminated 2/1/87)	—
Mario Cuomo— Empire Leadership Fund (4/24/87)	—	—	$108,570	0
Edward Kennedy— Fund for a Democratic Majority	$1,243,543	$1,395,850	$112,753	$392,764

1987 is consistent with the generalization that leadership PACs established by aspiring presidential nominees are a major part of pre-candidacy activity and fund-raising during the early campaign.

Fund-raising success using presidential campaign committees during the early candidacy period and extending through the pre-election year and the early nomination period likewise is associated with candidate survival, viability, and success in the early nomination process. As Table 5.4 presents, there were eight candidates for the 1988 Democratic presidential nomination who

TABLE 5.4
Summary Analysis of Candidates Grouped by Viability
with Associated Levels of Early Candidacy Fund-Raising Success
1988 Presidential Election Cycle
Democrats

Candidates Grouped by Viability	1987		1988	
	First Half	Total	January	February
Viable Through Early Nom. Process:				
Michael Dukakis	$4,232,634	$10,201,543	$804,840	$1,248,401
Richard Gephardt	$2,145,300	$4,323,825	$212,703	$1,072,157
Paul Simon	$906,201	$3,797,166	$534,259	$1,018,841
Active Through Early Nom. Process:				
Bruce Babbitt	$1,128,739	$1,748,132	$252,665	$168,308
Al Gore	$1,419,067	$3,827,460	$180,746	$1,041,401
Gary Hart	$2,145,032	$2,219,997	$70,304	$18,366
Rev. Jesse Jackson	$1,025,297 (9 months)	$1,990,732	$610,037	$879,472
Withdrawing Before Early Nom. Process:				
Joseph Biden	$3,232,157	$3,763,248	$4,600	$5,507
Withdrawing Before Formal Announcement:				
Bill Bradley	—	—	—	—
Dale Bumpers	—	—	—	—
Bill Clinton	—	—	—	—
Mario Cuomo	—	—	—	—
Edward Kennedy	—	—	—	—
Sam Nunn	—	—	—	—
Charles Robb	—	—	—	—
Patricia Schroeder	—	—	—	—

established presidential campaign committees, and three of the four candidates who were among the most successful in pre-election year and early election year fund-raising through these campaign committees—Dukakis, Gephardt, and Simon—also proved to be the three candidates whose performance in the early nomination process classified them as viable. Dukakis's early candidacy fund-raising totaled $10,201,543, by far the largest total among the Democratic candidates, and Gephardt and Simon's pre-election year totals of $4,323,825 and $3,797,166 respectively ranked second and fourth. The other four Democratic candidates who remained active through the early nomination process generally had substantially lower pre-election year fund-raising totals, including Hart's $2,219,997, Jackson's $1,990,732, and Babbitt's $1,748,132, although Gore was an exception in that his pre-election year fund-raising total of $3,827,460 was in the range of the viable candidates despite the fact that his early primary and caucus performance did not classify him as a viable candidate. Biden's fund-raising total of $3,763,248 was about equal to Gore's and yet he was neither viable nor active through the early nomination process, but in this case his early withdrawal was a result of a scandal that fund-raising success could not mitigate. In short, during the early candidacy phase just as during the pre-candidacy phase, the level of fund-raising success did indeed prove to be associated with which candidates achieved viability in the early nomination process, which candidates remained active through the early nomination process, and which ones were forced to withdraw. Consistent with the hypothesized relationship between early candidacy fund-raising success and candidate survival, viability, and success through the early nomination process, the more a candidate raised through a presidential campaign committee during the early candidacy phase, the more likely it was for that candidate to be viable through the early nomination process or, for those whose success was more limited, to at least remain active through the early nomination process.

The momentum in fund-raising achieved by the candidates for the 1988 Democratic nomination in the early candidacy phase also proved to be significant to candidate viability and success. As Table 5.5 presents, the three candidates classified as viable through the early nomination process—Dukakis, Gephardt, and Simon—all had positive ratios in their second half of 1987 to first half of 1987 fund-raising totals, with Dukakis presenting the largest absolute dollar figures, $5,968,910 to $4,232,634, and with Simon having the greatest ratio, $2,890,966 to $906,201. These three candidates who are classified as viable also had strong positive fund-raising momentum ratios for February 1988 to January 1988, for instance Dukakis whose totals were $1,248,401 in February 1988 to $804,840 in January 1988. Interestingly, these momentum ratios among viable candidates were consistently positive for the second half of 1987 as compared with the first half and for February 1988 as compared with January 1988, but were not consistently positive for the fourth quarter of 1987 versus the third quarter, suggesting that fund-raising momentum over the course of the entire pre-election year is more important to a candidate than a late surge in fund-raising momentum at the close of the pre-election year. These momentum ratios were mixed among the four candidates classified as simply active through the early nomination process, namely Babbitt, Gore, Hart, and Jackson, although Babbitt and Hart both had generally negative ratios indicating the absence of momentum. Gore and Jackson generally enjoyed positive ratios, indicating momentum, but for the second half of the pre-election year and the early part of the election year itself, not

TABLE 5.5
Analysis of Candidates Grouped by Viability
with Associated Levels of Early Candidacy Fund-Raising Momentum
1988 Presidential Election Cycle
Democrats

Candidates Grouped by Viability	2nd Half 1987 / 1st Half 1987	4th Qtr 1987 / 3rd Qtr 1987	Feb 1988 / Jan 1988
Viable Through Early Nom. Process:			
Michael Dukakis	$5,968,910	$2,560,674	$1,248,401
	$4,232,634	$3,408,236	$804,840
Richard Gephardt	$2,178,526	$1,125,748	$1,072,157
	$2,145,300	$1,052,778	$212,703
Paul Simon	$2,890,966	$1,788,095	$1,018,841
	$906,201	$1,102,871	$534,259
Active Through Early Nom. Process:			
Bruce Babbitt	$667,393	$383,035	$168,308
	$1,128,739	$284,358	$252,665
Al Gore	$2,410,042	$1,172,299	$1,041,401
	$1,419,067	$1,237,743	$180,746
Gary Hart	$74,964	$43,815	$18,366
	$2,145,032	$31,149	$70,304
Rev. Jesse Jackson	NA	$970,460	$879,472
	NA		$610,037
Withdrawing Before Early Nom. Process:			
Joseph Biden	$531,091	$23,890	$5,507
	$3,232,157	$507,201	$4,600

the whole pre-election year, again suggesting that a late surge in momentum is not as valuable as a year-long advance. Momentum in early candidacy fund-raising therefore is clearly important to candidate viability and success, but the overall figure for fund-raising must be significant if a candidate is to be viable, and momentum throughout the pre-election year is more important for candidate viability and success than a sudden surge in fund-raising late in the pre-election year.

Yet another measure of early candidacy fund-raising success is the amount of cash-on-hand available to a candidate at crucial junctures in the campaign, most notably at the end of 1987 as the pre-election year comes to a close, and also at the end of February 1988 as the formal nomination process moves into high gear. As Table 5.6 summarizes, the candidates ranked first, third, and fourth in cash-on-hand as of December 31, 1987—Dukakis, Gephardt, and Simon—proved to be the three candidates who achieved viability through the early nomination process, with Gore—who actually ranked second—remaining active through the early nomination process but not reaching the threshold for viability. The other candidates who only remained active through the early nomination process, including Babbitt, Hart and Jackson, had lower cash-on-hand totals as of December 31, 1987, with Gore's total of $894,074 in cash-on-hand being the only exception. A similar pattern is evident in cash-on-hand as of February 29, 1988, with the three candidates who achieved viability through the early nomination process generally having higher cash-on-hand totals, with Hart's third-ranking cash-on-hand total standing in contrast to his status as an active although not viable candidate. Thus, while fund-raising totals in and of themselves surely are the best predictors of candidate viability and success, dollars that are raised generally are only helpful to a candidate if they are still available to be spent, and cash-on-hand totals are the best measure of a candidate's available financial resources. The cash-on-hand totals for the 1988 Democratic candidate field support the generalization that the candidates with the most cash-on-hand as of December 1987 and February 1988 went on to achieve viability and success in the early nomination process.

TABLE 5.6
Analysis of Candidates Grouped by Viability
with Associated Levels of Cash-on-Hand
1988 Presidential Election Cycle
Democrats

Candidates Grouped by Viability	Cash-on-Hand as of 12/31/87	Cash-on-Hand as of 2/29/88
Viable Through Early Nom. Process:		
Michael Dukakis	$2,180,729	$2,920,432
Richard Gephardt	$781,841	$450,037
Paul Simon	$202,033	$760,756
Active Through Early Nom. Process:		
Bruce Babbitt	$87,114	$247,768
Al Gore	$894,074	$340,927
Gary Hart	$123,525	$488,967
Rev. Jesse Jackson	$5,677	$170,015
Withdrawing Before Early Nom. Process:		
Joseph Biden	$21,715	$10,774

The level of federal matching funding received by each candidate is a final significant measure of fund-raising success. This federal matching figure obviously can represent a major infusion of new funds into each candidate's campaign, and because only the first $250 of each contribution is matchable, it also is a measure of the level of participation at small and medium-size contribution levels that a candidate is able to attract. As Table 5.7 documents, the three Democratic candidates with the highest levels of federal matching funding as of January 1988—Dukakis, Gephardt, and Simon—also were the three candidates achieving viability in the early nomination process. Gore's total of $1,852,053 in federal matching funding in January 1988 was a close fourth to these three leading candidates, but his candidacy failed to achieve viability and he simply remained as an active candidate through the early nomination process. This same pattern persisted in the ranking of candidates in terms of federal matching funding in February 1988, with the exception that Gore's total in federal matching funding as an active candidate actually surpassed Gephardt's total as a viable candidate, although by only about $83,000. Overall, a candidate's level of federal matching funding certainly is an additional measure of fund-raising success, indicating not only the amount in new funds provided to candidates as the formal nomination process begins but also revealing the level of popular participation in a candidate's fund-raising. The levels of federal matching funding received by the 1988 Democratic candidate

TABLE 5.7
**Analysis of Candidates Grouped by Viability
with Associated Levels of Federal Matching Funding
1988 Presidential Election Cycle
Democrats**

Candidates Grouped by Viability	Federal Matching Funding on 1/31/88	Federal Matching Funding on 2/29/88
Viable Through Early Nom. Process:		
Michael Dukakis	$3,493,419	$1,569,597
Richard Gephardt	$1,910,832	$268,757
Paul Simon	$1,875,017	$364,011
Active Through Early Nom. Process:		
Bruce Babbitt	$742,065	$89,592
Al Gore	$1,852,053	$352,177
Gary Hart	$937,325	$179,317
Rev. Jesse Jackson	$598,021	$119,328
Withdrawing Before Early Nom. Process:		
Joseph Biden	0	0

field supports the generalization that the candidates with the highest totals in federal matching funding relative to the other candidates also are the candidates who achieve viability and success in the early nomination process.

In sum, the 1988 Democratic early nomination campaign presents a strong initial case study illustrating the extent to which success in early campaign fund-raising is crucial to a candidate's prospects for survival, viability, and success in the early presidential nomination process. At both the pre-candidacy and early candidacy phases, the level of success which a candidate achieves in fund-raising clearly is related to the candidate's capability to achieve viability, or at least to remain active, through the early nomination process. The role of leadership PACs as shadow campaign committees also is evident in the 1988 Democratic contest as almost all of the major candidates utilized this mechanism to support pre-candidacy activity and early fund-raising. Further examination of fund-raising by the candidate field in the 1988 Democratic early nomination campaign also establishes the importance of fund-raising momentum, a comparably strong total in cash-on-hand, and comparably strong federal matching funding as additional measures of a candidate's fund-raising success, and as predictors of candidate viability and success. Thus pre-candidacy and early candidacy fund-raising success among the candidate field seeking the 1988 Democratic presidential nomination was predictive of candidate survival, viability, and success, thereby supporting the pivotal role of money, the ability to generate more money, and the achievement of fund-raising success as predictors of candidate survival, viability, and success in the post-reform era early presidential nomination process.

Republican Campaign Fund-Raising in 1988

The early campaign for the 1988 Republican nomination, like the 1988 Democratic nomination contest, provides a striking case study of the impact of the money primary on the modern presidential selection process. As was the case on the Democratic side, there was a proliferation of leadership PACs and other organizational entities such as foundations, other tax-exempt organizations, and state-based political committees that were established very early in the 1988 Republican campaign. As Table 5.8 summarizes, of the thirteen active and potential Republican candidates in 1988, nine utilized a leadership PAC, and four of these nine also utilized some other organizational entity in addition to their leadership PAC. All four of the candidates categorized as viable through the early nomination process as well as both of the candidates categorized as active through the early nomination process utilized a leadership PAC, with three of the four viable candidates utilizing an additional organizational entity and one of the two candidates who were active through

TABLE 5.8
Summary Analysis of Candidates Grouped by Viability
with Associated Number of Candidate Leadership PACs
and Other Early Fund-Raising Entities
1988 Presidential Election Cycle
Republicans

Candidates Grouped by Viability	Number of Candidates	Other Early Entities	Leadership PACs	Neither
Viable Through Early Nom. Process:	4	3	4	0
Active Through Early Nom. Process:	2	1	2	0
Withdrawing Before Early Nom. Process:	—	—	—	—
Withdrawing Before Formal Announcement:	4	0	2	2
Other Potential Candidates:	3	0	1	2

the early nomination process also utilizing an additional organizational entity. Moreover, consistent with the generalization that PACs and other organizational entities are important for pre-candidacy and early candidacy success, of the four candidates who withdrew before a formal announcement and the three potential candidates, only three utilized a pre-candidacy committee, in each case a leadership PAC, with the other four not utilizing any pre-candidacy committee or organization whatsoever. Thus a pre-candidacy committee, and in fact a leadership PAC, was part of the early campaign of every candidate who achieved viability through the early nomination process or who remained active through the early nomination process in the 1988 Republican pre-nomination campaign. Among the candidates and would-be candidates for the 1988 Republican nomination, just as among their Democratic counterparts, in short, the prevalence of pre-candidacy committees and in particular leadership PACs is indicative of the critical importance of early fund-raising as a central part of the early campaign and the indispensable importance of fund-raising success for candidate survival, viability, and success through the early nomination process.

A wide variety of pre-candidacy committees and other organizational entities were utilized for this pre-candidacy fund-raising in the 1988 Republican pre-nomination campaign. Moreover, the success of these pre-candidacy fund-raising efforts was even more impressive among the Republican candidates than among their Democratic counterparts. A large number of leadership PACs and other organizational entities were employed by the emerging Republican field in the 1988 election cycle, with many candidates having both a leadership PAC and another organizational entity and with some of these entities dating back to the early 1980s or even the 1970s. As already noted, all four of the Republican candidates classified as viable through the early nomination process utilized PACs as part of their early campaign. Indicative of the early fund-raising success achieved by these ultimately viable Republican candidates utilizing leadership PACs were the remarkable totals they raised during 1986 alone, with front-runner George H. Bush's Fund for America's Future raising over $5 million, Jack Kemp's Campaign for a New Majority raising over $2 million, and Robert Dole's Fund for a Conservative Majority raising over $1 million—fund-raising success that dwarfed early campaign fund-raising through leadership PACs on the Democratic side in 1986. The fourth viable candidate, Pat Robertson, also utilized a PAC as part of this early campaign and raised modest totals that peaked at $367,349 in 1986. But Robertson's early campaign also had even more valuable entities such as his Freedom Council, a foundation that raised $1,577,380 during 1985 alone, and the candidate's long-standing affiliation with the Christian Broadcasting Network which provided a loan of $4.6 million. Thus all four viable candidates achieved strong early fund-raising totals, generally but not always utilizing leadership PACs as their primary fund-raising vehicle.

A much lower level of pre-candidacy fund-raising success is evident in the second category of the candidate field, namely those who remained as active candidates but who proved not to be viable through the early nomination process. The two candidates classified as active through the early nomination process both utilized leadership PACs, namely Pierre du Pont's Pete du Pont for President and Alexander Haig's Committee for America, but both of these candidates fell short of the $1 million threshold in 1986 fund-raising, early leadership PAC-raised support that certainly was noteworthy but that trailed well behind the early fund-raising of the candidates who ultimately proved to be viable. But both du Pont and Haig also utilized an alternate organizational entity along with their PACs during this pre-candidacy period. There were seven other potential candidates for the 1988 Republican nomination, including four who withdrew before a formal announcement and three more who never moved beyond simply being potential candidates, but only three of these seven candidates utilized entities for pre-candidacy fund-raising and in every case these entities were leadership PACs. Both Howard Baker's Republican Majority Fund and Donald Rumsfeld's Citizens for American Values also fell short of the $1 million threshold in fund-raising during 1986, modest fund-raising success that would have been competitive on the Democratic side, but compared with the Republican candidate field was unimpressive. In fact, these modest fund-raising results may even have foreshadowed both potential candidates' subsequent early withdrawal. Also quite significantly, all four of the Republican candidates who did not utilize any pre-candidacy fund-raising entity also were among the would-be contenders who in fact withdrew before a formal announcement of candidacy or never moved beyond a potential candidacy.

More detailed analysis of 1988 Republican pre-candidacy campaign fund-raising demonstrates even more dramatically than the early Democratic campaign just how critical fund-raising success during the pre-candidacy campaign is to candidate survival, viability, and success. As Table 5.9 summarizes, almost the entire field of would-be candidates engaged in early fund-raising, with the leadership PAC being the organizational entity relied upon most generally and with significant fund-raising activity beginning as early as 1985 and reaching its height in 1986—two years before the beginning of the presidential election year. As already noted, three of the four candidates categorized as viable through the early nomination process—Bush, Dole, and Kemp—raised substantial dollars

TABLE 5.9
Summary Analysis of Candidates Grouped by Viability
with Associated Levels of Pre-Candidacy Fund-Raising Success
1988 Presidential Election Cycle
Republicans

Candidates Grouped by Viability	Early Fund-Raising		Leadership PAC		
	Pre-1986	1986	1985	1986	1987
Viable Through Early Nom. Process:					
George H. Bush			$3,949,581	$5,226,402	$1,177,912
Robert Dole			$1,371,226	$1,174,518	$601,929
Jack Kemp	$359,000	$450,000	$1,156,422	$2,037,013	$207,526
Pat Robertson	$1,577,380		$160,880	$367,349	$66,086
Active Through Early Nom. Process:					
Pierre du Pont			—	$877,872	—
Alexander Haig			—	$617,541	$409,639
Withdrawing Before Early Nom. Process:					
Withdrawing Before Formal Announcement:					
Howard Baker	$2,302,261 (1983)		$741,229	$687,366	$449,890
Patrick Buchanan					
Paul Laxalt					
Donald Rumsfeld				$813,010	$356,441

during these pre-candidacy campaigns. Bush's amazing early fund-raising totals of $3,949,581 in 1985 and $5,226,402 in 1986 far exceeded his Republican competitors, just as was the case with Dukakis on the Democratic side, with his 1986 total actually exceeding the combined 1986 totals of the three other Republican candidates who proved to be viable through the early nomination process. But perhaps signaling the prospect of a competitive start to the formal nomination process was the level of early fund-raising achieved by Dole, who raised $1,371,226 in 1985 and $1,174,518 in 1986, and Kemp who raised $1,156,422 in 1985 and $2,037,013 in 1986. Robertson's questionable reliance upon his close affiliation with the Christian Broadcasting Network made his poor fund-raising results through his PAC—just $160,880 in 1985 and $367,349 in 1986—much less important than would have been the case absent this affiliation.

Forming a second tier of candidates with much less impressive fund-raising results are two Republicans—du Pont and Haig—who ultimately proved to be able to remain active through the early nomination process but whose leadership PAC fund-raising was far below the levels of the top tier of Republican contenders. Both of these candidates did not begin pre-candidacy fund-raising until 1986, with du Pont raising $877,872 and Haig raising $617,541 during this crucial early campaign year. These comparatively lower early fund-raising totals certainly gave advance indication that these two Republican candidates would not be viable against opponents whose early fund-raising was two-, three-, and even four- or five-times greater. Among the would-be candidates for the 1988 Republican nomination who withdrew before any formal announcement were two candidates—Howard Baker and Donald Rumsfeld—whose early fund-raising during 1986 totaled $687,366 and $813,010 respectively, fund-raising results that placed them in the same dollar range as candidates who ultimately were able to remain active through the early nomination process. Baker's strength as a potential candidate was made all the greater by the fact that his leadership PAC, the Republican Majority Fund, actually dated to 1980 and had raised in excess of $2 million in some of its more active years. It should be noted that Baker's withdrawal occurred because of his selection as Chief of Staff to President Reagan, and Rumsfeld in all likelihood was positioning himself for his subsequent appointment in President George H. Bush's new administration, rationales completely apart from the political and fund-raising dynamics of the early 1988 campaign. In sum, leadership PACs as well as alternate pre-candidacy entities were utilized broadly within the 1988 Republican candidate field, and their level of success during the two- and three-year period prior to the presidential election year certainly provided an early indication of the strength of the final Republican candidate field in 1988. Aside from early candidate withdrawals motivated by other political choices, the Republican contenders who achieved the most successful early and ongoing pre-candidacy fund-raising generally also were the candidates who proved to be viable as the early nomination process began.

Leadership PACs established by would-be candidates for the 1988 Republican nomination clearly played a major part in the early phase of the pre-nomination campaign. In fact, the use of PACs for early campaign fund-raising was universal among the competitive Republican candidate field, and the level of early fund-raising success achieved by these Republican candidate leadership PACs was unprecedented, far exceeding the Democratic candidate leadership PACs in this presidential election cycle. Moreover, as was also the case on the Democratic side, simply the pattern in the level of activity of these Republican candidate leadership PACs supports the generalization that they were established to support pre-presidential candidacy activity and to engage in early campaign fund-raising. As Table 5.10 documents, eight early aspirants

TABLE 5.10
Comparison of Contributions to Presidential Candidate Leadership PACs
Prior to and During Presidential Election Years
1988 Presidential Election Cycle
Republicans

Candidate and Leadership PAC	1985	1986	1987	1988
George H. Bush— Fund for America's Future (4/25/85)	$3,949,581	$5,226,402	$1,177,912	$607,996
Robert Dole— Fund for a Conservative Majority, fka Campaign America (3/1/78)	$1,371,226	$1,174,518	$601,929	$375,112
Jack Kemp— Campaign for a New Majority, fka Campaign for Prosperity (circa 1982)	$1,156,422	$2,037,013	$207,526	$415,177
Pat Robertson— Americans for the Republic fka Committee for Freedom (6/25/85)	$160,880	$367,349	$66,086	$170,763
Pierre du Pont—Pete du Pont for President (6/3/86)	—	$877,872	—	—
Alexander Haig— Committee for America (4/2/86)	—	$617,541	$409,639	0
Howard Baker— Republican Majority Fund	$741,229	$687,366	$449,890	$684,499
Donald Rumsfeld— Citizens for American Values (12/23/85)	—	$813,010	$356,441	$74,000

for the 1988 Republican presidential nomination established leadership PACs in advance of the announced candidacy period, in six cases as early as 1985 or before, and in the other two cases in 1986. Quite significantly, as was also the case with six of the eight candidates on the Democratic side in the 1988 presidential election cycle, fund-raising by seven of these eight Republican candidate-affiliated leadership PACs reached its height during 1986, the year before the pre-election year when fund-raising by formal presidential campaign committees generally begins. Total fund-raising activity among these eight leadership PACs during 1986 ranged from a low of $367,349 in the case of Robertson's PAC to a high of $5,226,402 in the case of Bush's PAC. Also quite significantly, as would be expected if these PACs indeed were functioning as pre-candidacy fund-raising entities, the fund-raising totals for all eight of these leadership PACs fell off substantially in 1987, the pre-election year when campaign fund-raising efforts could be expected to shift to the official presidential campaign committees. This overall pattern in leadership PAC fund-raising from 1985 through 1987 is consistent with the generalization that leadership PACs established by aspiring presidential nominees are a major part of pre-candidacy activity and fund-raising during the early campaign.

The early candidacy period of the pre-nomination campaign, in particular the pre-election year when announced candidates begin utilizing formal presidential campaign committees, builds upon the fund-raising efforts which aspiring candidates launched during their pre-candidacy campaigns. The level of fund-raising success achieved during this early candidacy phase using presidential campaign committees is associated very closely with candidate survival, viability, and success in the early nomination process. As Table 5.11 summarizes, just six of the original field of thirteen would-be and potential candidates for the 1988 Republican presidential nomination established presidential campaign committees, and the four candidates who were the most successful in pre-election year and early election year fund-raising through these campaign committees—Bush, Robertson, Dole, and Kemp—also proved to be the candidates whose performance in the early nomination process categorized them as viable. All four of these leading contenders for the 1988 Republican nomination achieved fund-raising totals during the pre-election year of 1987 that were staggering relative to any campaign up to that time. Bush's 1987 fund-raising total of $18,801,408 certainly led the field, but both Robertson and Dole were not far behind, with 1987 totals of $14,203,223 and $14,044,166 respectively. Kemp's 1987 fund-raising total of $7,170,234 ranked last among the leading four Republican contenders, but his performance in the opening nomination contests also categorized his candidacy as viable through the early nomination process. The next tier of Republican contenders certainly had far less impressive pre-election year fund-raising results, including du Pont who raised

TABLE 5.11
Summary Analysis of Candidates Grouped by Viability
with Associated Levels of Early Candidacy Fund-Raising Success
1988 Presidential Election Cycle
Republicans

Candidates Grouped by Viability	1987		1988	
	First Half	Total	January	February
Viable Through Early Nom. Process:				
George H. Bush (7/86 to 6/87)	$9,380,285	$18,801,408	$767,893	$1,158,031
Robert Dole	$3,716,216	$14,044,166	$1,169,695	$1,308,134
Jack Kemp (11/86 to 6/87)	$3,172,936	$7,170,234	$1,040,271	$991,716
Pat Robertson	—	$14,203,223	$1,277,682	$2,256,525
Active Through Early Nom. Process:				
Pierre du Pont	$1,409,089	$3,743,111	$478,941	$348,977
Alexander Haig	$458,357	$1,250,770	$40,333	$27,398
Withdrawing Before Early Nom. Process:				
Withdrawing Before Formal Announcement:				
Howard Baker	—	—	—	—
Patrick Buchanan	—	—	—	—
Paul Laxalt	—	—	—	—
Donald Rumsfeld	—	—	—	—

$3,743,111 and Haig who raised $1,250,770, and as expected their early performance in the formal nomination process categorized them as active but not viable through the early nomination process. The remaining field of early would-be candidates for the Republican nomination, including the four who withdrew before any formal announcement, never established presidential campaign committees and did not do any official presidential campaign fundraising whatsoever during 1987. Thus, consistent with the hypothesized relationship between early candidacy fund-raising success and candidate survival, viability, and success through the early nomination process, the candidates who raised the most during the early candidacy period indeed proved to be the candidates whose performance categorized them as viable or active through the early nomination process. In fact, the Republican candidates in the 1988 presidential election cycle who raised the most through a presidential campaign committee during the early candidacy period proved to be viable through the opening of the formal nomination process, and the candidates

Chapter 5

who ranked next in overall fund-raising success at least proved to be able to remain active through the early nomination process.

Momentum in fund-raising is a further measure of fund-raising success, and the level of fund-raising momentum achieved by candidates for the 1988 Republican nomination during the pre-election year was associated with candidate viability and success. As Table 5.12 presents, the four candidates categorized as viable through the early nomination process—Bush, Dole, Kemp, and Robertson (whose ratio is estimated from available data)—all had positive ratios in their second half of 1987 to first half of 1987 fund-raising totals, with Bush having the highest absolute dollar figure for the year as a whole, $9,421,123 to $9,380,284, but with Dole very close behind and also reflecting the highest ratio, $10,327,950 to $3,716,216. The momentum of campaign fund-raising continued to build among the leaders in the Republican field as

TABLE 5.12
Analysis of Candidates Grouped by Viability
with Associated Levels of Early Candidacy Fund-Raising Momentum
1988 Presidential Election Cycle
Republicans

Candidates Grouped by Viability	2nd Half 1987 / 1st Half 1987	4th Qtr 1987 / 3rd Qtr 1987	Feb 1988 / Jan 1988
Viable Through Early Nom. Process:			
George H. Bush	$9,421,123	$6,206,290	$1,158,031
	$9,380,284	$3,214,834	$767,893
Robert Dole	$10,327,950	$6,345,035	$1,308,134
	3,716,216	$3,982,915	$1,169,695
Jack Kemp	$4,016,574	$1,939,638	$991,716
	$3,172,936	$2,076,936	$1,040,271
	(7 months)		
Pat Robertson	$3,132,940 (4th Qtr)	$3,132,940	$2,256,525
	$11,070,283	N.A.	$1,277,682
	(1st, 2nd, 3rd Qtrs)		
Active Through Early Nom. Process:			
Pierre du Pont	$2,334,023	$1,260,963	$348,977
	$1,409,089	$1,073,060	$478,941
Alexander Haig	$792,413	$352,579	$27,398
	$458,357	$439,834	$40,333
Withdrawing Before Early Nom. Process:			

the pre-election year progressed, with front-runner Bush and principal challenger Dole both having high momentum ratios for the fourth quarter as compared with the third quarter of 1987, a pattern of a late pre-election year surge not evident on the Democratic side in 1988. A late surge in fund-raising also was demonstrated by Robertson, whose loss of momentum in the fourth quarter of 1987 was balanced by a surprising positive momentum ratio of $2,256,525 raised in February 1988 as compared with $1,277,682 raised in January 1988. Candidates in the active Republican field such as du Pont and Haig who achieved much lower absolute dollar figures and less impressive momentum ratios for the second half of 1987 to the first half of 1987, for instance du Pont's $2,334,023 to $1,409,089, and Haig's $792,413 to $458,357, actually remained active but were not classified as viable through the early nomination process, again consistent with the hypothesized impact of fund-raising success on candidate survival, viability, and success through the early nomination process. These momentum ratios were even more mixed and in fact were generally negative for the fourth quarter to the third quarter of 1987 and for February 1988 to January 1988 for both du Pont and Haig, again consistent with the expectation that candidates with weaker fund-raising would prove not to be viable even if they remained active through the early nomination process. In short, momentum in early candidacy fund-raising is clearly associated with candidate survival, viability, and success in the 1988 Republican early nomination process. As was the case in the early 1988 Democratic nomination campaign, Republican candidates whose overall fund-raising figures were significant both in absolute dollar totals and as ratios also were the candidates who proved to achieve viability and success in the early nomination process. While momentum throughout the pre-election year was most important as an indicator of fund-raising success, the candidates in the 1988 Republican pre-nomination campaign who continued to build their momentum during the fourth quarter of 1987 and through February of 1988 also were the candidates who were categorized as viable through the early nomination process.

Another measure of early candidacy fund-raising success is the amount of cash-on-hand available to a candidate, especially at crucial junctures in the campaign such as the end of 1987, the pre-election year, and also the end of February 1988, as the formal nomination process approached its height. As Table 5.13 summarizes, three of the top four candidates ranked by cash-on-hand as of the end of 1987—Bush, Dole, and Kemp—also were categorized as viable candidates based on their actual performance in the early nomination process. Moreover, Robertson's cash-on-hand figure jumped substantially in February 1988, reaching $7,412,321, the highest of any candidate including Bush, a pattern consistent with the expectation that candidates with the

TABLE 5.13
Analysis of Candidates Grouped by Viability
with Associated Levels of Cash-on-Hand
1988 Presidential Election Cycle
Republicans

Candidates Grouped by Viability	Cash-on-Hand as of 12/31/87	Cash-on-Hand as of 2/29/88
Viable Through Early Nom. Process:		
George H. Bush	$5,704,342	$6,704,924
Robert Dole	$2,208,683	$836,446
Jack Kemp	$127,982	$59,686
Pat Robertson	$105,850	$7,412,321
Active Through Early Nom. Process:		
Pierre du Pont	($208,888)	$225,289
Alexander Haig	$136,260	$6,245
Withdrawing Before Early Nom. Process:		

strongest fund-raising also would prove—as Robertson did—to be classified as viable through the early nomination process. The candidates in the active 1988 Republican candidate field with low cash-on-hand, both as of the end of 1987 and the end of February 1988, including du Pont and Haig, remained in the race but had low vote totals in the opening nomination contests, categorizing their candidacies as active but not viable, again consistent with the pattern demonstrated by the 1988 Democratic candidate field. In short, consistent with the expectation that candidates with the strongest fund-raising will achieve viability and success, the 1988 Republican candidates who had the highest cash-on-hand totals in December 1987 and February 1988 indeed achieved viability and success in the early nomination process.

A final measure of fund-raising success is the level of federal matching funding received by each candidate, a figure reflecting both the amount of new funding available to the candidate as the formal nomination process opens as well as the breadth of the candidate's base of $250 and below contributors. As Table 5.14 presents, the top four candidates with the highest totals in federal matching funding in both January 1988 and February 1988 also proved to be the viable candidates in the early nomination process. These four candidates, including Bush, Dole, Kemp, and Robertson, received federal matching funding in January 1988 ranging from Robertson's $6,455,898 and Bush's $6,374,982 to Kemp's $3,893,846, and these same four candidates likewise received the largest totals in federal matching funding in February 1988. The two Republican candidates in 1988 with comparatively much lower totals

TABLE 5.14
Analysis of Candidates Grouped by Viability
with Associated Levels of Federal Matching Funding
1988 Presidential Election Cycle
Republicans

Candidates Grouped by Viability	Federal Matching Funding on 1/31/88	Federal Matching Funding on 2/29/88
Viable Through Early Nom. Process:		
George H. Bush	$6,374,982	$237,348
Robert Dole	$5,566,330	$657,096
Jack Kemp	$3,893,846	$612,609
Pat Robertson	$6,455,898	$785,883
Active Through Early Nom. Process:		
Pierre du Pont	$2,208,522	$91,980
Alexander Haig	$292,934	$146,451
Withdrawing Before Early Nom. Process:		

in federal matching funding, namely du Pont and Haig who received $2,208,522 and $292,934 respectively in January 1988, also failed to meet the test for viability even as they continued to be active candidates when the formal nomination process opened. Thus, as the hypothesized relationship between fund-raising success and candidate viability predicts, and as was the case with the 1988 Democratic candidate field, the levels of federal matching funding received by the 1988 Republican candidates proved to be related to candidate viability and success. Republican candidates receiving comparatively greater totals in federal matching funding also were the candidates who indeed achieved viability and success when the early nomination process began to unfold.

The 1988 Republican early nomination campaign, like the 1988 Democratic early nomination campaign, is a case study showing the extent to which success in early campaign fund-raising is essential to candidate survival, viability, and success in the opening presidential nomination contests. Examination of the 1988 Republican candidate field during both the pre-candidacy and early candidacy phases provides compelling evidence that the candidates who were strongest in their pre-candidacy and early candidacy fund-raising also achieved viability in the early nomination process. The role of leadership PACs was even greater among the 1988 Republican candidate field, with every viable or active candidate utilizing a leadership PAC to support pre-candidacy activity and early fund-raising and with the Republican candidates raising substantially more through these leadership PACs than their Democratic counterparts. Other measures of fund-raising success, such as fund-raising momentum, the amount of cash-on-hand, and the level of federal matching funding, all also proved to be predictive of which candidates would achieve viability and success in the early nomination process. Thus, fund-raising success during both the pre-candidacy and early candidacy phases of the 1988 Republican early nomination campaign, just as was the case with the 1988 Democratic early nomination campaign, was associated consistently with candidate survival, viability, and success in the early nomination process. Money, the development of an effective fund-raising program, and overall fund-raising success during the early nomination campaign all were associated with candidate survival, viability, and success in the opening contests of the 1988 Republican nomination process, providing yet additional strong support for the central place of the money primary and its requirement of fund-raising success as the first and perhaps most challenging test for aspiring presidential nominees in the post-reform presidential nomination process.

Campaign Fund-Raising in the 2000 Early Nomination Campaign

The 2000 presidential nomination contest's early campaign took the money primary to a new level of intensity and decisiveness in the early presidential selection process. As the most recent presidential election and the eighth presidential election of the post-reform era, and with the quarter century old framework of campaign finance reform severely eroded, the 2000 presidential election stands as a milestone in the evolution of the money primary that exists today. Money and fund-raising efforts to generate more money now stand as the first and greatest challenge for any aspiring presidential nominee. Moreover, with the trend toward front-loading of the primary and caucus calendar established and on the Republican side even more advanced, would-be candidates for either major party's nomination in 2000 had no alternative but to plan early and ongoing campaign fund-raising with the goal of amassing all or almost all of the funding needed to conduct a nationwide nomination campaign before the formal nomination process even began. Perhaps even more significantly, by the 2000 campaign the FECA framework had deteriorated substantially relative to just twelve years before, with numerous new loopholes in the system of campaign finance reform having opened and the trend toward money and the raising of money as the first arbiter of presidential nominee selection having advanced further still. The extraordinary importance of pre-candidacy activity and fund-raising and in particular of leadership PACs and other organizational entities in the early campaign is further indication of the dominance which the money primary had achieved by the 2000 campaign. In fact, so much of the 2000 pre-nomination campaign occurred during the pre-candidacy and early candidacy phases that the pre-election year may well have become the decisive phase in presidential nominee selection. In short, as dramatic as the final chapter of the 2000 presidential election proved to be, the early campaign in this most recent election stands as an equally striking beginning to a new era in which the money primary and the requirements of fund-raising success may well constitute a fundamentally new system for presidential nominee selection.

Democratic Campaign Fund-Raising in 2000

The early campaign for the 2000 Democratic presidential nomination, while distinct in that an incumbent Vice President was seeking his party's presidential nomination, included a money primary that was critical to the unfolding nomination contest. A strong indication of the rise of the money primary in the Democratic pre-nomination period was the proliferation of leadership PACs and other organizational entities that began operation very early in the 2000 Democratic campaign. As Table 5.15 summarizes, the 2000 Democratic candidate field included seven active or potential candidates, and five of them utilized a leadership PAC as a pre-candidacy committee. Moreover, the two Democratic candidates who proved to be viable through the opening nomination process—Al Gore and Bill Bradley—both utilized leadership PACs, with Bradley also having a tax-exempt foundation. At the other end of the spectrum, among the four candidates who ultimately withdrew from the nomination contest even before making a formal announcement, two had a leadership PAC as a pre-candidacy committee and two others did not. One other would-be candidate in the 2000 Democratic nomination contest never went beyond being a potential candidate but nonetheless had a leadership PAC, a fact that more than anything else was what identified him as a potential candidate in the first place. Thus a pre-candidacy committee and in fact a leadership PAC was part of the early campaign of most of the 2000 Democratic field and certainly of the two candidates who achieved viability in the early nomination process. This rise in the use of leadership PACs by aspiring presidential candidates, and the reliance by some candidates on other organizational entities as well, represents an important response by candidates to the emergence of fund-raising as a pivotal pre-candidacy activity and the necessity for an even earlier start in order to ensure survival, viability, and success.

TABLE 5.15
**Summary Analysis of Candidates Grouped by Viability
with Associated Number of Candidate Leadership PACs
and Other Early Fund-Raising Entities
2000 Presidential Election Cycle
Democrats**

Candidates Grouped by Viability	Number of Candidates	Other Early Entities	Leadership PACs	Neither
Viable Through Early Nom. Process:	2	1	2	0
Active Through Early Nom. Process:	—	—	—	—
Withdrawing Before Early Nom. Process:	—	—	—	—
Withdrawing Before Formal Announcement:	4	0	2	2
Other Potential Candidates:	1	0	1	0

The leadership PAC clearly was the preferred vehicle for pre-candidacy activity and early candidacy fund-raising in the 2000 Democratic nomination campaign. All five of the candidates or potential candidates for the 2000 Democratic nomination who had a pre-candidacy committee utilized a leadership PAC for this purpose. Moreover, only one of these candidates also utilized another organizational entity as well as a PAC, namely Bill Bradley. His foundation, the Fair Tax Foundation, dated back to 1984 when he was a Senator and also had served as a pre-candidacy organization leading up to his first presidential nomination bid in 1988. Following Bradley's departure from the U.S. Senate in 1996, the Fair Tax Foundation provided a platform for his continuing public presence, and later that year he augmented this capability with the establishment of a more politically focused leadership PAC. The increasing longevity of the leadership PACs utilized by presidential aspirants in the 2000 presidential election cycle also is noteworthy, with Gephardt's Effective Government Committee dating back to 1984—four quadrennial election cycles earlier—and Bradley's Time Future, Inc., dating back to 1996. Two other leadership PACs, Gore's Leadership '98 and Kerrey's Building America's Conscience and Kids—dated to early 1998, a year before the pre-election year. Only two candidates in the 2000 Democratic nomination contest did not utilize a leadership PAC or any pre-candidacy committee, namely the Rev. Jesse Jackson and John Kerry, and both of these potential candidates withdrew from the contest even before making a formal announcement. In short, consistent with the new political environment of an extended early campaign and a newly dominant money primary, leadership PACs were the means by which most candidates launched pre-candidacy activity in their extended pursuit of the 2000 Democratic nomination.

The pre-candidacy phase of the 2000 Democratic nomination contest, while relatively narrow in terms of its candidate field, nonetheless proved to be intensive and competitive. Moreover, early fund-raising by the principal Democratic candidate, Al Gore, was particularly aggressive and effective. As Table 5.16 notes, Gore's leadership PAC—Leadership '98—raised $4,262,940 during 1998, by far the largest total of any Democratic candidate or potential candidate during this year preceding the pre-election year. Vice President Gore's candidacy as a sitting Vice President and the heir to a still popular President certainly did a great deal to discourage additional candidates, with four other potential challengers withdrawing before their formal announcements. These early withdrawals aside, most of the activity during the 2000 Democratic nomination contest's early campaign emanated from the Gore campaign as it endeavored to establish an insurmountable lead in early fund-raising that in turn might give his candidacy the aura of inevitability. Bradley's fund-raising total for 1998 was just $398,291, less than one-tenth of Gore's total for the same year. While Bradley's actual vote totals in the early nomination process categorized him along with Gore as a viable candidate for the

TABLE 5.16
**Summary Analysis of Candidates Grouped by Viability
with Associated Levels of Pre-Candidacy Fund-Raising Success
2000 Presidential Election Cycle
Democrats**

Candidates Grouped by Viability	Early Fund-Raising		Leadership PAC		
	Pre-1998	1998	1997	1998	1999
Viable Through Early Nom. Process:					
Al Gore			—	$4,262,940	0
Bill Bradley			$91	$398,291	$7,050
Active Through Early Nom. Process:					
Withdrawing Before Early Nom. Process:					
Withdrawing Before Formal Announcement:					
Richard Gephardt			$371,793	$971,062	$363,325
Rev. Jesse Jackson					
Bob Kerrey			—	$284,788	$135,128
John Kerry					

Democratic nomination, with Bradley in fact being Gore's sole challenger for the Democratic nomination, it is notable that his early fund-raising results certainly would not have suggested this. In fact, as Table 5.16 also notes, Richard Gephardt's early fund-raising through his PAC totaled $971,062, substantially exceeding Bradley's total, and Bob Kerrey's early fund-raising totaled $284,788, about $100,000 short of Bradley's total, yet both of these candidates ended up withdrawing before a formal announcement. In short, Gore's intensive and very successful early fund-raising, as expected, was followed by victories in the early nomination process that made him not only a viable candidate but the confirmed front-runner. While Bradley's lackluster early fund-raising gave little indication of the highly competitive challenge he ultimately would mount, his failure to mount significant early fund-raising may well have been an early indication that his campaign ultimately would be unprepared to successfully challenge the enormous advantages of the sitting Vice President.

The pattern in fund-raising by leadership PACs as the primary vehicle for pre-candidacy activity and early fund-raising in the 2000 nomination campaign points clearly to their role as shadow campaign committees for aspiring presidential candidates. As Table 5.17 presents, the two candidates categorized as viable—Gore and Bradley—and two of the four candidates who withdrew—Gephardt and Kerrey—all utilized leadership PACs during their pre-candidacy campaigns. That these PACs actually were intended as vehicles to support pre-candidacy presidential campaign activity is evident simply from

TABLE 5.17
Comparison of Contributions to Presidential Candidate Leadership PACs
Prior to and During Presidential Election Years
2000 Presidential Election Cycle
Democrats

Candidate and Leadership PAC	1997	1998	1999	2000
Al Gore—				
Leadership '98 (2/19/98)	—	$4,262,940	0	0
Bill Bradley—				
Time Future, Inc. (8/13/96)	$91	$398,291	$7,050	$164,340
Richard Gephardt—				
Effective Government Committee (1984)	$371,793	$971,062	$363,325	$487,225
Bob Kerrey—				
Building America's Conscience and Kids PAC (3/25/98)	—	$284,788	$135,128	$21,497

the pattern of their fund-raising which for all four candidates peaked during 1998, the year prior to the pre-election year. Quite significantly, in the following year these PACs which were affiliated with newly announced presidential candidates had precipitous declines in total fund-raising, with Gore's PAC discontinuing fund-raising altogether and Bradley's PAC fund-raising dropping from $398,291 to $7,050. As noted relative to this pattern during the 1988 campaign, these declines in PAC fund-raising during the pre-election year are to be expected as candidates shift their energies and contributors shift their dollars to fund-raising efforts by the same candidates' official presidential campaign committees. It is interesting to note, however, that PACs connected with would-be presidential candidates who declined to run exhibited less precipitous declines in fund-raising from 1998 to 1999, with Gephardt's PAC fund-raising dropping from $971,062 to $363,325 and Kerrey's from $284,788 to $135,128. The fact that both of these candidates had withdrawn and therefore did not establish presidential campaign committees may explain why they chose to continue their PAC fund-raising at least at some level even as the presidential nomination campaign continued. In short, even with its relatively narrow candidate field, the 2000 Democratic nomination contest's pre-candidacy phase included significant early fund-raising by PACs during the year before the pre-election year, a pattern supporting the conclusion that leadership PACs indeed are a major part of pre-candidacy activity and early fund-raising during the early campaign.

Continued fund-raising success during the early candidacy period, continuing through the pre-election year of 1999 and extending into the nomination period itself, likewise is associated with candidate survival, viability, and success in the early nomination process. By the pre-election year when candidate fund-raising was being conducted by presidential campaign committees, however, the 2000 Democratic candidate field had narrowed to just two candidates, Gore and his lone challenger, Bradley. As Table 5.18 presents, both of these candidates mounted massive and highly successful fund-raising efforts throughout 1999, and by year-end Gore had amassed a total of $28,186,946, while Bradley was close behind at $27,419,838. The pace of this fund-raising was quite different, however, with Gore having enormous momentum from the pre-candidacy period as 1999 opened and reaching $17,537,396 by mid-year. Bradley, on the other hand, began 1999 building upon a very limited pre-candidacy effort, and had reached only $11,710,632 by mid-year. The story of Bradley's challenge to Gore was the strength of his fund-raising during the second half of 1999, pulling almost even with Gore by December 1999 and as a result raising significant questions about Gore's effectiveness and electability. Bradley's fund-raising success continued into the early nomination period itself, with Bradley out-fund-raising Gore by $1,308,059 to $588,630 in January

TABLE 5.18
Summary Analysis of Candidates Grouped by Viability
with Associated Levels of Early Candidacy Fund-Raising Success
2000 Presidential Election Cycle
Democrats

Candidates Grouped by Viability	1999		2000	
	First Half	*Total*	*January*	*February*
Early Nom. Process:				
Al Gore	$17,537,396	$28,186,946	$588,630	$1,798,828
Bill Bradley	$11,710,632	$27,419,838	$1,308,059	$710,295
Active Through				
Early Nom. Process:				
Withdrawing Before				
Early Nom. Process:				
Withdrawing Before				
Formal Announcement:				
Richard Gephardt	—	0	—	—
Rev. Jesse Jackson				
Bob Kerrey	—	—	—	—
John Kerry				

2000, a pattern that then was reversed when Gore out-fund-raised Bradley by $1,798,828 to $710,295 in February 2000. In short, the fund-raising campaigns of the two candidates for the 2000 Democratic nomination during the pre-election year of 1999 and early 2000 mirrored this race's highly contested early campaign, with Bradley's very strong showing for a time representing a credible challenge to the incumbent Vice President whose nomination had seemed all but certain just months earlier.

Momentum in fund-raising also was an important part of the early campaign leading up to the 2000 Democratic nomination contest, just as fund-raising success itself was integral to the candidates' standing during the pivotal pre-election year. As Table 5.19 details, both Gore and Bradley had impressive fund-raising totals for 1999 as a whole, each surpassing all previous records for fund-raising during the pre-election year in a Democratic contest. But while Gore had momentum through the first half of the year, by the second half the tide had shifted to Bradley who out-fund-raised Gore by the slim margin of $7,309,314 to $6,754,343 in the third quarter and by the wide margin of $8,399,893 to $3,895,207 in the fourth quarter. As a result, Gore's momentum ratios for the second half to the first half of 1999 and the fourth quarter to the third quarter of 1999 were both unfavorable, while Bradley's momentum ratios for the same periods were highly favorable, especially his

TABLE 5.19
Analysis of Candidates Grouped by Viability
with Associated Levels of Early Candidacy Fund-Raising Momentum
2000 Presidential Election Cycle
Democrats

Candidates Grouped by Viability	2nd Half 1999 / 1st Half 1999	4th Qtr 1999 / 3rd Qtr 1999	Feb 2000 / Jan 2000
Viable Through Early Nom. Process:			
Al Gore	$10,649,550	$3,895,207	$1,798,828
	$17,537,396	$6,754,343	$588,630
Bill Bradley	$15,709,207	$8,399,893	$710,295
	$11,710,632	$7,309,314	$1,308,059
Active Through Early Nom. Process:			
Withdrawing Before Early Nom. Process:			
Withdrawing Before Formal Announcement:			
Richard Gephardt	—	—	—
Rev. Jesse Jackson	—	—	—
Bob Kerrey	—	—	—
John Kerry	—	—	—

second half to first half ratio of $15,709,207 to $11,710,632. Bradley's fund-raising momentum did not carry through into the early nomination period, however, with Gore re-establishing his momentum with a February to January 2000 momentum ratio of $1,798,828 to $588,630, while Bradley's fund-raising trailed off during the same crucial time period. Thus, just as fund-raising success itself was a critical dimension of the overall Gore–Bradley contest, so too were their respective levels of momentum in fund-raising. While Gore's early dominance in fund-raising as well as his quest for the nomination itself were quickly threatened when Bradley began gaining in his dollar totals and had momentum in his favor, Bradley ultimately proved to be unable to maintain his momentum as Gore re-established his earlier fund-raising lead and the advantage of fund-raising momentum.

Each candidate's cash-on-hand is a further measure of fund-raising success, and in the 2000 Democratic nomination contest it was especially important because Gore's fund-raising was very early and hence his spending could have been unduly accelerated as well. An examination of a candidate's cash-on-hand therefore is invaluable as a measure of the extent to which dollars generated through successful early fund-raising are still available to be spent on a campaign. As Table 5.20 indicates, as of the end of the pre-election year in December 1999, Bradley's cash-on-hand was well ahead of Gore's, $8,320,943 to $5,734, 782, certainly also a reflection of the amazing fund-raising by Bradley through the second half of 1999. Yet by February 2000 this disparity was reversed, with Gore's $4,139,937 comparing very favorably with Bradley's $2,957,650. These mixed cash-on-hand totals for Gore and Bradley in the 2000 Democratic nomination contest are consistent with the generalization that an advantage in cash-on-hand is important to candidate viability and success. While Bradley's lead at the important pre-election year-end juncture raised serious questions about Gore's inevitability, Gore's recovery and his advantage over Bradley in cash-on-hand as of February 2000 supports the generalization that having the most cash-on-hand as the nomination period opens is associated with viability and success in the early nomination process.

A candidate's level of federal matching funding is a final measure of fund-raising success, providing an important read on a candidate's breadth of support with matchable contributions. The federal matching funding figures for the 2000 Democratic nomination contest were unusually important, with the close Gore–Bradley race in total fund-raising tilting toward Gore in terms of federal matching funding. As Table 5.21 presents, Gore's federal matching funding as of January 31, 2000, surpassed Bradley's, $5,544,497 to $4,178,817. In fact, this difference in contributions eligible for federal matching funding

TABLE 5.20
Analysis of Candidates Grouped by Viability
with Associated Levels of Cash-on-Hand
2000 Presidential Election Cycle
Democrats

Candidates Grouped by Viability	Cash-on-Hand as of 12/31/99	Cash-on-Hand as of 2/29/00
Viable Through Early Nom. Process:		
Al Gore	$5,734,782	$4,139,937
Bill Bradley	$8,320,943	$2,957,650
Active Through Early Nom. Process:		
Withdrawing Before Early Nom. Process:		
Withdrawing Before Formal Announcement:		
Richard Gephardt	—	—
Rev. Jesse Jackson		
Bob Kerrey	—	—
John Kerry	—	—

TABLE 5.21
Analysis of Candidates Grouped by Viability
with Associated Levels of Federal Matching Funding
2000 Presidential Election Cycle
Democrats

Candidates Grouped by Viability	Federal Matching Funding on 1/31/00	Federal Matching Funding on 2/29/00
Viable Through Early Nom. Process:		
Al Gore	$5,544,497	$270,852
Bill Bradley	$4,178,817	$204,138
Active Through Early Nom. Process:		
Withdrawing Before Early Nom. Process:		
Withdrawing Before Formal Announcement:		
Richard Gephardt	—	—
Rev. Jesse Jackson		
Bob Kerrey	—	—
John Kerry	—	—

in and of itself accounts for Gore's recovery in terms of cash-on-hand at this vital juncture when the formal nomination process was just beginning. Gore's advantage in contributions eligible for federal matching funding continued in February 2000, when Gore received $270,852 while Bradley received just $204,138. Gore's advantage in federal matching funding, like his slight advantage in fund-raising in general, positioned him well as the formal nomination process opened, providing additional support for the generalization that being ahead in this important measure of fund-raising success is related to viability and success in the early nomination process.

In sum, the 2000 Democratic early nomination campaign provides another case study of the impact of successful early campaign fund-raising on a candidate's prospects for survival, viability, and success in the early presidential nomination process. At the pre-candidacy phase, when the field of potential candidates totaled seven, the incumbent Vice President's strength in early fund-raising coupled with President Clinton's continued popularity had a powerful winnowing effect, reducing the candidate field to just two announced candidates. Leadership PACs were the preferred vehicle for this pre-candidacy fund-raising, with both Bradley and Gore utilizing PACs but with Gore's organization far out-performing Bradley's at this early stage. At the early candidacy phase, with only one candidate challenging the front-runner, successful fund-raising again loomed as a decisive factor, with Gore and

Bradley head-to-head in a race for financial support. While during the first half of the pre-election year Gore was well ahead of Bradley in fund-raising, by the second half of the year Bradley had almost caught up, and the momentum certainly had shifted in Bradley's favor. The credible challenge which Bradley presented to Gore, and especially the closeness of their competition for fund-raising success, ultimately proved to be the dominant headline of the 2000 Democratic campaign. In such a closely balanced race, Gore's slight advantage in terms of successful fund-raising was made evident by additional measures of fund-raising success such as momentum in fund-raising, the amount of cash-on-hand, and the level of federal matching funding, all areas in which Gore proved to be slightly ahead of Bradley. Thus, in the 2000 Democratic early nomination campaign, just as in both parties' 1988 early nomination campaigns, successful pre-candidacy and early candidacy fund-raising indeed was predictive of candidate survival, viability, and success in the early nomination process, providing further confirmation of the central importance of money and the early pursuit of money in the selection of presidential nominees.

Republican Campaign Fund-Raising in 2000

The 2000 Republican nomination contest stands as an additional case study that is consistent with the overall evolution of the post-reform era pre-nomination period and also as a new milestone in the continued advance of significant trends in the presidential nominee selection process. This Republican nomination race was the most expensive presidential nomination campaign on record, and as a result fund-raising had a pivotal place in the campaign from beginning to end. Fund-raising had an especially critical role during the Republicans' early campaign, beginning as early as 1996 and 1997, both making and breaking candidacies and perhaps even determining the ultimate presidential nominee. Also setting the 2000 Republican race apart, as noted earlier, was its extraordinary candidate field, both in the total size of this field at the outset—at least sixteen candidates and potential candidates—and the extent to which the field developed and changed during the early campaign. Moreover, an array of trends in the evolution of the early campaign continued and in fact advanced significantly with the 2000 Republican nomination race. The proliferation of leadership PACs, their ever earlier use by presidential aspirants, and the use of an array of other organizational entities as shadow campaign committees reached new heights with the 2000 Republican race. The deterioration of the framework of campaign finance reform also reached a new level, and campaign spending by would-be and active candidates and the campaign fund-raising to support it also escalated to record levels. Most significantly, the early campaign and most notably its relentless impact in winnowing out candidates and forming the final candidate field, became more important than ever.

Candidates and would-be candidates utilizing leadership PACs and other organizational entities as vehicles for pre-candidacy activity and fund-raising exploded in numbers and level of activity during the early campaign for the 2000 Republican nomination. As Table 5.22 summarizes, of the sixteen potential candidates, fourteen utilized some form of pre-candidacy committee and twelve of these utilized a leadership PAC in the 2000 election's early campaign. In addition, nine of the fourteen candidates who utilized some form of pre-candidacy committee established a foundation or other organizational entity, with seven of these having a leadership PAC as well. All three of the candidates categorized as viable through the early nomination process utilized pre-candidacy committees, with one of these three utilizing both a leadership PAC and an additional organizational entity. Ironically, the eventual nominee, George W. Bush, was the only candidate categorized as viable who did not utilize a leadership PAC, relying instead on his state-registered political committee—the Governor Bush Committee—as in effect his pre-candidacy committee. In addition, all of the candidates who remained as active candidates through the early nomination process but who were not categorized as viable also utilized pre-candidacy committees, with two of these candidates relying exclusively on their leadership PAC and the third having an additional political committee as well as a PAC. Finally, even the candidates who ended up withdrawing before the formal nomination process began or who withdrew before making a formal

TABLE 5.22
**Summary Analysis of Candidates Grouped by Viability
with Associated Number of Candidate Leadership PACs
and Other Early Fund-Raising Entities
2000 Presidential Election Cycle
Republicans**

Candidates Grouped by Viability	Number of Candidates	Other Early Entities	Leadership PACs	Neither
Viable Through Early Nom. Process:	3	3	1	0
Active Through Early Nom. Process:	3	1	3	0
Withdrawing Before Early Nom. Process:	5	2	4	1
Withdrawing Before Formal Announcement:	5	3	4	1
Other Potential Candidates:	—	—	—	—

announcement of candidacy utilized leadership PACs as well as other organizational entities, with eight of the ten candidates in these two categories having one or more pre-candidacy committees, and five having both a leadership PAC as well as an alternate organizational entity. Consistent with the generalization that these PACs and other organizational entities are important for pre-candidacy and early candidacy success, the two candidates who failed to have any pre-candidacy committee both proved to be unsuccessful, with Elizabeth Dole withdrawing after her announcement of candidacy but before the opening of the nomination process and Tommy Thompson withdrawing before making any formal announcement. In short, the proliferation of pre-candidacy committees and in particular leadership PACs among the 2000 Republican candidate field is consistent with the generalization that these entities are important to pre-candidacy and early candidacy fund-raising success and the conclusion that early fund-raising success is critical to candidate survival, viability, and success in the early nomination process.

The variety evident in the many pre-candidacy committees and other organizational entities active in advance of the 2000 Republican early nomination campaign also was impressive. As was the case in 1988, moreover, the success of these pre-candidacy fund-raising efforts was even more impressive among the Republican candidates than among their Democratic counterparts. Most Republican candidates in 2000 had both a leadership PAC and another organizational entity to support their nascent campaigns. Most of these entities were established during the four-year period leading up to the 2000 nomination period, with at least five being established at the beginning of this quadrennial cycle, namely Forbes' Americans for Hope, Growth and Opportunity (which originally was a tax-exempt foundation), Bauer's Campaign for Working Families, Ashcroft's Spirit of America PAC, Kasich's Pioneer PAC, and Kemp's Freedom and Free Enterprise PAC, timing that certainly links their establishment to the anticipated presidential campaign. Moreover, some of these PACs were tremendously successful in their early fund-raising, especially during 1998, most notably Bauer's Campaign for Working Families which raised $5,064,724, Quayle's Campaign America which raised $3,661,634, Ashcroft's Spirit of America PAC which raised $2,576,807, and Kasich's Pioneer PAC which raised $1,122,801. Among the three candidates categorized as viable through the early nomination process, all three had at least one pre-candidacy committee that was enormously successful in early fund-raising, again especially during 1998, with Bush's Governor Bush Committee raising $9,739,132, Forbes' Americans for Hope, Growth and Opportunity raising $13 million in 1997 and 1998, and McCain's Senate Campaign Committee making a $2 million transfer to his pre-candidacy effort. Many organizational entities besides leadership PACs also were utilized in advance of the 2000 Republican nomination process, including foundations such as Alexander's Republican Exchange Satellite Network, Wilson's Black Bear Forum, and Forbes' Americans for Hope, Growth and Opportunity Foundation (before he changed it to a PAC), federal political committees such as McCain's Senate Campaign Committee and Hatch's Committee for Republican Leadership, and non-federal political committees such as Kasich's New Century PAC. It is important to note that simply having a successful leadership PAC or other organizational entity did not necessarily guarantee that a would-be candidate would survive the pre-candidacy phase let alone move from early candidacy to viability and success in the opening nomination contests. Even some candidates who had successful PAC activity and fund-raising ended up withdrawing before the early nomination process, such as Quayle whose Campaign America raised $3,661,634 in 1998, or withdrawing even before making a formal announcement of candidacy, such as Ashcroft whose Spirit of America PAC raised $2,576,807 in 1998 and Kasich whose Pioneer PAC raised $1,122,801 in 1998. Nonetheless, and consistent with the generalization that early fund-raising is of critical importance, the three candidates who ultimately proved to be viable in the early nomination process—Bush, Forbes, and McCain—all had pre-candidacy committees or other early campaign entities that generally were more successful in early fund-raising than the committees for the rest of the Republican candidates who were active in the early campaign.

A general overview of the early campaign for the 2000 Republican nomination confirms the critical importance of early fund-raising success and significant early funding to candidate survival, viability, and success. As Table 5.23 summarizes, almost the entire field of would-be Republican candidates engaged in pre-candidacy fund-raising, with leadership PACs being the organizational entity utilized almost across the board and certainly being the entity on which financial data was publicly accessible. Two of the three candidates categorized as viable through the early nomination process—Bush and Forbes—raised substantial dollars during their pre-candidacy campaign, and the third candidate—McCain—made a major infusion of $2 million from his Senatorial campaign committee into his new presidential campaign committee. Bush actually did not need to establish a special pre-candidacy committee because his state-based gubernatorial committee served as his platform for launching his presidential campaign. While a good deal of the $10,156,915 he raised in 1996–1997 and the $9,739,132 he raised in 1998 was for his gubernatorial re-election campaign, much of his political activity during this period also was focused on his presidential ambitions. The campaign organization and infrastructure which he built as Governor of Texas, especially his fund-raising apparatus, along with the start-up funding he accumulated, provided a strong start to his presidential campaign in early 1999. Forbes' early fund-raising through his foundation, which later became a PAC, totaled $13 million during 1997–1998, likewise an

TABLE 5.23
Summary Analysis of Candidates Grouped by Viability
with Associated Levels of Pre-Candidacy Fund-Raising Success
2000 Presidential Election Cycle
Republicans

Candidates Grouped by Viability	Early Fund-Raising		Leadership PAC		
	Pre-1998	1998	1997	1998	1999
Viable Through Early Nom. Process:					
George W. Bush	$10,156,915 (1996–1997)	$9,739,132			
Steve Forbes	$13,000,000 (1997–1998)		$250	$100,122	$240
John McCain		$2,000,000			
Active Through Early Nom. Process:					
Gary Bauer			$2,016,798	$5,064,724	$1,388,862
Orrin Hatch			$117,150	$90,850	$5,000
Alan Keyes			0	$1,253	$420
Withdrawing Before Early Nom. Process:					
Lamar Alexander			$790,340	$686,920	$51,500
Patrick Buchanan			0	0	0
Elizabeth Dole					
Dan Quayle			$2,189,404	$3,661,634	$140,581
Robert Smith			$29,228	$257,398	$9,779
Withdrawing Before Formal Announcement:					
John Ashcroft			$235,500	$2,576,807	$533,922
John Kasich			$811,317	$1,122,801	$140,488
Jack Kemp			$525,550	$397,625	$22,015
Tommy Thompson					
Pete Wilson					

extraordinarily well-financed start to his campaign. Early fund-raising success and significant up-front funding thus were a common denominator among all three of the 2000 Republican contenders who proved to be viable candidates once the formal nomination process commenced.

The remainder of the 2000 Republican candidate field comparatively speaking had much more limited fund-raising capabilities and resources but were quite varied in their actual funding levels going into the early campaign. Among the candidates who proved to be able to remain active through the early nomination process were Gary Bauer, Orrin Hatch, and Alan Keyes, but of these three only Bauer had early fund-raising success, raising $5,064,724 in 1998 through his leadership PAC. The other two active candidates, Hatch and Keyes, raised comparatively very little early money, and while Hatch never caught on as a candidate, Keyes' ideological agenda ensured at least a core of strong supporters. An additional tier of candidates who all withdrew after their formal announcement but before the early nomination process included two candidates with strong early fund-raising during 1998, including Quayle whose PAC raised $3,661,634 and Alexander whose PAC raised $686,920. But also in this group were some candidates with very weak early fund-raising, including Buchanan and Dole who raised no early money, and Robert Smith whose early fund-raising was quite modest. Finally, and surprisingly, the last tier of Republican candidates included several with strong early fund-raising during 1998, namely Ashcroft who raised $2,576,807 and Kasich who raised $1,122,801, again an indication that simply raising money in and of itself certainly does not ensure success. In sum, the complexity of this picture of early fund-raising notwithstanding, the conclusion that significant early fund-raising is integral to candidate viability and success in the early nomination process is well supported. Other candidates with successful yet more modest fund-raising totals achieved varying levels of success as candidates. Yet achieving fund-raising success in and of itself did not ensure a successful candidacy, as several well-financed Republican candidates who withdrew early from the 2000 race can attest; successful early fund-raising therefore might well be regarded as essential but not sufficient for viability and success in the formal nomination process.

The role of leadership PACs as in effect shadow campaign committees for aspiring presidential candidates is evident from the pattern of fund-raising by these entities, a pattern that was reflected in the early campaign for the 2000 Republican nomination just as it was reflected in the early 2000 Democratic contest and the early races in both parties in 1988 as well. As Table 5.24 presents, the ten leadership PACs affiliated with presidential aspirants in the early campaign for the 2000 Republican contest on which financial data is available followed a similar pattern, with PAC fund-raising either beginning in 1997 or

TABLE 5.24
Comparison of Contributions to Presidential Candidate Leadership PACs
Prior to and During Presidential Election Years
2000 Presidential Election Cycle
Republicans

Candidate and Leadership PAC	1997	1998	1999	2000
Steve Forbes—				
Americans for Hope, Growth and Opportunity (9/17/97)	$250	$100,122	$240 (Terminated 10/10/99)	—
Gary Bauer—				
Campaign for Working Families (11/26/96)	$2,016,798	$5,064,724	$1,388,862	$1,095,082
Orrin Hatch—				
Capitol Committee (1/1/93)	$117,150	$90,850	$5,000	$40,500
Alan Keyes—				
Life and Liberty PAC (1993)	0	$1,253	$420	$37,326
Lamar Alexander—				
Campaign for a New American Century (6/10/93)	$790,340	$696,920	$51,500	0 (Terminated 6/20/00)
Patrick Buchanan—				
America First PAC	0	0	0	0
Dan Quayle—				
Campaign America	$2,189,404	$3,661,634	$140,581	$2,000
Robert Smith—				
Live Free or Die PAC	$29,228	$257,398	$9,779	$730,730
John Ashcroft—				
Spirit of America PAC (7/5/96)	$235,500	$2,576,807	$533,922	$2,868
John Kasich—				
Pioneer PAC (12/18/96)	$811,317	$1,122,801	$140,488	$208,070
Jack Kemp—				
Freedom and Free Enterprise PAC (2/18/97)	$525,550	$397,625	$22,015 (Terminated 8/31/99)	—

1998, or dating from an earlier year, reaching its height during 1998 (or in one case during 1997), and then falling off radically during 1999, the pre-election year. This pattern, as was the case in the other early campaigns under study, is especially significant when it is understood that this peak in PAC fund-raising in 1998 is during the year before the pre-election year and hence is the last year before candidates and contributors shift their attention to the official presidential campaign committee established by each announced candidate. Typical of this pattern was Bauer's Campaign for Working Families PAC, in which fund-raising went from $2,016,798 during 1997 to a high of $5,064,724 during 1998, and then fell back to $1,388,862 during the pre-election year of 1999. As would be expected if these PACs were functioning as pre-candidacy fund-raising entities for the 2000 nomination contest, not a single PAC affiliated with a Republican candidate or would-be candidate increased its fund-raising once 1998 concluded and the pre-election year of 1999 commenced. Instead, as would be expected of PACs functioning as pre-candidacy committees, support for these candidate-affiliated PACs dropped precipitously in 1999, while at the same time fund-raising began in earnest through each of these candidates' newly established presidential campaign committees. This overall pattern in PAC fund-raising from 1997 to 1999 is consistent with the generalization that aspiring presidential candidates established these leadership PACs as a major part of their pre-candidacy fund-raising campaigns during the early campaign for the 2000 Republican presidential nomination.

Candidate fund-raising during the early candidacy period of 1999 was pivotal to the development and outcome of the 2000 Republican pre-nomination campaign. In fact, building upon the pre-candidacy fund-raising that preceded it, this early candidacy fund-raising period represented the height of the 2000 Republican early nomination contest, both by substantially narrowing the candidate field and by launching the front-runners on their way. As Table 5.25 summarizes, most of the original candidate field from the pre-candidacy period proceeded into this early candidacy period, including thirteen of the original field of sixteen potential candidates. This field of thirteen candidates established presidential campaign committees and engaged in early candidacy fund-raising, regardless of whether they ultimately proved to be viable candidates or alternatively were active through the early nomination process or withdrew either before or after publicly announcing their candidacies. Quite significantly, the three candidates who were the most successful in their early candidacy fund-raising—Bush, Forbes, and McCain—also proved to be the candidates whose performance in the early nomination process categorized them as viable. In fact, two of these candidates—Bush and Forbes—had fund-raising totals for the pre-election year of 1999 that eclipsed the rest of the candidate field, with Bush raising an

TABLE 5.25
Summary Analysis of Candidates Grouped by Viability
with Associated Levels of Early Candidacy Fund-Raising Success
2000 Presidential Election Cycle
Republicans

Candidates Grouped by Viability	1999		2000	
	First Half	Total	January	February
Viable Through Early Nom. Process:				
George W. Bush	$37,035,945	$67,316,260	$1,673,644	$2,858,745
Steve Forbes	$9,430,899	$33,834,499	$7,289,459	$2,542,306
John McCain	$4,303,585	$13,622,787	$2,525,256	$11,171,963
Active Through Early Nom. Process:				
Gary Bauer	$3,434,071	$6,842,243	$363,896	$170,099
Orrin Hatch	0	$2,099,726	$122,541	$51,837
Alan Keyes	$1,914,712	$3,557,662	$650,843	$805,046
Withdrawing Before Early Nom. Process:				
Lamar Alexander	$2,093,731	$2,424,881	0	0
Patrick Buchanan	$2,407,080	$5,050,986	$290,327	$284,615
Elizabeth Dole	$3,513,942	$5,141,082	$35,552	$28,976
Dan Quayle	$3,388,378	$4,205,064	$179	0
Robert Smith	$1,511,375	$1,943,642	0	0
Withdrawing Before Formal Announcement:				
John Ashcroft	—	—	—	—
John Kasich	$1,711,293	$1,784,459	$35	$25
Jack Kemp	—	—	—	—
Tommy Thompson	—	—	—	—
Pete Wilson	$19,950	$19,950	0	0

amazing total of $67,316,260 and Forbes reporting a total of $33,834,499, most of which reflected self-funding. The third candidate who ultimately proved to be viable, McCain, raised $13,622,787 during 1999, nowhere near Bush's or Forbes' totals but twice the total of the next highest candidate.

The next tier of Republican contenders had far less impressive pre-election year fund-raising totals, including Bauer who raised $6,842,243, Keyes whose total was $3,557,662, and Hatch who raised $2,099,726, and consistent with expectations their early performance in the formal nomination process categorized them as active although not viable. An even lower tier of the Republican candidate field who withdrew even before reaching the opening nomination contests raised totals during 1999 that were comparable to the totals raised by candidates who remained active, with these withdrawing candidate totals ranging from Dole at $5,141,082 and Buchanan at $5,050,986 to Alexander at $2,424,881 and Smith at $1,943,642. Also as would be expected, the two candidates who actually withdrew even before making a formal announcement raised lower totals during 1999, including Kasich at $1,784,459 and Wilson at just $19,950. Thus the 2000 Republican early campaign provided further support for the hypothesized relationship between early candidacy fund-raising success and candidate survival, viability, and success in the early nomination process. As was the case in both parties' 1988 nomination campaigns and in the 2000 Democratic nomination campaign, the Republican candidates and potential candidates in the 2000 presidential election cycle who raised the most through a presidential campaign committee during the early candidacy period, and in general during the pre-candidacy period before it, also proved to be viable through the opening of the formal nomination process. Moreover, and likewise consistent with the hypothesized relationship, candidates who ranked next in overall fund-raising success proved to be able to remain active through the early nomination process or, as was the case with the 2000 race, withdrew in the closing months of the pre-election year.

A further measure of fund-raising success is momentum in fund-raising, and the level of momentum in fund-raising achieved by candidates for the 2000 Republican nomination during the pre-election year was clearly associated with candidate viability and success. As Table 5.26 presents, the three candidates who proved to be viable through the early nomination process—Bush, Forbes, and McCain—had ratios measuring their fund-raising momentum that are consistent with the hypothesized fund-raising success—candidate viability relationship. While Bush's momentum ratio for the second half of 1999 to the first half of 1999 was not actually positive, the extraordinarily high dollar amounts involved—$30,280,315 for the second half to $37,035,945 for the first half—reflect the reality that his tremendous early success in fund-raising was evidence of his campaign's strength and that raising over $30 million on top of $37 million obviously did not reflect a lagging fund-raising effort. Both of the other viable candidates in the 2000 Republican field—Forbes and McCain—had strong positive momentum ratios comparing the second half of 1999 to the first half of 1999, with Forbes' momentum ratio at $24,403,600 to $9,430,899, and McCain's momentum ratio at $9,303,904 to $4,303,585. Bush and McCain both also enjoyed positive momentum ratios as the pre-election year moved into the early nomination campaign period, with the momentum ratio comparing February 2000 to January 2000 for Bush being $2,858,745 to $1,673,644 and for McCain soaring to a very impressive $11,171,963 to $2,525,256. Candidates in the lower tiers grouped by viability reflected not only progressively lower absolute totals in dollars raised during 1999 but also progressively less favorable momentum ratios.

TABLE 5.26
Analysis of Candidates Grouped by Viability
with Associated Levels of Early Candidacy Fund-Raising Momentum
2000 Presidential Election Cycle
Republicans

Candidates Grouped by Viability	2nd Half 1999 / 1st Half 1999	4th Qtr 1999 / 3rd Qtr 1999	Feb 2000 / Jan 2000
Viable Through Early Nom. Process:			
George W. Bush	$30,280,315	$10,200,140	$2,858,745
	$37,035,945	$20,080,174	$1,673,644
Steve Forbes	$24,403,600	$13,215,028	$2,542,306
	$9,430,899	$11,188,572	$7,289,459
John McCain	$9,303,904	$6,261,561	$11,171,963
	$4,303,585	$3,042,343	$2,525,256
Active Through Early Nom. Process:			
Gary Bauer	$3,408,161	$1,486,340	$170,099
	$3,434,071	$1,921,821	$363,896
Orrin Hatch	$2,099,726	$860,479	$51,837
	0	$1,239,247	$122,541
Alan Keyes	$1,643,000	$1,058,293	$805,046
	$1,914,712	$584,707	$650,843
Withdrawing Before Early Nom. Process:			
Lamar Alexander	$331,150	0	0
	$2,093,731	$331,150	0
Patrick Buchanan	$2,639,908	$1,205,156	$284,615
	$2,407,080	$1,434,752	$290,327
Elizabeth Dole	$1,627,140	$314,900	$28,976
	$3,513,942	$1,312,240	$35,552
Dan Quayle	$816,686	$22,510	0
	$3,388,378	$794,176	$179
Robert Smith	$432,268	$7,185	0
	$1,511,375	$425,083	0
Withdrawing Before Formal Announcement:			
John Ashcroft	NA	NA	NA
John Kasich	$73,165	$240	$25
	$1,711,293	$72,925	$35
Jack Kemp	—	—	—
Tommy Thompson	—	—	—
Pete Wilson	0	0	0
	$19,950	0	0

Among the candidates who remained active through the early nomination process, namely Bauer, Hatch, and Keyes, the absolute dollar figures for each six month period were in the strong range of $1.5 million to $3.5 million, but the momentum ratios generally were unfavorable, for instance Bauer whose ratio was $3,408,161 for the second half of 1999 as compared to $3,434,071 for the first half of 1999, and Keyes whose ratio was $1,643,000 for the second half of 1999 as compared to $1,914,712 for the first half of 1999. Interestingly, this momentum ratio for candidates who remained active but were not viable through the early nomination process in general fell off further in early 2000, with Bauer's falling to $170,099 for February 2000 as compared to $363,896 for January 2000. Candidates in the lowest tiers, namely those who withdrew before the early nomination process or who withdrew before a formal announcement, had the weakest fund-raising momentum ratios. In fact, among the candidates who withdrew before the early nomination process were several with very unfavorable ratios for the second half of 1999 compared to the first half of 1999, most notably Alexander's $331,150 to $2,093,731, Dole's $1,627,140 to $3,513,942, and Quayle's $816,686 to $3,388,378, with the only positive momentum ratio being Buchanan's $2,639,908 to $2,407,080. In the tier of candidates who withdrew even before a public announcement of candidacy, the momentum ratios as expected were extraordinarily weak, for instance Kasich's highly unfavorable ratio of $73,165 to $1,711,293. In short, as was the case in both parties' early campaigns in the 1988 nomination campaign and in the Democratic early campaign in 2000, the Republican early campaign in 2000 provides further support for the hypothesized relationship between fund-raising success measured by momentum in fund-raising and candidate viability and success in the early nomination process. Momentum in early candidacy fund-raising in the 2000 Republican early campaign clearly was associated with candidate viability and success in the early nomination process.

The cash-on-hand available to candidates, especially at crucial junctures in the campaign such as the end of 1999, the pre-election year, and also the end of February 2000 as the formal nomination process reached its height, is yet another measure of a candidate's fund-raising success. As Table 5.27 summarizes, of the top five candidates in terms of cash-on-hand at the end of 1999, three—Bush, McCain, and Forbes—were categorized as viable candidates based on their actual performance in the early nomination process. These cash-on-hand totals as of year-end 1999 for candidates who later proved to be viable were substantially higher than the other candidates in the 2000 Republican field, most notably Bush's staggering cash-on-hand total of $31,384,042. The other two candidates who were viable through the early nomination process, McCain and Forbes, had cash-on-hand totals as of the end of 1999 of $1,507,918 and $796,720 respectively, ahead of all but two of the other candidates in the Republican field. Cash-on-hand totals for Republican candidates in the other categories of candidates

TABLE 5.27
Analysis of Candidates Grouped by Viability
with Associated Levels of Cash-on-Hand
2000 Presidential Election Cycle
Republicans

Candidates Grouped by Viability	Cash-on-Hand as of 12/31/99	Cash-on-Hand as of 2/29/00
Viable Through Early Nom. Process:		
George W. Bush	$31,384,042	$10,583,185
Steve Forbes	$796,720	$529,828
John McCain	$1,507,918	$1,348,002
Active Through Early Nom. Process:		
Gary Bauer	$212,860	$127,345
Orrin Hatch	$173,571	$780
Alan Keyes	$809,235	$256,982
Withdrawing Before Early Nom. Process:		
Lamar Alexander	0	0
Patrick Buchanan	$288,920	$201,316
Elizabeth Dole	$54,396	$20,523
Dan Quayle	$178,651	$67,414
Robert Smith	$243,708	$210,552
Withdrawing Before Formal Announcement:		
John Ashcroft	NA	NA
John Kasich	$1,088,600	$987,853
Jack Kemp	—	—
Tommy Thompson	—	—
Pete Wilson	$76,295	$76,295

grouped by viability certainly were generally far less than in the top category of viable candidates, as the hypothesized relationship between fund-raising success and candidate viability would suggest. Among the Republican candidates categorized as active through the early nomination process, cash-on-hand totals as of year-end 1999 generally were much lower than for the candidates in the viable grouping, with only Keyes having a total—$809,235—in the same range as one of the viable candidates, but with Bauer having $212,860 and Hatch at just $173,571. Contrary to the hypothesized relationship, Republican candidates in the lowest categories of viability, including withdrawals before the early nomination process and withdrawals before a formal announcement, did not have progressively lower cash-on-hand totals but instead had incrementally higher totals—like Smith's $243,708 and Kasich's $1,088,600. Yet these departures from the expected pattern in cash-on-hand in all likelihood were a result of unspent campaign balances resulting from early withdrawals. Finally, cash-on-hand totals as of the end of February 2000 reflected the same general pattern as in December 1999, with the three candidates categorized as viable having substantial cash-on-hand balances and with the remaining Republican candidate field reflecting a range of much lower cash-on-hand totals. In short, consistent with the hypothesis that candidates with the strongest fund-raising will achieve viability and success, the 2000 Republican candidates whose successful fund-raising was reflected in strong cash-on-hand totals indeed emerged as the viable and successful candidates in the 2000 Republican nomination contest.

The level of federal matching funding received by each candidate is a final measure of fund-raising success by the field of candidates for the 2000 Republican nomination. As Table 5.28 presents, the distribution of candidates

TABLE 5.28
Analysis of Candidates Grouped by Viability
with Associated Levels of Federal Matching Funding
2000 Presidential Election Cycle
Republicans

Candidates Grouped by Viability	Federal Matching Funding on 1/31/00	Federal Matching Funding on 2/29/00
Viable Through Early Nom. Process:		
George W. Bush	0	0
Steve Forbes	0	0
John McCain	$2,098,786	$102,527
Active Through Early Nom. Process:		
Gary Bauer	$1,985,453	$91,991
Orrin Hatch	0	0
Alan Keyes	$616,630	$30,373
Withdrawing Before Early Nom. Process:		
Lamar Alexander	0	0
Patrick Buchanan	$1,188,057	$58,037
Elizabeth Dole	0	0
Dan Quayle	$1,052,999	$51,440
Robert Smith	0	0
Withdrawing Before Formal Announcement:		
John Ashcroft	NA	NA
John Kasich	NA	NA
Jack Kemp	—	—
Tommy Thompson	—	—
Pete Wilson	0	0

grouped by viability was consistent with the expectation that the candidates with higher levels of federal matching funding in general would emerge as viable or at least active through the early nomination process. The candidate with the highest total in federal matching funding was McCain, who received $2,098,786 in January 2000 and $102,527 in February 2000, and as expected he proved to be among the candidates who emerged as viable through the early nomination process. While Bush and Forbes likewise were categorized as viable, neither received any federal matching funding, in Bush's case because he declined it in order not to be bound by spending ceilings, and in Forbes' case because he self-funded his campaign. Candidates in the next two tiers grouped by viability generally qualified for less federal matching funding, again as the hypothesized relationship between fund-raising success and viability predicts. Bauer, who remained active through the early nomination process, qualified for $1,985,453 in federal matching funding, while Buchanan and Quayle, both of whom withdrew before the early nomination process, qualified for just $1,188,057 and $1,052,999 respectively. While Keyes received just $616,630 in federal matching funding and nonetheless was in a higher category as an active candidate, his highly ideological campaign accounts for his survival in spite of limited resources. Thus, consistent with the hypothesized relationship between fund-raising success and candidate viability, the levels of federal matching funding received by candidates for the 2000 Republican nomination indeed were related to candidate viability and success, with the candidates qualifying for the most federal matching funding indeed proving to be viable and active through the early nomination process.

In sum, the 2000 Republican early nomination campaign provides a fourth case study of the critical role of the early campaign and in particular early campaign fund-raising for candidate survival, viability, and success in the early presidential nomination process. In fact, much of the action in the 2000 Republican contest was during the early campaign, with a field of potential candidates that originally numbered sixteen being narrowed to thirteen as a result of potential candidates who withdrew at the pre-candidacy phase, and then to just six—with the opening of the formal nomination process still months away. Indeed the impact of fund-raising on the 2000 Republican early nomination campaign was greater than in any previous early presidential nomination process, with potential candidates declining to announce their candidacies and announced candidates withdrawing before a single caucus or primary vote was cast, in almost every case citing problems in fund-raising as their reason. The towering presence throughout the early campaign both as the presumed nominee for most of the race and as the acknowledged nominee by early March—George W. Bush—was unquestionably the candidate with the most successful fund-raising in the history of presidential nomination politics. Bush's decision to decline federal matching funding in order to fund his entire nomination campaign through fund-raising represented a new high watermark in the erosion of the FECA campaign finance reform framework and was indicative of the tremendous success of his early fund-raising effort. The two other candidates who proved to be viable contenders in the early Republican nomination contest, Forbes and McCain, also were successful in generating substantial dollars to mount their challenges, Forbes by self-funding his campaign, and McCain by utilizing his Senate campaign committee and then achieving solid success in early campaign fund-raising through his presidential campaign committee. Thus, in the 2000 Republican early nomination contest as in the other early nomination campaigns included in this study, successful pre-candidacy and early candidacy fund-raising had a decisive impact on candidate survival, viability, and success in the early nomination process, underscoring again the ever increasing and in fact pivotal importance of money in the presidential nomination process.

Summary

Fund-raising success indeed is predictive of candidate survival, viability, and success in the early presidential nomination process. The early campaigns for the Democratic and Republican presidential nominations in both 1988 and 2000, the two all non-incumbent presidential election years of the post-reform era, provide compelling case studies supporting this generalization. Fund-raising success in the early campaign, which generally extends through the pre-election year, is found to be critical to candidate survival, viability, and success in the early presidential nomination process, confirming the first hypothesis of this study. Moreover, fund-raising success during the pre-candidacy period itself, extending over the months and even years prior to the pre-election year, likewise is critical in order to establish the organizational and fund-raising base that is essential for ongoing fund-raising success and, in turn, for candidate survival, viability, and success in the early presidential nomination process, confirming this study's second hypothesis as well. In examining these two hypotheses, fund-raising during both the pre-candidacy and early candidacy phases of presidential campaigns is studied as the independent variable and candidate performance in the early nomination process is studied as the dependent variable. Besides pre-candidacy and early candidacy fund-raising totals, early candidacy fund-raising success is examined utilizing a variety of measures, each important aspects of campaign fund-raising. Momentum in fund-raising is found to be strongly related to candidate survival, viability, and success in the early nomination process. Cash-on-hand totals and federal matching funding totals, both also measures of fund-raising success, likewise are found to be related to candidate survival, viability, and success in the early nomination process. Thus to a degree not generally recognized, success in pre-candidacy as well as early candidacy fund-raising is predictive of a candidate's prospects in the early presidential nomination process. Fund-raising success, the first and most important dimension of the money primary, therefore is an integral and indeed generally decisive factor in the early presidential nomination process.

Notes

1. William G. Mayer, *The Divided Democrats: Ideological Unity, Party Reform, and Presidential Elections* (Boulder, Colo.: Westview, 1996), 35–41.

2. Michael G. Hagen and William G. Mayer, "The Modern Politics of Presidential Selection: How Changing the Rules Really Did Change the Game," in *In Pursuit of the White House: How We Choose Our Presidential Nominees*, ed. William G. Mayer (New York: Chatham House Publishers, Inc., 2000), 21, 40, and Anthony Corrado, "Financing the 2000 Elections," in *The Election of 2000*, ed. Gerald M. Pomper (New York: Chatham House Publishers, Inc., 2001), 98.

3. Anthony Corrado, *Paying for Presidents: Public Financing in National Elections* (New York: The Twentieth Century Fund Press, 1993), 49.

4. Anthony Corrado, *Campaign Finance Reform* (New York: The Century Foundation Press, 2000), 12–14.

5. Rhodes Cook, "The Nominating Process," in *The Elections of 1988*, ed. Michael Nelson (Washington, D.C.: Congressional Quarterly Press, 1989), 61.

6. Anthony Corrado, "Financing the 2000 Elections," 94.

7. Corrado, *Campaign Finance Reform*, 54.

8. Robert F. Bauer, *Soft Money Hard Law: A Guide to the New Campaign Finance Law* (Washington, D.C.: Perkins Coie, LLP, 2002), 22, 68, 103.

9. Cook, "The Nominating Process," 32.

10. Corrado, "Financing the 2000 Elections," 97-100.

11. Anthony Corrado, *Creative Campaigning: PACs and the Presidential Selection Process* (Boulder, Colo.: Westview Press, Inc., 1992), 77.

12. Corrado, "Financing the 2000 Elections," 93–95.

13. Bruce Ackerman and Sam Ayres, *Voting with Dollars: A New Paradigm for Campaign Finance* (New Haven, Conn.: Yale University Press, 2002), 162–63.

14. Corrado, "Financing the 2000 Elections," 98.

15. Cook, "The Nominating Process," 29–31.

16. Corrado, *Creative Campaigning*, 92–95.

17. Cook, "The Nominating Process," 25–26.

6

Media Coverage of Campaign Fund-Raising Success and Candidate Viability

MEDIA COVERAGE OF PRESIDENTIAL ELECTION CAMPAIGNS is an integral part of presidential electoral politics, and since the presidential nomination reforms and the proliferation of presidential primaries, media coverage of presidential nomination campaigns has become increasingly extensive as well. This media coverage commences at ever earlier points in the campaign, is increasingly focused and intense, and can be relentless when scandal or controversy arises. Moreover, media coverage of campaign fund-raising to finance the increasingly expensive process of seeking the presidential nomination likewise has increased substantially. For the media in general, for the print media in particular, and especially for major newspapers with national circulations, the topic of campaign fund-raising by candidates and would-be candidates for the presidency combines national politics and political personalities with money and the excitement of political competition, all in the pursuit of an office that always has attracted enormous popular interest—the presidency. To a significant degree, this media coverage serves not only to cover candidates and potential candidates in general but also to evaluate their standing and credibility as prospective presidential nominees.[1] In addition, because actual milestones and contests with measurable results are few and far between during the ever lengthening early campaign leading up to actual voting in primaries and caucuses, it is perhaps inevitable that the media has fastened upon regular coverage of campaign fund-raising as a means for covering presidential nomination campaigns.[2] In short, just as the media cover presidential nomination campaigns in general, the media increasingly are focusing attention on campaign fund-raising by candidates and potential candidates during the ever longer pre-candidacy and early candidacy campaigns preceding the formal presidential nomination process.

Media coverage of campaign fund-raising by candidates seeking their party's presidential nomination therefore is a vital aspect of the early nomination campaign and the money primary, a dimension beyond campaign fund-raising itself that in effect is an echo of campaign fund-raising. In fact, just as successful campaign fund-raising must be at the top of any presidential aspirant's list of priorities, favorable media coverage of campaign fund-raising must be regarded as vitally important as well. To be sure, a successful fund-raising effort is of paramount importance to an aspiring presidential nominee, both for the money it provides to launch and conduct a campaign and for the capability it represents as a continuing source of funds as a campaign moves into high gear. But success in fund-raising also brings a degree of credibility and standing to a candidate that no other campaign resource can provide, and favorable media coverage of campaign fund-raising is indispensable to achieving this credibility and standing.[3] A candidate whose early fund-raising is successful therefore benefits twice, both by a flow of money as an immediate campaign resource, and by positive media coverage of campaign fund-raising that in turn brings greater candidate credibility and standing. On the other hand, a candidate whose early fund-raising is meager suffers a double setback, both from diminished funding for the campaign, and potentially from unfavorable media coverage of these flagging campaign prospects. Media coverage of campaign fund-raising as an echo of campaign fund-raising itself thus has enormous potential for advancing a presidential aspirant's early campaign and merits careful attention in this study of the money primary.

The data analysis which follows examines media coverage of campaign fund-raising in the early presidential nomination campaign that extends from the beginning of the pre-election year through January of the election year when the formal nomination process begins. Consistent with this study's focus on the 1988 and 2000 presidential election cycles as case studies of the money primary in the early presidential nomination process, this analysis of media coverage of campaign fund-raising includes two periods: the early campaign period for the 1988 presidential election, extending from January 1987 through January 1988; and the early campaign period for the 2000 presidential election, extending from January 1999 through January 2000. Three distinct categories of media coverage of presidential nomination campaign fund-raising are examined: horse race coverage comparing candidates in terms of their fund-raising success; candidate focused coverage that evaluates individual candidates' fund-raising success; and general coverage of campaign fund-raising and the issue of campaign finance in national politics. Data on media coverage of fund-raising in each of these categories for each of the thirteen-month-long periods under study is summarized on a month-by-month basis as well as for the entire period. The pertinent data collected includes which of the three categories each news article falls into; the month and year in which it appeared; and its length measured in word count. In addition, for both the horse race coverage and the candidate focused coverage, an evaluation is made as to whether the spin of this coverage was generally positive, negative, or neutral. Media coverage in three major newspapers is included in this analysis, namely *The New York Times* and *The Washington Post*, because they are recognized as newspapers of record, and *The Wall Street Journal*, because of its status as the recognized newspaper for business and financial news.

Media Coverage of Campaign Fund-Raising in the 1988 Early Nomination Campaign

The 1988 early nomination campaign and its two major party nomination contests offer a first and in effect a base-line case study of media coverage of campaign fund-raising in the early nomination process. Media coverage of the overall 1988 presidential campaign was record-breaking and even trend-setting in many respects, but it was during the early nomination campaign that this presidential election cycle's most significant developments in media coverage occurred.[4] Because 1988 was the first all non-incumbent presidential election in almost three decades, both parties had active early nomination campaigns, providing ample opportunity for unprecedented media coverage of the early campaign as well as the nomination campaign which followed. But new standards for appropriate media coverage also were forged as a result of the 1988 presidential election's early nomination campaign, and media activism carried to new levels even altered the candidate field and changed the dynamics of the nomination race itself. Especially notable is the example of Gary Hart responding to reports of his alleged womanizing with the suggestion to follow him, a challenge which led to exposure of his marital infidelity, producing a scandal which drove the front-runner from the race and set a new standard for media coverage of candidates' personal lives.[5] The 1988 presidential election cycle and its early nomination campaign also was a period during which the media directed more attention to campaign fund-raising and campaign finance. As the early campaign leading up to 1988 saw the introduction and expansion of varied new approaches to campaign fund-raising—including the proliferation of leadership PACs and pre-candidacy committees, the use of foundations and other organizational entities for political purposes, and the increased sophistication of campaign fund-raising utilizing campaign consultants—media attention increasingly was drawn to early campaign fund-raising and its significance in the overall campaign.[6] The net result was a surge in media coverage of the 1988 presidential election's early nomination campaign from the perspective of campaign fund-raising, heightening the awareness of attentive voters and newspaper readers in general to presidential campaign fund-raising and especially to the individual fortunes of front-runners and other candidates seeking fund-raising success during the early campaign.

The extent of media coverage of campaign fund-raising during the 1988 nomination race's early campaign is evident simply from its overall volume as well as its distribution over the course of the entire 1987 pre-election year. As Table 6.1 presents, both *The New York Times* and *The Washington Post* featured regular coverage of early presidential nomination campaign fund-raising during the thirteen month period leading up to the opening of the formal nomination process. *The New York Times* had 66 news articles with a total of 59,005 words on presidential campaign fund-raising during this period, an average of 5 articles per month. Coverage in *The Washington Post* was even more extensive, totaling 94 articles with 70,009 words, an average of 7 articles per month. By contrast, as Table 6.1 also presents, *The Wall Street Journal's* coverage of presidential campaign fund-raising was much more limited, totaling just 21 articles with 18,627 words. This coverage of campaign fund-raising extended throughout the thirteen months of the pre-election year and the immediate pre-nomination period, with almost every month having at least several articles. Yet it is significant that there were peaks in coverage in certain months, generally at the end of each quarter, namely in April 1987, June–July 1987, October 1987, and December 1987–January 1988. In the case of *The New York Times*, these peaks in media coverage of campaign fund-raising included 7 articles in April 1987, 10 articles in June 1987, 9 articles in October 1987, and 8 articles in January 1988. *The Washington Post's* more extensive coverage of campaign fund-raising also had these peaks, with 12 articles in April 1987, 8 articles in June 1987, 13 articles in October 1987, 10 articles in December 1987, and 12 more articles in January 1988. *The Wall Street Journal's* limited coverage did not reflect these quarterly peaks, aside from a slight increase to 3 articles in June 1987, 4 articles in December 1987, and 3 more articles in January 1988. Aside from the volume of media coverage, which establishes a baseline for comparison with future early campaign periods, the pattern of peaking each quarter clearly relates to the financial disclosure reports which each announced candidate must submit on a quarterly basis under FECA. These disclosure reports can be seen as early campaign events, milestones that attract media attention to campaign fund-raising and that in effect create op-

TABLE 6.1
Overview of Media Coverage of Candidate and Campaign Fund-Raising
1988 Presidential Election Cycle
January 1987–January 1988

	The New York Times		The Washington Post		The Wall Street Journal	
	Articles	Words	Articles	Words	Articles	Words
January 1987	1	1,422	6	4,388	1	183
February 1987	3	3,671	3	1,523	—	—
March 1987	—	—	—	—	—	—
April 1987	7	3,880	12	10,804	1	577
May 1987	7	8,684	7	4,733	2	2,052
June 1987	10	10,306	8	4,678	3	2,455
July 1987	4	3,565	4	1,957	—	—
August 1987	3	2,034	4	3,165	2	1,462
September 1987	4	3,616	7	4,877	2	1,722
October 1987	9	6,966	13	8,803	2	2,697
November 1987	3	2,149	8	7,135	1	1,120
December 1987	7	5,815	10	8,437	4	4,811
January 1988	8	6,897	12	9,509	3	1,548
Totals:	66	59,005	94	70,009	21	18,627

portunities to compare candidates and potential candidates not only in terms of their progress but also in terms of their standing relative to one another.

Analysis of media coverage of campaign fund-raising during the early campaign indicates that this coverage is not homogeneous but rather can be differentiated into distinct categories which each reflect significant patterns of their own. The three categories of media coverage of presidential nomination campaign fund-raising evident from this analysis include horse race coverage that compares candidates' fund-raising; candidate focused coverage that evaluates individual candidates' fund-raising; and general coverage of campaign fund-raising and the issue of campaign finance. Tables 6.2, 6.3, and 6.4 compare media coverage categorized into these three distinct groupings for *The New York Times, The Washington Post,* and *The Wall Street Journal,* revealing important patterns in these categories of coverage that are evident in all three newspapers. Comparing the three categories of media coverage, it is clear that these print media are most interested in candidate focused coverage of campaign fund-raising which reports on a particular candidate's fund-raising efforts. *The New York Times* concentrated slightly more on candidate focused coverage by publishing 32 articles with a total of 27,366 words over the thirteen month period, and *The Washington Post* concentrated even moreso on this candidate focused coverage with 59 articles and 43,574 words. General

TABLE 6.2
Analysis of Media Coverage of Candidate and Campaign Fund-Raising
1988 Presidential Election Cycle
The New York Times
January 1987–January 1988

	Horse Race Coverage of Campaign Fund-Raising		Coverage of Individual Candidate Fund-Raising		General Coverage of Campaign Fund-Raising	
	Articles	*Words*	*Articles*	*Words*	*Articles*	*Words*
January 1987	—	—	—	—	1	1,422
February 1987	—	—	1	527	2	3,144
March 1987	—	—	—	—	—	—
April 1987	1	605	2	941	4	2,334
May 1987	1	765	3	5,470	3	2,449
June 1987	1	989	4	2,702	5	6,615
July 1987	1	663	1	683	2	2,219
August 1987	—	—	2	1,106	1	928
September 1987	1	1,354	2	1,034	1	1,228
October 1987	2	1,611	5	4,638	2	717
November 1987	—	—	1	773	2	1,376
December 1987	—	—	4	3,049	3	2,766
January 1988	—	—	7	6,443	1	454
Totals:	7	5,987	32	27,366	27	25,652

coverage of campaign fund-raising and campaign finance ran second as a focus of media coverage, with *The New York Times*' total of 27 articles and 25,652 words running close to its volume of candidate focused coverage, but with *The Washington Post*'s coverage totaling 33 articles and 25,196 words, about half of the volume of its candidate focused coverage. Horse race coverage of campaign fund-raising which compared candidates with one another in terms of their fund-raising success ran a distant third in volume of coverage, with *The New York Times* publishing 7 articles with 5,987 words and *The Washington Post* publishing 2 articles with 1,239 words. Media coverage in *The Wall Street Journal* also generally reflected this distribution pattern among the three categories, although candidate focused campaign fund-raising coverage and general campaign fund-raising coverage were more evenly balanced in volume, and horse race coverage comparing the candidates' fund-raising success was almost non-existent. Overall this categorization of media coverage of early campaign fund-raising reflects the media's primary interest in covering individual candidates, even as additional coverage addresses the issue of campaign fund-raising in general. This focus on the individual candidate certainly reflects the media's framing of campaign fund-raising as a significant

TABLE 6.3
Analysis of Media Coverage of Candidate and Campaign Fund-Raising
1988 Presidential Election Cycle
The Washington Post
January 1987–January 1988

	Horse Race Coverage of Campaign Fund-Raising		Coverage of Individual Candidate Fund-Raising		General Coverage of Campaign Fund-Raising	
	Articles	*Words*	*Articles*	*Words*	*Articles*	*Words*
January 1987	—	—	2	1,020	4	3,368
February 1987	—	—	1	654	2	869
March 1987	—	—	—	—	—	—
April 1987	—	—	7	4,952	5	5,852
May 1987	—	—	2	1,486	5	3,247
June 1987	—	—	5	3,054	3	1,624
July 1987	1	813	2	836	1	308
August 1987	—	—	2	1,952	2	1,213
September 1987	—	—	7	4,877	—	—
October 1987	1	426	10	7,135	2	1,242
November 1987	—	—	6	5,944	2	1,191
December 1987	—	—	7	6,199	3	2,238
January 1988	—	—	8	5,465	4	4,044
Totals:	2	1,239	59	43,574	33	25,196

indicator of each candidate's credibility and standing in the unfolding early nomination campaign.

The timing of media coverage of campaign fund-raising over the thirteen months leading up to the opening of the formal nomination process in 1988 also reflects significant patterns and provides a further base-line for comparison with media coverage of fund-raising in future early campaigns. As Tables 6.2, 6.3, and 6.4 also reflect, the volume of media coverage clearly builds as the pre-election year progresses. This increase in media coverage as the year unfolds is especially evident with respect to candidate focused coverage, with *The New York Times* publishing 10 articles during the first half of 1987 as compared with 15 articles during the second half of 1987, and with *The Washington Post* publishing 17 articles during the first half of 1987 as compared with 34 articles during the second half in 1987. Moreover, this candidate focused coverage also builds even during the second half of 1987, with *The New York Times* publishing 5 articles during the third quarter as compared with 10 articles during the fourth quarter, and with *The Washington Post* publishing 11 articles during the third quarter as compared with 23 articles during the fourth quarter. The opposite trend is evident with media coverage of general

Chapter 6

TABLE 6.4
Analysis of Media Coverage of Candidate and Campaign Fund-Raising
1988 Presidential Election Cycle
The Wall Street Journal
January 1987–January 1988

	Horse Race Coverage of Campaign Fund-Raising		Coverage of Individual Candidate Fund-Raising		General Coverage of Campaign Fund-Raising	
	Articles	Words	Articles	Words	Articles	Words
January 1987	—	—	1	183	—	—
February 1987	—	—	—	—	—	—
March 1987	—	—	—	—	—	—
April 1987	—	—	—	—	1	577
May 1987	1	1,636	1	416	—	—
June 1987	—	—	2	1,223	1	1,232
July 1987	—	—	—	—	—	—
August 1987	—	—	1	366	1	1,096
September 1987	—	—	1	945	1	777
October 1987	—	—	—	—	2	2,697
November 1987	—	—	—	—	1	1,120
December 1987	—	—	3	3,009	1	1,802
January 1988	1	951	2	597	—	—
Totals:	2	2,587	11	6,739	8	9,301

campaign fund-raising during 1987, with a higher volume of this general coverage occurring during the first half of 1987 as compared with the second half of 1987. Specifically, general coverage of campaign fund-raising in *The New York Times* included 15 articles during the first half of 1987 and declined to 11 articles during the second half of 1987, while general campaign fund-raising coverage in *The Washington Post* included 19 articles during the first half of 1987 as compared with just 10 articles during the second half. *The Wall Street Journal*'s patterns in media coverage of different categories of campaign fund-raising were less pronounced but generally reflected a slight increase in both candidate focused coverage and general campaign fund-raising coverage as 1987 progressed. This analysis of media coverage of campaign fund-raising confirms the extent of this media coverage throughout the pre-election year of 1987 as well as the progressive building of this media coverage of campaign fund-raising, especially media coverage of individual candidates' fund-raising success, during the latter part of the year. Each of these patterns is consistent with the hypothesized impact of media coverage of campaign fund-raising success on candidate survival, viability, and success in the early presidential nomination process.

Horse race coverage of campaign fund-raising during the 1988 election's early campaign, while limited in volume, merits special analysis. As Tables 6.5, 6.6, and 6.7 present, during the thirteen month period from January 1987 through January 1988, the overall volume of media coverage of early campaign fund-raising framed in terms of a horse race was quite small, including 7 articles and 8 candidate comparisons in *The New York Times*, 2 articles and 4 candidate comparisons in *The Washington Post*, and 2 articles and 5 candidate comparisons in *The Wall Street Journal*. Quite significantly, almost all of this media coverage of campaign fund-raising framed as a horse race focused on candidates who subsequently proved to be viable in the opening contests of the nomination process. In fact, of the 11 articles and 17 candidate comparisons appearing in these three newspapers during the pre-nomination period studied, all but 2 of them focused on candidates who proved to be viable in the early nomination process. An analysis of candidate comparisons in these horse race articles presented in the appendices shows 15 references to candidates who proved to be viable, just 1 reference to a candidate who only remained active through the early nomination process, and only 1 reference to a candidate who withdrew. These appendices also indicate that most of the candidate references in this horse race coverage not only were viable candidates but perceived front-runners, with 6 references to Dukakis in this horse race coverage and 6 references to Bush; the other 5 references were divided

TABLE 6.5
Summary Analysis of Horse Race Coverage of Campaign Fund-Raising
1988 Presidential Election Cycle
The New York Times
January 1987–January 1988

		1st Qtr 1987	2nd Qtr 1987	3rd Qtr 1987	4th Qtr 1987	Jan 1988	Overall
Viable Through	Pos	—	2	2	3	—	7
Early Nom.	Neg	—	—	—	—	—	—
Process:	Neu	—	—	—	—	—	—
Active Through	Pos	—	—	—	—	—	—
Early Nom.	Neg	—	—	—	—	—	—
Process:	Neu	—	—	—	—	—	—
Withdrawing	Pos	—	1	—	—	—	1
Before Early	Neg	—	—	—	—	—	—
Nom. Process:	Neu	—	—	—	—	—	—
Withdrawing	Pos	—	—	—	—	—	—
Before Formal	Neg	—	—	—	—	—	—
Announcement:	Neu	—	—	—	—	—	—

Note: This table refers to candidates compared in horse race coverage of campaign fund-raising, numbers that generally are greater than the number of horse race articles.

TABLE 6.6
Summary Analysis of Horse Race Coverage of Campaign Fund-Raising
1988 Presidential Election Cycle
The Washington Post
January 1987–January 1988

		1st Qtr 1987	2nd Qtr 1987	3rd Qtr 1987	4th Qtr 1987	Jan 1988	Overall
Viable Through	Pos	—	—	1	3	—	4
Early Nom.	Neg	—	—	—	—	—	—
Process:	Neu	—	—	—	—	—	—
Active Through	Pos	—	—	—	—	—	—
Early Nom.	Neg	—	—	—	—	—	—
Process:	Neu	—	—	—	—	—	—
Withdrawing	Pos	—	—	—	—	—	—
Before Early	Neg	—	—	—	—	—	—
Nom. Process:	Neu	—	—	—	—	—	—
Withdrawing	Pos	—	—	—	—	—	—
Before Formal	Neg	—	—	—	—	—	—
Announcement:	Neu	—	—	—	—	—	—

Note: This table refers to candidates compared in horse race coverage of campaign fund-raising, numbers that generally are greater than the number of horse race articles.

TABLE 6.7
Summary Analysis of Horse Race Coverage of Campaign Fund-Raising
1988 Presidential Election Cycle
The Wall Street Journal
January 1987–January 1988

		1st Qtr 1987	2nd Qtr 1987	3rd Qtr 1987	4th Qtr 1987	Jan 1988	Overall
Viable Through	Pos	—	1	—	—	3	4
Early Nom.	Neg	—	—	—	—	—	—
Process:	Neu	—	—	—	—	—	—
Active Through	Pos	—	—	—	—	—	—
Early Nom.	Neg	—	1	—	—	—	1
Process:	Neu	—	—	—	—	—	—
Withdrawing	Pos	—	—	—	—	—	—
Before Early	Neg	—	—	—	—	—	—
Nom. Process:	Neu	—	—	—	—	—	—
Withdrawing	Pos	—	—	—	—	—	—
Before Formal	Neg	—	—	—	—	—	—
Announcement:	Neu	—	—	—	—	—	—

Note: This table refers to candidates compared in horse race coverage of campaign fund-raising, numbers that generally are greater than the number of horse race articles.

among Biden, Hart, and Dole, each of whom received 1, and Robertson, who received 2. Interestingly, all but 1 of these candidate references in news articles with a horse race frame were positive. Thus, while horse race coverage of early campaign fund-raising in the 1988 presidential election cycle certainly was quite limited in volume, it clearly concentrated on the viable candidates and in fact the perceived front-runners, providing each of them with a boost in standing and credibility relative to other candidates in their respective party nomination races.

Media coverage of campaign fund-raising that was candidate focused and covered individual candidates' fund-raising during the early campaign leading up to the 1988 nomination process was much more substantial than the horse race coverage but also much more broadly distributed over the candidate field and not limited just to the candidates who later proved to be viable. In *The New York Times*, as Table 6.8 presents, there were 33 candidate focused articles on early campaign fund-raising during the thirteen month period under study, with 11 articles focused on candidates who proved to be viable, 20 focused on candidates who simply remained as active candidates, and just 2 focused on candidates who withdrew even before a public announcement of candidacy.[7] These articles were broadly distributed among the individual candidates within the viable and active candidate groupings, with literally every candidate being the focus of at least 1 article and with most being the focus of

TABLE 6.8
Summary Analysis of Coverage of Individual Candidate Fund-Raising
1988 Presidential Election Cycle
The New York Times
January 1987–January 1988

		1st Qtr 1987	2nd Qtr 1987	3rd Qtr 1987	4th Qtr 1987	Jan 1988	Overall
Viable Through	Pos	—	2	1	2	—	5
Early Nom.	Neg	—	1	2	1	1	5
Process:	Neu	—	—	—	1	—	1
Active Through	Pos	1	—	1	2	1	5
Early Nom.	Neg	—	5	—	4	6	15
Process:	Neu	—	—	—	—	—	—
Withdrawing	Pos	—	—	—	—	—	—
Before Early	Neg	—	—	—	—	—	—
Nom. Process:	Neu	—	—	—	—	—	—
Withdrawing	Pos	—	1	—	—	—	1
Before Formal	Neg	—	—	1	—	—	1
Announcement:	Neu	—	—	—	—	—	—

Note: This table refers to candidates covered in candidate focused coverage of individual candidate fund-raising, numbers that sometimes are greater than the number of candidate focused articles.

2 or more. Even the perceived front-runners, Dukakis and Bush, were the focus of about the same number of articles—namely 2 apiece—as the other candidates who were categorized as viable candidates along with them. This media coverage of individual candidates' fund-raising did tend to be more positive among the perceived front-runners, with 3 positive articles to just 1 negative article, and among the viable candidates in general, with 5 positive articles to 4 negative articles, as compared with other active candidates who overall received just 5 positive articles to 15 negative articles. Hart's highly unfavorable media coverage, both in general and of his fund-raising, certainly affected these article totals, with his thirteen month total for candidate focused fund-raising coverage totaling 11 negative articles to just 1 positive article. Thus media coverage of campaign fund-raising that was candidate focused in *The New York Times* was significant and broadly distributed among candidates who proved to be either viable or at least active through the early nomination process, with the candidates receiving the more frequent positive coverage tending to be the same candidates who were either perceived front-runners or categorized as viable through the early nomination process.

The same general pattern in media coverage of campaign fund-raising that is candidate focused also is evident in media coverage in *The Washington Post* and to an extent in *The Wall Street Journal*, with media coverage generally being broadly distributed over the candidate field and not limited just to the candidates who later proved to be viable. In *The Washington Post*, as Table 6.9 presents, there were 59 candidate focused articles on early campaign fund-raising during the thirteen month period under study, with 22 articles focused on candidates who proved to be viable, 29 articles focused on candidates who simply remained as active candidates, and 8 articles focused on other candidates. As Table 6.10 presents, the same is true although in more limited numbers with *The Wall Street Journal*'s coverage, with the overall total of 10 candidate focused articles on early campaign fund-raising including 3 articles focused on candidates who proved to be viable, 5 articles on candidates who simply remained as active candidates, and just 2 articles on other candidates. Moreover, with *The Washington Post*, and as was the case with *The New York Times*, these articles were broadly distributed among the individual candidates within the viable and active candidate groupings, with most viable and active candidates receiving at least 1 article and many receiving 2 or 3. And again, as with *The New York Times*, the perceived front-runners—Dukakis and Bush—were the focus of either the same number of articles or even fewer articles as the rest of the viable and active candidates. In the case of *The Wall Street Journal*, its much smaller number of candidate focused articles also was broadly distributed, although Hart did receive 5 of the 6 Democratic candidate focused articles. As was also the case with *The New York Times*, this media coverage of campaign fund-raising in both *The Washington Post* and *The Wall Street Journal* was more positive toward the perceived front-runner

TABLE 6.9
Summary Analysis of Coverage of Individual Candidate Fund-Raising
1988 Presidential Election Cycle
The Washington Post
January 1987–January 1988

		1st Qtr 1987	2nd Qtr 1987	3rd Qtr 1987	4th Qtr 1987	Jan 1988	Overall
Viable Through	Pos	—	—	4	3	—	7
Early Nom.	Neg	—	3	2	8	—	13
Process:	Neu	1	—	—	—	1	2
Active Through	Pos	—	1	—	4	—	5
Early Nom.	Neg	—	8	—	7	6	21
Process:	Neu	2	—	—	—	1	3
Withdrawing	Pos	—	1	—	—	—	1
Before Early	Neg	—	—	—	—	—	—
Nom. Process:	Neu	—	—	—	—	—	—
Withdrawing	Pos	—	—	4	1	—	5
Before Formal	Neg	—	1	1	—	—	2
Announcement:	Neu	—	—	—	—	—	—

Note: This table refers to candidates covered in candidate focused coverage of individual candidate fund-raising, numbers that sometimes are greater than the number of candidate focused articles.

candidates—with Dukakis receiving 3 positive articles to 1 negative article and Bush receiving 2 positive articles to 1 negative article—and to a lesser extent also was relatively more positive toward viable candidates—who received 9 positive articles to 14 negative articles, with Robertson's total of 7 negative articles in *The Washington Post* skewing these totals somewhat. The comparable ratio of positive to negative articles in both *The Washington Post* and *The Wall Street Journal* among candidates who simply remained active through the early nomination process was 6 positive articles to 25 negative articles, a much higher level of negative coverage than the viable candidates received. Thus, as was the case with *The New York Times'* coverage of campaign fund-raising that was candidate focused, candidate focused coverage of campaign fund-raising in *The Washington Post* and *The Wall Street Journal* likewise was broadly distributed among the candidates who proved to be either viable or at least active through the early nomination process. It is especially noteworthy that positive coverage of individual candidates' fund-raising was more frequent with candidates who were the perceived front-runners or, to a lesser extent, with candidates who later proved to be viable through the early nomination process.

Thus media coverage of campaign fund-raising in the 1988 election's early presidential nomination campaign was a significant part of the media's overall coverage of this nomination process and extended through the pre-election year of 1987 and into January 1988 as well. As would be expected based upon

TABLE 6.10
Summary Analysis of Coverage of Individual Candidate Fund-Raising
1988 Presidential Election Cycle
The Wall Street Journal
January 1987–January 1988

		1st Qtr 1987	2nd Qtr 1987	3rd Qtr 1987	4th Qtr 1987	Jan 1988	Overall
Viable Through	Pos	—	1	1	—	—	2
Early Nom.	Neg	—	—	—	1	—	1
Process:	Neu	—	—	—	—	—	—
Active Through	Pos	—	—	—	1	—	1
Early Nom.	Neg	—	1	—	1	2	4
Process:	Neu	—	—	—	—	—	—
Withdrawing	Pos	—	—	—	—	—	—
Before Early	Neg	—	—	—	—	—	—
Nom. Process:	Neu	—	—	—	—	—	—
Withdrawing	Pos	—	—	—	—	—	—
Before Formal	Neg	—	—	1	—	—	1
Announcement:	Neu	1	1	—	—	—	2

Note: This table refers to candidates covered in candidate focused coverage of individual candidate fund-raising, numbers that sometimes are greater than the number of candidate focused articles.

FECA's requirement that candidates submit quarterly financial disclosure reports, this media coverage in the three newspapers included in this study peaked in terms of the volume of coverage at the end of each quarter. According to this analysis of 1988's early nomination campaign, this media coverage of campaign fund-raising was not homogeneous but can be differentiated into horse race coverage, candidate focused coverage, and general coverage of the issue of campaign finance. Moreover, consistent with this study's hypothesis that media coverage of campaign fund-raising success in effect constitutes an echo of fund-raising success itself, candidate focused coverage of campaign fund-raising comprised the largest category of this media coverage, with quarterly peaks in the volume of this coverage being particularly pronounced. While horse race coverage of campaign fund-raising was found to be a small part of media coverage of campaign fund-raising in general, it also is significant that this horse race coverage concentrated on candidates who proved to be viable in the early nomination process and in particular the perceived front-runners, and that this coverage generally was positive and therefore a boost to the prospects of these candidates. To be sure, the extent to which media coverage of campaign fund-raising in 1988's early nomination campaign concentrated on candidate focused coverage is a particularly significant finding of this analysis. This media coverage was found to be broadly distributed among the groupings of candidates, especially among candidates who proved to be viable or who at least remained active through the early nomination process. But consistent with the hypothesized relationship between positive media coverage of a candidate's fund-raising and candidate viability through the early nomination process, the candidates who most often received positive coverage of campaign fund-raising were the same candidates who proved to be viable candidates through the early nomination process.

In sum, media coverage of campaign fund-raising indeed was found to constitute a significant dimension of the 1988 election's early campaign, with candidate focused coverage of campaign fund-raising being especially prominent and indeed related to the quarterly schedule of candidate financial disclosure reports. As the hypothesized relationship between media coverage of a candidate's success in early campaign fund-raising and candidate survival, viability, and success in the early nomination process predicts, moreover, candidates receiving a greater volume of positive horse race coverage as well as more positive candidate focused coverage indeed are the same candidates who later proved to be viable and even victorious in the opening contests of the presidential nomination process.

Media Coverage of Campaign Fund-Raising in the 2000 Early Nomination Campaign

The 2000 early nomination campaign and both major party nomination contests provide a second case study of media coverage of campaign fund-raising in the early nomination process that is very important to this analysis. Coming twelve years after the 1988 early nomination campaign, and representing the beginning of the eighth presidential election cycle of the post-reform era, the 2000 early nomination campaign is indicative of the extent to which media coverage of presidential nomination campaigns in general and early campaign fund-raising in particular has emerged as a major dimension of the presidential nomination process. This second case study is especially valuable for this analysis because of the additional set of data on media coverage of early campaign fund-raising which it introduces, permitting trends in the growth and dynamics of media coverage to be identified and understood. Moreover, the 2000 presidential nomination process represented a new milestone in the evolution of the post-reform era nomination system, with the front-loading of the primary and caucus schedule continuing to advance and with candidates and potential candidates making myriad strategic adjustments in response.[8] Most notably, the framework of campaign finance reform reached the point of near disintegration with the 2000 presidential election cycle, creating new incentives and opportunities for uncontrolled campaign fund-raising by presidential aspirants.[9] The rise of early campaign fund-raising as a pivotal factor during the pre-candidacy and early candidacy phases of nascent presidential campaigns, and the emergence of the money primary as a decisive step in presidential nominee selection, therefore are particularly prominent in the 2000 early nomination campaign. Media coverage of campaign fund-raising likewise reached a new height with the 2000 early campaign, confirming the media's vital role as a dimension of the money primary.

The volume of media coverage of campaign fund-raising during the 2000 nomination race's early campaign was much higher than during 1988's early campaign. Overall media coverage in the three newspapers studied nearly doubled, increasing from a total of 181 articles and 147,641 words during 1988's early campaign to a total of 310 articles and 302,546 words during 2000's early campaign. This enormous increase, both in the number of articles and in the total word count and average length, was reflected in all three major newspapers studied. As Table 6.11 presents, this increase in media coverage is especially impressive in the case of *The New York Times* in which media coverage of campaign fund-raising expanded from 66 articles and 59,005 words in 1988's early campaign to 132 articles and 125,641 words in 2000's early campaign—a more than 100 percent increase. As Table 6.11 also presents, coverage also increased in *The Washington Post*—which was in the forefront of media coverage of early campaign fund-raising even in 1988— rising from 94 articles and 70,009 words in 1988's early campaign to 115 articles and 133,140 words in 2000's early campaign. Even *The Wall Street Journal*, which gave very little attention to campaign fund-raising or even campaign finance just twelve years earlier, began offering major coverage by the 2000 early campaign. As Table 6.11 also presents, this coverage of campaign fund-raising during the early campaign in *The Wall Street Journal* increased from just 21 articles and 18,627 words in 1988's early campaign to 63 articles and 43,765 words in 2000's early campaign—a three-fold increase, the highest rate of growth in coverage among the three newspapers studied. Thus media coverage of early campaign fund-raising in the three newspapers included in this study extended throughout the pre-election year of 1999 and into the pre- nomination period of January 2000, a pattern also reflected in 1987 and early 1988, with each of these thirteen months having several articles and frequently 10 or more articles in each newspaper. By the 2000 election's early campaign, in short, media coverage of campaign fund-raising by candidates and potential candidates for the presidential nomination had become a major agenda item for the media and an integral part of the early presidential nomination process.

TABLE 6.11
Overview of Media Coverage of Candidate and Campaign Fund-Raising
2000 Presidential Election Cycle
January 1999–January 2000

	The New York Times		The Washington Post		The Wall Street Journal	
	Articles	Words	Articles	Words	Articles	Words
January 1999	5	5,077	11	10,460	3	706
February 1999	—	—	3	3,753	—	—
March 1999	5	5,042	11	11,338	3	3,358
April 1999	8	4,986	12	21,141	12	12,710
May 1999	12	13,349	8	9,773	3	1,786
June 1999	10	9,092	9	10,528	4	2,337
July 1999	22	21,632	21	19,373	4	3,535
August 1999	10	7,265	7	7,401	2	971
September 1999	11	8,849	10	8,933	4	1,464
October 1999	12	14,188	10	16,498	9	6,635
November 1999	12	8,196	4	5,088	6	3,433
December 1999	13	13,098	2	1,774	7	4,170
January 2000	12	14,867	7	7,080	6	2,660
Totals:	132	125,641	115	133,140	63	43,765

The extensive year-long media coverage of early campaign fund-raising in the 2000 presidential election also presents a number of significant patterns in the frequency and volume of media coverage, just as was also evident in the 1988 early campaign. The extent of media coverage of early campaign fund-raising had peaks in terms of the frequency and volume of coverage, with these peaks generally occurring immediately after each quarter of the year and especially immediately after mid-year and year-end. In the case of *The New York Times*, while there was no clear peak in early 1999, coverage peaked at 22 articles and 21,632 words in July 1999, a substantial increase over the 10 articles and 9,092 words in June 1999; then during the second half of 1999, while the frequency of coverage was fairly steady at about 12 articles per month, the volume of coverage peaked at 14,188 words in October 1999 from 8,849 words the month before, and peaked again at 13,098 words in December 1998 and 14,867 words in January 2000, up from just 8,196 words in November 1999. This quarterly pattern was even more evident in *The Washington Post*'s coverage, with coverage growing from 11 articles and 11,338 words to 12 articles and 21,141 words in April 1999, from 9 articles and 10,528 words to 21 articles and 19,373 words in July 1999, from 10 articles and 8,933 words to 10 articles and 16,498 words in October 1999, and from 2 articles and 1,774 words to 7 articles and 7,080 words in January 2000. Even *The Wall Street Journal*'s coverage of early campaign fund-raising had this quarterly pattern of peaks in coverage, with clear peaks evident in April 1999, July 1999, October 1999, and December 1999–January 2000. As was clear during the 1987 pre-election year as well, these quarterly peaks in coverage followed a pattern corresponding with the schedule of quarterly candidate financial disclosure reports filed with the FEC, in effect constituting an echo of candidate fund-raising success in terms of media coverage of that fund-raising success.

A further significant pattern in this media coverage of campaign fund-raising during the early nomination campaign is the overall timing of this coverage over the course of the pre-election year. Similar to the pattern during the 1987 pre-election year when the volume of this media coverage built as the year progressed, the volume of media coverage of early campaign fund-raising during the 1999 pre-election year likewise was greater during the second half of the year as compared with the first half. As Table 6.11 presents, *The New York Times* published 80 articles during the second half of 1999, as compared with 40 articles during the first half of 1999, and *The Wall Street Journal* published 32 articles during the second half of 1999, as compared with 25 articles during the first half of 1999. Yet this pattern for 1999 is not as uniformly progressive with respect to the increased volume of media coverage of campaign fund-raising as the year moves into its closing months, as was the case in 1987, with the 1999 pre-election year reflecting a shifting of media coverage from the fourth quarter of the year to the third quarter, an average of three months earlier in the pre-election year cycle. As is evident from a close examination of Table 6.11, both *The New York Times* and *The Washington Post* published a higher number of articles in the third quarter of 1999 as compared to the fourth quarter, the opposite of the pattern in 1987 when the fourth quarter of 1987 had a higher number of articles than the third quarter. Indicative of this shift in media coverage to an earlier juncture in the campaign, namely from the fourth quarter to the third quarter, was the timing of coverage in *The New York Times*, which published 43 articles in the third quarter and just 37 articles in the fourth quarter, as well as in *The Washington Post* which published 38 articles in the third quarter and just 16 articles in the fourth quarter. Thus while media coverage of campaign fund-raising in general during the pre-election year of 1999 reflected a generally progressive trend toward a greater volume of coverage during the second half of 1999 as compared with the first half, a shift toward earlier coverage is present within this general trend, with the greater volume of overall media coverage occurring during the third quarter of 1999 as compared with during the fourth quarter of 1999.

Categorization of media coverage of campaign fund-raising during the thirteen month early campaign leading up to the 2000 presidential nomination process into three distinct categories, as was the case with 1988's early campaign, identifies additional patterns and trends. Utilizing the same system of categorization employed with media coverage of campaign fund-raising from 1988's early campaign, this analysis separates media coverage of campaign fund-raising into three categories: horse race coverage that compares candidates' fund-raising; candidate focused coverage that evaluates particular candidates' fund-raising; and general coverage of campaign fund-raising and the issue of campaign finance. Tables 6.12, 6.13, and 6.14 summarize this three-part categorization for the three newspapers included in this study, a breakdown showing the significant frequency and volume of media coverage in all three categories of coverage. A major focus of media coverage of early campaign fund-raising in the 2000 election reflected in this categorization is general coverage of campaign fund-raising and campaign finance, a topic that ranked second in the 1988 election's early campaign media coverage. This heightened media attention to campaign finance is most evident in *The New York Times*, with coverage of general campaign fund-raising and campaign finance increasing from 27 articles and 25,652 words in the 1988 election cycle

TABLE 6.12
Analysis of Media Coverage of Candidate and Campaign Fund-Raising
2000 Presidential Election Cycle
The New York Times
January 1999–January 2000

	Horse Race Coverage of Campaign Fund-Raising		Coverage of Individual Candidate Fund-Raising		General Coverage of Campaign Fund-Raising	
	Articles	Words	Articles	Words	Articles	Words
January 1999	—	—	1	1,330	4	3,747
February 1999	—	—	—	—	—	—
March 1999	2	2,361	1	532	2	2,149
April 1999	2	1,042	—	—	6	3,944
May 1999	—	—	2	5,199	10	8,150
June 1999	2	2,254	2	921	6	5,917
July 1999	2	1,866	11	9,422	9	10,344
August 1999	—	—	3	2,479	7	4,786
September 1999	—	—	4	3,401	7	5,448
October 1999	1	958	3	4,030	8	9,200
November 1999	—	—	4	3,402	8	4,794
December 1999	2	1,559	—	—	11	11,539
January 2000	1	96	2	3,223	9	11,548
Totals:	12	10,136	33	33,939	87	81,566

Chapter 6

TABLE 6.13
Analysis of Media Coverage of Candidate and Campaign Fund-Raising
2000 Presidential Election Cycle
The Washington Post
January 1999–January 2000

	Horse Race Coverage of Campaign Fund-Raising		Coverage of Individual Candidate Fund-Raising		General Coverage of Campaign Fund-Raising	
	Articles	Words	Articles	Words	Articles	Words
January 1999	—	—	8	7,655	3	2,805
February 1999	—	—	2	1,736	1	2,017
March 1999	—	—	6	7,412	5	3,926
April 1999	3	4,692	5	11,628	4	4,821
May 1999	—	—	6	6,491	2	3,282
June 1999	3	4,169	5	5,990	1	369
July 1999	5	5,294	11	10,205	5	3,874
August 1999	—	—	2	2,959	5	4,442
September 1999	—	—	8	7,541	2	1,392
October 1999	2	2,184	2	3,241	6	11,073
November 1999	—	—	3	3,444	1	1,644
December 1999	1	1,206	1	568	—	—
January 2000	—	—	4	4,606	3	2,474
Totals:	14	17,545	63	73,476	38	42,119

to 87 articles and 81,566 words in the 2000 election cycle, a more than three-fold increase. Campaign finance also was the highest priority in *The Wall Street Journal* in which coverage of general campaign fund-raising and campaign finance increased from 8 articles and 9,301 words in the 1988 election cycle to 35 articles and 22,007 words in the 2000 election cycle, likewise exceeding its horse race and candidate focused coverage.

Candidate focused coverage of campaign fund-raising also continued to be a priority during the early campaign leading up to the 2000 election cycle, ranking as the highest category of coverage in *The Washington Post*—as was the case in the 1988 election cycle as well—and ranking as the second highest category of coverage in both *The New York Times* and *The Wall Street Journal*. In *The Washington Post*, candidate focused coverage of campaign fund-raising totalled 63 articles and 73,476 words, continuing its pattern from 1988's early campaign when candidate focused coverage also exceeded either campaign finance or horse race coverage. Finally, as was also the case during the 1988 election's early campaign, horse race coverage comparing candidates with one another in terms of their fund-raising success ran a distant third in all three newspapers, with the frequency and volume of this horse race coverage gen-

TABLE 6.14
Analysis of Media Coverage of Candidate and Campaign Fund-Raising
2000 Presidential Election Cycle
The Wall Street Journal
January 1999–January 2000

	Horse Race Coverage of Campaign Fund-Raising		Coverage of Individual Candidate Fund-Raising		General Coverage of Campaign Fund-Raising	
	Articles	Words	Articles	Words	Articles	Words
January 1999	—	—	—	—	3	706
February 1999	—	—	—	—	—	—
March 1999	1	306	—	—	2	3,052
April 1999	2	1,894	6	7,109	4	3,707
May 1999	—	—	1	829	2	957
June 1999	1	369	1	756	2	1,212
July 1999	2	1,608	2	1,927	—	—
August 1999	—	—	1	648	1	323
September 1999	2	944	1	343	1	177
October 1999	—	—	2	1,812	7	4,823
November 1999	1	720	—	—	5	2,887
December 1999	—	—	3	1,283	4	1,450
January 2000	1	410	1	800	4	2,474
Totals:	10	6,251	18	15,507	35	22,007

erally ranging anywhere from one-third to one-fifth of either candidate focused coverage or general coverage of campaign fund-raising. Thus the media's coverage of campaign fund-raising during the 2000 election's early campaign reflected significantly increased attention to general campaign fund-raising and campaign finance, with *The New York Times* and *The Wall Street Journal* making campaign finance their dominant topic for campaign fund-raising coverage. Candidate focused coverage, while not as dominant as in the 1988 election's early campaign, continued to be the focus of considerable media attention in all three newspapers, especially *The Washington Post* in which candidate focused coverage of campaign fund-raising dominated its coverage of the 2000 election's early campaign fund-raising just as it dominated its coverage of the 1988 election's early campaign fund-raising.

This analysis categorizing media coverage of campaign fund-raising over the thirteen months leading up to the opening of the formal nomination process in 2000 in terms of horse race, candidate focused, and campaign finance coverage also reveals additional patterns in the timing of this coverage that are significant. The shift in media coverage of campaign fund-raising to earlier in the pre-election year exhibited in aggregate data on media coverage in *The New York Times* and *The Washington Post* (see Table 6.11) in actuality is a shift that is entirely in the category of candidate focused coverage. While this candidate focused coverage continues to be greater in the second half of the pre-election year of 1999 as compared with the first half of 1999, as also was the case in the pre-election year of 1987, the coverage in 1999 in both *The New York Times* and *The Washington Post* was much greater in the third quarter than the fourth quarter of the year. As Table 6.12 presents, candidate focused coverage of campaign fund-raising in *The New York Times* totaled 18 articles and 15,302 words in the third quarter of 1999 as compared with just 7 articles and 7,432 words in the fourth quarter of 1999. Likewise in *The Washington Post*, as Table 6.13 presents, candidate focused coverage of campaign fund-raising totaled 21 articles and 18,705 words in the third quarter of 1999 as compared with 6 articles and 7,253 words in the fourth quarter of 1999. Moreover, this greater level of early candidate focused coverage in *The Washington Post* also extended to the first half as compared to the second half of 1999, with candidate focused coverage totaling 32 articles and 40,912 words in the first half of 1999 as compared with 27 articles and 27,958 words in the second half of 1999. Thus media coverage of early campaign fund-raising in the 2000 early nomination campaign not only extended throughout the entire pre-election year of 1999 but in general increased progressively as the year proceeded, timing that also was evident in media coverage of campaign fund-raising in the 1988 election's early campaign. Yet quite distinct timing is evident with candidate focused coverage of campaign fund-raising in the 2000 election's early campaign, with this coverage not only being much greater in frequency and volume but also occurring earlier in the pre-election year of 1999 relative to twelve years before. Consistent with the advance of the early campaign in presidential nomination politics and the rise of the money primary as a vital dimension of that campaign, candidate focused coverage of campaign fund-raising not only increased substantially during 1999 as a whole but shifted to significantly earlier in the year.

Horse race coverage of campaign fund-raising during the 2000 election's early campaign exhibited significant patterns that are similar to the horse race coverage of campaign fund-raising during the 1988 election's early campaign. This horse race coverage of campaign fund-raising was a distant third in both frequency and volume compared with candidate focused and general fund-raising coverage, indicating that the limited media attention given to horse race coverage of campaign fund-raising in the 1988 election's early campaign was evident in the 2000 election's early campaign as well. Quite significantly, as Tables 6.15, 6.16, and 6.17 present, all of this media coverage of campaign fund-raising framed as a horse race concentrated on candidates who subsequently proved to be viable in the opening contests of the nomination cam-

TABLE 6.15
Summary Analysis of Horse Race Coverage of Campaign Fund-Raising
2000 Presidential Election Cycle
The New York Times
January 1999–January 2000

		1st Qtr 1999	2nd Qtr 1999	3rd Qtr 1999	4th Qtr 1999	Jan 2000	Overall
Viable Through	Pos	3	6	3	4	3	19
Early Nom.	Neg	—	—	1	2	1	4
Process:	Neu	1	—	—	—	—	1
Active Through	Pos	—	—	—	—	—	—
Early Nom.	Neg	—	—	—	—	—	—
Process:	Neu	—	—	—	—	—	—
Withdrawing	Pos	—	—	—	—	—	—
Before Early	Neg	—	—	—	—	—	—
Nom. Process:	Neu	—	—	—	—	—	—
Withdrawing	Pos	—	—	—	—	—	—
Before Formal	Neg	—	—	—	—	—	—
Announcement:	Neu	—	—	—	—	—	—

Note: This table refers to candidates compared in horse race coverage of campaign fund-raising, numbers that generally are greater than the number of horse race articles.

TABLE 6.16
Summary Analysis of Horse Race Coverage of Campaign Fund-Raising
2000 Presidential Election Cycle
The Washington Post
January 1999–January 2000

		1st Qtr 1999	2nd Qtr 1999	3rd Qtr 1999	4th Qtr 1999	Jan 2000	Overall
Viable Through	Pos	—	8	5	4	—	17
Early Nom.	Neg	—	1	2	2	—	5
Process:	Neu	—	—	—	—	—	—
Active Through	Pos	—	—	—	—	—	—
Early Nom.	Neg	—	—	—	—	—	—
Process:	Neu	—	—	—	—	—	—
Withdrawing	Pos	—	—	—	—	—	—
Before Early	Neg	—	—	—	—	—	—
Nom. Process:	Neu	—	—	—	—	—	—
Withdrawing	Pos	—	—	—	—	—	—
Before Formal	Neg	—	—	—	—	—	—
Announcement:	Neu	—	—	—	—	—	—

Note: This table refers to candidates compared in horse race coverage of campaign fund-raising, numbers that generally are greater than the number of horse race articles.

TABLE 6.17
Summary Analysis of Horse Race Coverage of Campaign Fund-Raising
2000 Presidential Election Cycle
The Wall Street Journal
January 1999–January 2000

		1st Qtr 1999	2nd Qtr 1999	3rd Qtr 1999	4th Qtr 1999	Jan 2000	Overall
Viable Through	Pos	1	5	4	2	1	13
Early Nom.	Neg	—	2	3	—	—	5
Process:	Neu	—	—	—	—	—	—
Active Through	Pos	—	—	—	—	—	—
Early Nom.	Neg	—	—	—	—	—	—
Process:	Neu	—	—	—	—	—	—
Withdrawing	Pos	—	—	—	—	—	—
Before Early	Neg	—	—	—	—	—	—
Nom. Process:	Neu	—	—	—	—	—	—
Withdrawing	Pos	—	—	—	—	—	—
Before Formal	Neg	—	—	—	—	—	—
Announcement:	Neu	—	—	—	—	—	—

Note: This table refers to candidates compared in horse race coverage of campaign fund-raising, numbers that generally are greater than the number of horse race articles.

paign. In fact, of the 36 articles and 64 candidate comparisons appearing in the three newspapers included in this analysis, literally every one focused on a candidate who proved to be viable in the early nomination process. The eventual nominees—Gore and Bush—received the majority of the candidate references in these horse race articles, with 45 of the 64 candidate references being to either Gore or Bush. As is detailed in the appendices, the overwhelming portion of this horse race coverage presented Gore, Bush, or the other viable candidates positively, a pattern also evident in the 1988 election's early campaign, with 49 of the 64 candidate references being made with a positive spin, only 14 of the 64 being made with a negative spin, and a single candidate reference being neutral. Interestingly, 13 of the 14 negative candidate references in the three newspapers studied concerned Gore, who received only 8 positive references as compared with 13 negative references in this horse race coverage of campaign fund-raising, generally unfavorable horse race coverage that occurred as Bradley's fund-raising was out-pacing Gore's and actually almost surpassing him.

Finally, and perhaps most significantly, horse race coverage of campaign fund-raising in the 2000 election's early campaign continued a pattern of focusing on candidates who proved to be viable that also is evident in the 1988 election's early campaign. As Table 6.18 summarizes, however, the frequency and volume of this horse race coverage in the 2000 election cycle was signifi-

TABLE 6.18
**Analysis Comparing Horse Race Coverage of Campaign Fund-Raising
1988 and 2000 Presidential Election Cycles
The New York Times, The Washington Post, and The Wall Street Journal**

	1988 Election Cycle			2000 Election Cycle		
	The New York Times	The Washington Post	The Wall Street Journal	The New York Times	The Washington Post	The Wall Street Journal
Viable Candidates:						
Positive	7	4	4	19	17	13
Negative	—	—	—	4	5	5
Neutral	—	—	—	1	—	—
Other Candidates:						
Positive	1	—	—	—	—	—
Negative	—	—	1	—	—	—
Neutral	—	—	—	—	—	—

Note: This table refers to candidates compared in horse race coverage of campaign fund-raising, numbers that generally are greater than the number of horse race articles.

cantly higher than twelve years earlier. Thus, while horse race coverage of the 2000 election's early campaign was limited relative to candidate focused coverage, it was substantially greater than during the 1988 election's early campaign while continuing to concentrate heavily on viable candidates and perceived front-runners. In general this coverage was highly favorable, providing ultimately viable candidates and especially perceived front-runners such as Bush with a boost in standing and credibility. But this horse race coverage was not always positive, with front-runner Gore suffering a rash of negative horse race articles from mid- to late-1999 as challenger Bradley and his fund-raising success threatened Gore's lead.

Media coverage of campaign fund-raising that was candidate focused and covered individual candidates' fund-raising during the early campaign leading up to the 2000 nomination process was a major category of coverage but unlike 1987 not necessarily the highest ranked category of coverage in all three newspapers examined in this study.[10] As already noted, candidate focused coverage of campaign fund-raising indeed was the highest of the three categories of coverage in *The Washington Post*, as was the case in 1987 as well, with coverage of campaign finance and horse race coverage of campaign fund-raising running far behind. Moreover, while coverage of campaign fund-raising and campaign finance was the highest ranked category of coverage in both *The New York Times* and *The Wall Street Journal* in 1999, candidate focused coverage nonetheless was a major category of coverage in both of these newspapers as well. Yet patterns in candidate focused coverage of campaign fund-raising in 1999 varied greatly among these three newspapers. In *The New York Times*, as Table 6.19 presents, candidate focused coverage of campaign fund-raising not only received a large share of coverage (see Table 6.12) but overwhelmingly this coverage was concentrated among the viable candidates. In fact, on the Republican side, 19 candidate focused articles covered Bush out of 20 candidate focused articles concerning viable candidates and a total of 22 candidate focused articles altogether. In *The Washington Post*, on the other hand, as Table 6.20 presents, a distribution of candidates received candidate focused coverage of campaign fund-raising, with 13 of the 66 candidate focused articles concerning candidates who did not prove to be viable. While limited in terms of the overall number of articles, this candidate focused coverage was distributed among all of the categories of candidate, including 2 articles focused on nonviable candidates who remained active through the early nomination process, 7 articles focused on candidates who withdrew before the early nomination process, and 4 articles focused on candidates who withdrew before a formal announcement of candidacy. *The Wall Street Journal's* candidate focused coverage also was distributed to some degree among the candidates, as Table 6.21 presents, with 5 of the 19 candidate focused articles concerning candidates who did not prove to be viable. Thus, while the substantial increase in overall coverage

TABLE 6.19
Summary Analysis of Coverage of Individual Candidate Fund-Raising
2000 Presidential Election Cycle
The New York Times
January 1999–January 2000

		1st Qtr 1999	2nd Qtr 1999	3rd Qtr 1999	4th Qtr 1999	Jan 2000	Overall
Viable Through	Pos	2	3	11	5	3	24
Early Nom.	Neg	—	—	3	1	—	4
Process:	Neu	—	—	3	1	—	4
Active Through	Pos	—	—	—	—	—	—
Early Nom.	Neg	—	—	—	—	—	—
Process:	Neu	—	—	—	—	—	—
Withdrawing	Pos	—	—	—	—	—	—
Before Early	Neg	—	1	1	—	—	2
Nom. Process:	Neu	—	—	—	—	—	—
Withdrawing	Pos	—	—	—	—	—	—
Before Formal	Neg	—	—	—	—	—	—
Announcement:	Neu	—	—	—	—	—	—

Note: This table refers to candidates covered in candidate focused coverage of individual candidate fund-raising, numbers that sometimes are greater than the number of candidate focused articles.

TABLE 6.20
Summary Analysis of Coverage of Individual Candidate Fund-Raising
2000 Presidential Election Cycle
The Washington Post
January 1999–January 2000

		1st Qtr 1999	2nd Qtr 1999	3rd Qtr 1999	4th Qtr 1999	Jan 2000	Overall
Viable Through	Pos	6	8	7	5	—	26
Early Nom.	Neg	—	4	14	—	4	22
Process:	Neu	2	1	1	1	—	5
Active Through	Pos	1	1	—	—	—	2
Early Nom.	Neg	—	—	—	—	—	—
Process:	Neu	—	—	—	—	—	—
Withdrawing	Pos	3	—	—	—	—	3
Before Early	Neg	—	2	1	—	—	3
Nom. Process:	Neu	1	—	—	—	—	1
Withdrawing	Pos	2	—	—	—	—	2
Before Formal	Neg	1	—	—	—	—	1
Announcement:	Neu	—	1	—	—	—	1

Note: This table refers to candidates covered in candidate focused coverage of individual candidate fund-raising, numbers that sometimes are greater than the number of candidate focused articles.

TABLE 6.21
Summary Analysis of Coverage of Individual Candidate Fund-Raising
2000 Presidential Election Cycle
The Wall Street Journal
January 1999–January 2000

		1st Qtr 1999	2nd Qtr 1999	3rd Qtr 1999	4th Qtr 1999	Jan 2000	Overall
Viable Through	Pos	—	3	3	4	1	11
Early Nom.	Neg	—	2	1	—	—	3
Process:	Neu	—	—	—	—	—	—
Active Through	Pos	—	—	—	—	—	—
Early Nom.	Neg	—	—	—	—	—	—
Process:	Neu	—	—	—	—	—	—
Withdrawing	Pos	—	1	—	—	—	1
Before Early	Neg	—	2	–	—	—	2
Nom. Process:	Neu	—	—	—	1	—	1
Withdrawing	Pos	—	—	—	—	—	—
Before Formal	Neg	—	1	—	—	—	1
Announcement:	Neu	—	—	—	—	—	—

Note: This table refers to candidates covered in candidate focused coverage of individual candidate fund-raising, numbers that sometimes are greater than the number of candidate focused articles.

of campaign fund-raising between the 1988 election's early campaign and the 2000 election's early campaign certainly is significant, the continued importance of candidate focused coverage among the three categories of coverage is significant as well. Differences in patterns of coverage among the three newspapers examined also are significant, most notably the top priority which *The Washington Post* gave to candidate focused coverage and the different degrees to which *The New York Times* and both of the other newspapers studied reflected the general pattern of candidate focused coverage being concentrated among only the viable candidates.

An analysis comparing candidate focused coverage of campaign fund-raising in the early campaigns preceding the 1988 and 2000 election campaigns indicates important trends that are particularly significant. As Table 6.22 presents, a comparison of candidate focused coverage published in the three newspapers in 1988 and 2000 reflects dramatic change, not only in terms of greatly increased candidate focused coverage but in a much greater concentration on candidates who proved to be viable in the early nomination process. While the absolute levels of coverage and the extent of the shift in focus to viable candidates varies, the overall magnitude of the shift between 1988 and 2000 toward concentrating coverage more on viable candidates is striking indeed. While this shift to focusing on viable candidates is greatest with *The New York Times*, it also is evident with *The Washington Post* and *The*

TABLE 6.22
Analysis Comparing Coverage of Individual Candidate Fund-Raising
1988 and 2000 Presidential Election Cycles
The New York Times, The Washington Post,* and *The Wall Street Journal

	1988 Election Cycle			*2000 Election Cycle*		
	The New York Times	*The Washington Post*	*The Wall Street Journal*	*The New York Times*	*The Washington Post*	*The Wall Street Journal*
Viable Candidates:						
Positive	5	7	2	24	26	11
Negative	5	13	1	4	22	3
Neutral	1	2	—	4	5	—
Other Candidates:						
Positive	6	11	1	—	7	1
Negative	16	23	5	2	4	3
Neutral	—	3	1	—	2	1

Note: This table refers to candidates covered in candidate focused coverage of individual candidate fund-raising, numbers that sometimes are greater than the number of candidate focused articles.

Wall Street Journal as well. Also impressive is the extent to which candidate focused coverage of viable candidates is proportionately more positive in 2000 than in 1988. Here again *The Washington Post* stands apart from the other two newspapers studied, not only in distributing its coverage more broadly among both viable and other candidates but in publishing a balance between articles with a positive and a negative spin. Yet overall the trend among all three newspapers examined not only is toward a greater concentration of candidate focused coverage on candidates who proved to be viable but toward coverage that is positive toward the candidates covered. This array of patterns and trends, including the growth in candidate focused coverage of campaign fundraising, its significantly increased concentration on viable candidates, and its tendency to be generally positive toward candidates who proved to be viable, all indicate the importance which the media ascribes to fund-raising success and are consistent with the emergence of the early campaign and especially the money primary as pivotal phases in the early presidential nomination process.

Thus media coverage of campaign fund-raising in the 2000 election's early presidential nomination campaign was significantly increased in frequency and volume relative to the 1988 election's early campaign, a trend that in and of itself underscores the increased attention of the media to the early campaign. Many of the patterns in media coverage of campaign fund-raising exhibited in the 1988 election's early campaign are present in the 2000 election's early campaign as well, including the peaks in coverage following each quarter during the pre-election year and the link to fund-raising success through candidate financial disclosure reports to the FEC which this pattern suggests. Also evident in media coverage of the 2000 election's early campaign, as in the 1988 election's early campaign twelve years earlier, is the distribution of media coverage of campaign fund-raising among horse race coverage, candidate focused coverage, and general campaign fund-raising and campaign finance coverage, a categorization that again is valuable in identifying significant trends in media coverage of fund-raising during the early campaign. The shifting of media coverage of campaign fund-raising and in particular candidate focused coverage of campaign fund-raising during the 2000 election's early campaign relative to the 1988 election's early campaign, especially from the fourth quarter to the third quarter of 1999 and in some cases even from the second half to the first half of 1999, is a particularly noteworthy indication of the rise of the early campaign. As was the case with the 1988 election's early campaign, horse race coverage of campaign fund-raising in the 2000 election's early campaign was concentrated among viable candidates and was almost exclusively positive aside from horse race coverage of Gore. Interestingly, while Gore received significant negative horse race coverage as his fund-raising

contest with Bradley tightened, this deviation only reinforces the generalization that horse race coverage is generally positive toward the candidate whose
fund-raising is successful. Finally, candidate focused coverage of campaign
fund-raising in the 2000 election's early campaign also exhibits patterns similar to the 1988 election's early campaign, including the shifting of candidate
focused coverage to earlier in the pre-election year. But most noteworthy of all
is a significant trend in the 2000 election's early campaign for candidate focused coverage of individual candidate fund-raising to be concentrated
among candidates who ultimately proved to be viable, rather than viable and
active candidates as was the case twelve years earlier, and for this coverage to
be positive far more often than negative. This finding not only supports the
value to individual candidates of positive media coverage in terms of achieving viability in the early nomination process but perhaps more than any other
finding of this media coverage analysis highlights the advancing importance
of the early campaign and the rise of the money primary as a pivotal phase in
the early presidential nomination process.

Summary

Media coverage of campaign fund-raising during the early campaign for the
presidential nomination is a pivotal dimension of the money primary and indeed a critical aspect of the early presidential nomination process. This examination of media coverage of campaign fund-raising during the early
campaigns for both the 1988 election and the 2000 election provides considerable support for the emergence of the early campaign and the money primary by identifying the connection between campaign fund-raising success
as reported in candidate financial disclosure reports to the FEC and the timing of media coverage of campaign fund-raising, with this media coverage in
effect constituting an echo of fund-raising success. While both the 1988 and
2000 election years' early campaigns had substantial media coverage of campaign fund-raising, the significant growth in the frequency and volume of
coverage over the twelve-year span between these early campaigns is indicative of the increasing importance of media coverage in early campaign presidential politics. The shifting of this media coverage in general and candidate
focused coverage of campaign fund-raising in particular to earlier in the pre-
election year in the 2000 election cycle is further confirmation of the emergence of this early campaign. Yet the strongest support for the part which
media coverage of campaign fund-raising has in the early campaign is provided by the analysis categorizing this media coverage as horse race coverage,
candidate focused coverage, or general campaign fund-raising and campaign

finance coverage, and comparing these findings over the two distinct election years examined as case studies. This analysis establishes the growth of candidate focused coverage of campaign fund-raising, its shift between the 1988 and 2000 election cycles to be concentrated primarily on viable candidates, and its generally positive spin in 2000 toward candidates whose fund-raising is successful, trends that are all consistent with media coverage's key role in candidate survival, viability, and success. Horse race coverage of campaign fund-raising, while generally much less in both frequency and volume, also is established as a significant part of media coverage of early campaign fund-raising. Candidates who receive media attention framed as horse race coverage of campaign fund-raising generally are presented favorably, and in the early campaigns in both the 1988 election and especially the 2000 election these candidates also are the ones who indeed proved to be viable in the early nomination process.

In sum, consistent with this study's third hypothesis regarding the media's role in the early campaign, media coverage of campaign fund-raising success was a significant part of the early nomination campaigns in 1988 and 2000 alike. Moreover, as the trends between the 1988 and 2000 election cycles established, media coverage of campaign fund-raising success has proven to be increasingly essential for candidates seeking to achieve viability and success in the early nomination process. This significantly increased role of media coverage of campaign fund-raising during the early campaign provides additional support for the money primary as a pivotal phase in the early campaign and in the overall presidential nomination process.

Notes

1. Thomas E. Patterson, *Out of Order* (New York: Vintage Books, 1994), 182–91.

2. William G. Mayer, "The Presidential Nominations," in *The Election of 2000*, ed. Gerald M. Pomper (New York: Chatham House Publishers, 2001), 24.

3. Nelson W. Polsby and Aaron Wildavsky, *Presidential Elections: Strategies and Structures of American Politics*, 10th ed. (New York and London: Chatham House Publishers, Inc., 2000), 101.

4. Rhodes Cook, "The Nominating Process," in *The Elections of 1988*, ed. Michael Nelson (Washington, D.C.: Congressional Quarterly Press, 1989), 32–34.

5. James Fallows, *Breaking the News: How the Media Undermine American Democracy* (New York: Vintage Books, 1997), 278.

6. Thomas E. Patterson, "The Press and Its Missed Assignment," in *The Elections of 1988*, ed. Michael Nelson (Washington, D.C.: Congressional Quarterly Press, 1989), 97–98.

7. The number of candidate focused articles in this analysis (Tables 6.8, 6.9, and 6.10) differs slightly from the total number of articles categorized as being focused on individual candidate fund-raising (Tables 6.2, 6.3, and 6.4) because some articles actually include separate candidate focused coverage of more than one candidate.

8. Mayer, "The Presidential Nominations," 12–16.

9. Anthony Corrado, "Financing the 2000 Elections," in *The Election of 2000*, ed. Gerald M. Pomper (New York: Chatham House Publishers, Inc., 2001), 94–95.

10. The number of candidate focused articles in this analysis (Tables 6.19, 6.20, 6.21, and 6.22) differs slightly from the total number of articles categorized as being focused on individual candidate fund-raising (Tables 6.12, 6.13, and 6.14) because some articles actually include separate candidate focused coverage of more than one candidate.

7

"The Money Primary" and Presidential Selection

CRUCIAL DIMENSION OF THE PRESIDENTIAL SELECTION PROCESS IN THE UNITED States is the process by which the choices available to voters are structured and determined. The pivotal importance of the nomination process in determining voter choices in the general election has been apparent for many years. Since the early 1970s when the presidential nomination reform process began to unfold, moreover, the importance of primaries and caucuses in the nomination process has received substantial attention as well. Increasingly, however, it is the period before the formal nomination process, during what is termed "the invisible primary" or "the early campaign," that the choices available to voters are decided. It is the early campaign, including the pre-candidacy and early candidacy phases and especially "the money primary," that constitutes the new politics of the early presidential nomination process and is the focus of this study.

The early campaign, in particular pre-candidacy and early candidacy fund-raising success, is crucial in defining the candidate field that emerges in each major party as the primary and caucus process begins and unfolds. This study examines fund-raising and media coverage of fund-raising as significant dimensions of pre-candidacy and early candidacy campaign activity, using the early presidential nomination contests of 1988 and 2000—the two all non-incumbent elections of the post-reform era—as case studies. Fund-raising data gathered from candidates' presidential campaign committee reports and leadership PAC reports to the Federal Election Commission comprise an important part of the data for this analysis. Data on media coverage of campaign fund-raising during the thirteen-month period leading up to the opening of the primary and caucus schedule, including coverage in *The New York Times*, *The Washington Post*, and *The Wall Street Journal*, provide a further important dimension to the analysis.

This study of the early presidential nominee selection process at both the pre-candidacy and early candidacy phases confirms the pivotal importance of money in establishing presidential candidate credibility and standing through the opening nomination contests. Fund-raising success, both at the early candidacy and pre-candidacy phases, is confirmed to be predictive of candidate survival, viability, and success in the early presidential nomination process. In particular, fund-raising success during the early candidacy phase, especially during the year prior to the presidential election year, is found to be associated with candidate survival, viability, and success through the opening nomination process, confirming this study's first and most important hypothesis. In addition, the extent of a candidate's success in fund-raising during the pre-candidacy phase which begins two or more years earlier, usually conducted through a leadership PAC and sometimes a non-profit entity or state-based committee, is found to be associated with candidates moving from pre-candidacy to announced candidacy and from simply survival to viability and success, confirming this study's second hypothesis. Indeed for most of the length of an unfolding presidential nomination campaign—in fact for the three or more years prior to the four to six weeks of a genuinely competitive nomination process—fund-raising success in terms of a candidate's total in dollars raised constitutes the principal means by which the prospects of competing candidacies are compared and even evaluated.

Complementing pre-candidacy and early candidacy fund-raising totals in predicting candidate survival, viability, and success is early candidacy fund-raising success defined in terms of key financial indicators during the pre-election year and up through the opening of the formal nomination process. Momentum in fund-raising during the pre-election year is found to be especially important, although the emergence of the early campaign means that the most successful candidates generally raise significant funding during the first half of the pre-election year, resulting in large absolute dollar totals throughout the year but not necessarily increasing momentum. Fund-raising momentum certainly is a mark of the emerging candidate, and candidates who proved to be viable or at least active through the early nomination process—and especially major challengers to front-runners—generally have increasing fund-raising momentum. Cash-on-hand totals, which are a measure of the extent to which resources raised through successful fund-raising are still available for use in the unfolding campaign, also are found to be predictive of candidate survival, viability, and success in the early nomination process. Front-runners without exception are found to have significant totals in cash-on-hand, and in general all viable candidates enter the opening nomination contests with substantial totals in cash-on-hand. And finally, the level of federal matching funding received in both January and February as the formal nomination process opens, funding which represents both a resource in and of itself but also reflects a candidate's breadth of support in contributions up to $250, likewise is found to be predictive of candidate survival, viability, and success in the early nomination process. In fact, aside from candidates who opted not to accept federal matching funding, candidates receiving the highest totals in federal matching funding almost without exception emerged as the viable and indeed the successful candidates in the early nomination process. Thus to a degree not generally recognized, success both in early fund-raising during the pre-election year and even in pre-candidacy fund-raising during the prior year or years is predictive of candidate survival, viability, and success in the early nomination process, findings that establish the significance of money and the money primary in early presidential selection.

A comparison of campaign fund-raising during the early campaigns leading up to the 1988 and 2000 nomination campaigns highlights important patterns and trends that are very significant for an understanding of the presidential nominee selection process. Consistent with the hypothesized emergence of the money primary as a pivotal phase in the early campaign, the pre-candidacy phase of the early nomination campaign underwent significant change from 1988 to 2000, with this pre-candidacy phase starting earlier, lasting longer, and becoming a period in the campaign when an increasing amount of campaign activity unfolds. Moreover, the early candidacy period and especially the first six to nine months of the pre-election year likewise are a time of increased activity, with a significant increase in the number of early withdrawals between 1988 and 2000, including the new phenomenon in 2000 of newly announced candidates withdrawing even before the opening nomination contests. Candidate approaches to early fund-raising likewise changed significantly between 1988 and 2000, with PACs and other pre-candidacy fund-raising entities being broadly utilized in both of these campaign years but with the level of PAC activity increasing substantially by the 2000 election's early campaign and with the number of candidates utilizing both a PAC and an additional organizational entity increasing as well. The undermining of the framework of campaign finance reform which began during the 1988 election cycle's early campaign reached the point of the FECA framework's near disintegration by the 2000 election's early campaign, with the level of pre-candidacy fund-raising and spending outside of the FECA regulatory structure escalating and with candidates even declining federal matching funding and the spending ceilings that go with it.

Comparison of these two early campaigns and their four major party pre-nomination campaigns also highlights interesting differences in fund-raising between the two major parties. The level of fund-raising in absolute dollar totals in both early campaigns was significantly higher in the Republican contests as compared with the Democratic contests in both 1988 and 2000, with the Republican candidates who emerged as viable generally raising twice the amount of the Democratic candidates who emerged as viable. As a result, not surprisingly, the winnowing impact of fund-raising and money was even greater in the Republican races as compared with the Democratic races, with even more Republicans than Democrats withdrawing early and citing problems with fund-raising as their reason. Quite interestingly, moreover, Republicans in general have proven to be ahead of their Democratic counterparts in fund-raising and especially innovations in fund-raising, with Republicans being the first to utilize leadership PACs (following the 1976 election cycle), to establish alternate organizational entities such as tax-exempt foundations (beginning in the 1988 election cycle), to opt out of the system of federal matching funding (most notably in the 1980, 1996, and 2000 election cycles), and even to self-fund their campaigns (in the 1996 and 2000 election cycles). Thus, while all of the major trends in early and increased fund-raising during both the pre-candidacy and early candidacy phases are shared in common in Democratic and Republican contests alike, comparison of the early campaigns in the two major parties highlights the degree to which money is even more critical for Republicans than Democrats who aspire to become their party's presidential nominee.

A second dimension to the money primary examined in this study is media coverage of campaign fund-raising. The extent to which a candidate receives coverage of successful fund-raising, whether the orientation of this coverage is positive or negative, and whether horse race coverage of campaign fund-raising compares a candidate favorably or unfavorably with other candidates all are found to be associated with candidate survival, viability, and success through the early nomination process, confirming this study's third hypothesis. Interestingly, aside from occasional media attention directed at fund-raising scandals or candidate withdrawals, media coverage of campaign fund-raising during the early campaign—both in terms of the volume of coverage and the extent of positive coverage—is increasingly concentrated on candidates with successful fund-raising and especially candidates who compare positively with other candidates in the media's horse race coverage of campaign fund-raising. Thus media coverage of campaign fund-raising success must be a vital part of a candidate's efforts to establish credibility and standing as a prospective presidential nominee. Candidates seeking the presidential nomination therefore of necessity must not only be successful in fund-raising but must receive media attention that communicates that fund-raising success during the long early campaign preceding the actual counting of votes and selection of delegates.

A variety of generalizations concerning media coverage of campaign fund-raising during the early campaign can be made by comparing the 1988 and 2000 elections' early campaigns, providing additional important support for the hypothesized relationship between media coverage and candidate survival, viability, and success through the opening nomination process. Analysis of this media coverage of campaign fund-raising in the early campaigns for the 1988 and 2000 nomination contests establishes three categories of coverage: horse race coverage comparing candidates' fund-raising; candidate focused coverage of individual candidates' fund-raising; and general campaign fund-raising and campaign finance coverage. Candidate focused coverage is a major category of media coverage in both early campaigns studied, a conclusion consistent with the role of reporting and even evaluating candidate success in fund-raising that is ascribed to the media by this study. In fact, *The Washington Post* had candidate focused coverage of campaign fund-raising as its highest category of coverage in the early campaigns of both the 1988 and 2000 elections while *The New York Times* had candidate focused coverage as its highest category in the 1988 election's early campaign and as its second highest category in the 2000 election's early campaign. Consistent with the increased importance of the early campaign and the emergence of the money primary as a critical phase is a shift in the timing of media coverage of campaign fund-raising between the 1988 and 2000 elections' early campaigns, with candidate focused coverage of campaign fund-raising shifting from the fourth to the third quarter and to an extent even from the second half to the first half of the pre-election year. Finally, and perhaps most significantly, comparison of the 1988 and 2000 elections' early campaigns also highlights a major shift in the distribution of media coverage, whether horse race or candidate focused coverage, with this coverage in 1988's early campaign being more generally distributed among candidates but by 2000's early campaign being concentrated on candidates who proved to be viable candidates. The fact that this horse race and candidate focused coverage in the 2000 election's early campaign also tended to be positive coverage of candidate success in fund-raising underscores the value of this coverage to candidates seeking to boost their credibility and standing during the early campaign.

Providing further support for the hypothesis that media coverage of campaign fund-raising is related to candidate survival, viability, and success, as well as for the rise of the money primary, are additional generalizations from this media coverage analysis. Patterns in the timing of this media coverage are especially noteworthy, both in establishing a stronger link between campaign fund-raising and media coverage and in highlighting the emergence of the early campaign and the money primary. The peak in media coverage of campaign fund-raising following each quarter of the pre-election year corresponds with the schedule of candidate financial disclosure reports to the FEC, and the presence of this pattern in both the 1988 and 2000 elections' early campaigns links campaign fund-raising with media coverage of campaign fund-raising. The shifting of this coverage in general to earlier in the pre-election year, from the fourth quarter to the third quarter and even from the second half to the first half, is a trend in the timing of media coverage that also is consistent with the early campaign and the emergence of the money primary. Moreover, notwithstanding interesting differences in media coverage of campaign fund-raising among the newspapers studied, this media coverage overall is consistent in supporting the hypothesized relationship between media coverage of campaign fund-raising and candidate survival, viability, and success in the early nomination process. While candidate focused coverage in the early campaign leading up to the formal nomination campaign is the highest priority in *The Washington Post* in both the 1988 and 2000 elections' early campaigns but only the second highest priority in *The New York Times* and *The Wall Street Journal* in the 2000 election's early campaign, it clearly is a major and growing category of coverage in all three newspapers studied. Further, while in the 2000 election's early campaign *The New York Times'* candidate focused coverage is concentrated on viable candidates and *The Washington Post* and *The Wall Street Journal*'s coverage is more broadly distributed, in all three newspapers there is a trend between the 1988 and 2000 elections' early campaigns toward candidate focused coverage of campaign fund-raising being increasingly concentrated among viable candidates. In addition, horse race coverage comparing candidates' fund-raising is concentrated among the viable candidates in both the 1988 and 2000 elections' early campaigns, but is much greater in frequency and volume by the 2000 election's early campaign. Thus an array of specific patterns and trends in media coverage of campaign fund-raising in the three newspapers studied provides yet additional support for media coverage of campaign fund-raising's relationship to candidate survival, viability, and success in the early nomination process and the advancing importance of the early campaign and the money primary in the early presidential nomination process.

Confirmation of this study's three hypotheses regarding the impact of early candidacy and pre-candidacy fund-raising and media coverage of early candidacy fund-raising has significant implications in terms of developing a better understanding of the early presidential nomination campaign. Because fund-raising success is established as pivotal at both the pre-candidacy and early candidacy phases of the campaign, candidates and potential candidates clearly have little choice but to begin active fund-raising at ever earlier points, and their singular objective must be to raise the highest total in contributions possible. Moreover, faced with spending ceilings once their candidacy is formally declared, would-be candidates have an incentive to delay their formal entrance into the nomination process and to continue their pre-candidacy campaign for as long as possible. At the pre-candidacy phase, therefore, most campaign fund-raising is conducted outside of the regulatory framework of campaign finance reform, with PACs (which at least are required to submit financial disclosure reports to the FEC) and other organizational entities (which in general are not) being utilized across the board by nascent presidential nomination campaigns without this early activity counting toward FECA spending ceilings. Even at the early candidacy phase, when presidential campaign committees that are subject to FECA regulation are the required vehicle for campaign fund-raising and spending, the continued availability of other organizational entities is just one of myriad ways candidates have developed for evading the campaign finance reform framework. Thus the competition for early and ongoing fund-raising success has created a money-driven early campaign in which the necessity of an early start and significant early dollar totals have resulted in long pre-candidacy and early candidacy phases to the early nomination campaign. And faced with FECA spending ceilings during the formal nomination process, candidates and would-be candidates are conducting increasingly lengthy pre-candidacy campaigns funded by an array of alternate organizational entities that have become platforms for activity during a largely unregulated yet very significant phase in early presidential selection.

This study's findings also highlight the critical importance of media coverage of campaign fund-raising during the early presidential nomination campaign, with the media not only reporting campaign fund-raising success but also comparing and evaluating campaign fund-raising success, a finding that also has significant implications. Media coverage of campaign fund-raising generally is candidate focused, covering individual candidates' fund-raising success, but some of this media attention also is horse race coverage comparing candidates' fund-raising success. The increasing concentration of this media coverage of campaign fund-raising on candidates who prove to be viable in the early nomination process, and the generally positive spin of this coverage, means that candidates whose early and ongoing fund-raising is successful can expect a further boost with positive media coverage of this campaign fund-raising success. Concomitantly, candidates whose early and ongoing fund-raising is lackluster suffer a further setback with either negative media coverage of their fund-raising or, more likely, no media coverage at all. The result of this media-driven dimension of the early campaign is that candidates and potential candidates must regard media attention, including media coverage of campaign fund-raising success, as a vital campaign asset. The media in general and newspapers in particular therefore have a pivotal mediating role during the early campaign, beyond their powerful mediating role during the nomination campaign as a whole, with candidates and would-be candidates relying upon the media for the boost in credibility and standing which only positive media coverage of fund-raising success can provide.

In terms of the overall presidential selection process, this study's confirmation of the critical importance of both fund-raising success and media coverage of fund-raising success highlights the rise of the money primary as a new and decisive step during the early campaign leading up to the formal presidential nomination campaign. Winning this money primary, including early and ongoing fund-raising success and positive media coverage of this fund-raising success, thus has become the foremost challenge for presidential aspirants in the early campaign. An obvious impact of the money primary is on the behavior of aspiring candidates for the presidential nomination who from the outset of the campaign, and in fact well before the campaign, have fund-raising and the building of a fund-raising organization as their highest campaign priority. Yet the impact of the money primary is equally great in defining the overall candidate field, with early announcements of candidacy, early withdrawals, and a substantially narrowed candidate field being the result. Less obvious but also significant is the impact of the money primary in terms of potential candidates who decide not to launch candidacies, with the would-be candidates who in the end decide not to run often being as important to the development of a candidate field and the dynamics of a nomination contest as those who do choose to run. The emergence of the money primary therefore has momentous implications for the presidential nomination process and presidential selection, with the development of the candidate field and the dynamics of the early campaign as a whole being more money-driven and media-focused than ever as a result. The overall candidate field and in particular the field of viable candidates, as well as the ultimate presidential nominees, undoubtedly are very different today compared with just two decades ago in large measure because of the new dynamic created by the money primary.

Finally, and most significantly, the rise of the money primary along with fund-raising and media coverage as its key components has significant implications for the post-reform era's goal to democratize the presidential nomination process and thereby achieve a greater level of popular control of the presidency. Fundamental democratic values such as providing electoral choice, ensuring deliberation, and achieving broad popular participation, all integral to the democratic electoral process which the presidential nominating reforms sought to ensure, are eviscerated as the money primary has emerged as dominant. Providing an adequate level of electoral choice is a key democratic value underlying the nomination process, and the criteria by which the candidate field is developed and narrowed and the final candidate field is defined are crucial to electoral choice. The money primary has had an enormous impact on the processes that determine electoral choice, with the identification and emergence of candidates, the development and narrowing of the candidate field, and the definition of the final field of viable and competitive candidates now all resulting in large part from the money primary rather than from democratic processes such as coalition building and the enlistment of popular support. The democratic value of a deliberative decision-making process also has suffered dramatically, with the lengthened pre-candidacy and early candidacy phases now being followed by a radically shortened formal public phase that begins with the opening nomination contests in late January and early February and generally is complete just four to six weeks later. The rapidity of this formal nomination process and the practical impossibility of new or surprise candidacies during this accelerated schedule certainly are inconsistent with the open deliberative process that a truly democratic system aspires to ensure.

Threatened most fundamentally by the rise of the money primary is the goal of greater popular participation in presidential nominee selection, a democratic ideal which the nominating reforms sought to ensure but that is now largely absent from the emerging presidential nomination process. Because the money primary has shifted presidential campaign activity to a much earlier and less public phase of the campaign, the real decisions regarding the overall candidate field and the ultimately viable candidates are now made absent consultation with the popular will. In addition, the trend toward front-loading the primary and caucus calendar as well as the accelerated determination of the inevitable nominee have made most of the primaries and caucuses as well as the preferences of a large segment of the electorate almost irrelevant to the final electoral result, in effect taking a nomination system that was designed to ensure broad popular participation and instead circumscribing the primary and caucus process and even preempting voter participation itself. Thus the rise of the money primary has serious implications for the democratic character of the presidential nomination process, with the selection process for nominees for the nation's highest office becoming significantly less democratic at a time when the stated objective is the opposite.

In sum, this study confirms the pivotal importance of the early campaign, including both the pre-candidacy and early candidacy phases, in the presidential nomination process. The money primary is at the center of this early campaign, with both fund-raising success and media coverage of fund-raising success proving to be indispensable as candidates move from pre-candidacy to early candidacy, as the winnowing process results in candidate withdrawals on the one hand and formal announcements of candidacy on the other hand, and as the opening nomination contests separate the viable candidates from the ones who are merely survivors. Quite significantly, candidate viability in the early presidential nomination process is found to be associated with both fund-raising success during the pre-candidacy and early candidacy phases of the early presidential nomination campaign and media coverage of fund-raising success. Moreover, the fact that campaign fund-raising success and media coverage of campaign fund-raising success are critical for candidate survival, viability, and success is indicative of the emergence of the money primary as a new phase in the ever evolving system of presidential selection. This money primary and its increasing dominance in early presidential selection represent the advent of what in effect is an "unreformed post-reform era" in the presidential nomination process, a development with profound long-term implications for the representation of fundamental democratic values in the identification and nomination of future Presidents.

Afterword

New Directions for
Presidential Nomination Reform

THE MONEY PRIMARY IN GENERAL and money and media coverage of fund-raising in particular have a monumental impact on the early presidential nomination process. Documenting this impact certainly contributes to understanding a critical early phase in the nomination campaign that is not part of the formal nomination process. But also critically important is the need to utilize this understanding of the role of money and media coverage of fund-raising to inform the ongoing debate on campaign finance and presidential nomination reform.

The reality of the contemporary presidential nomination process is that the momentous reforms that were the aftermath of the 1968 presidential nomination campaign have been overturned during the 1980s and 1990s. The impetus of this reform process was to open the presidential nomination process to more direct popular participation, removing political elites such as party leaders, elected officeholders, major contributors, and other influentials from the position of primacy in choosing presidential nominees which they maintained through 1968. But as well-intended as the reforms following the 1968 presidential election may have been, the more open and responsive process which the reforms sought to enshrine prevailed only through the 1972 and 1976 presidential elections and were effectively undermined and even overturned by the 1980s and 1990s. Quite amazingly, the perverse impact of money and media coverage of fund-raising in establishing or winnowing out presidential candidates and would-be candidates in the early campaign for the presidential nomination has returned control of presidential selection to political elites in general and, perhaps worse, to financial elites in particular.

The three-decades-old movement and continuing debate on campaign finance reform and presidential nomination process reform is well served by a
careful consideration of the enormous impact of money and media coverage
of fund-raising on the presidential nomination process. Campaign finance reform, now a perennial political debate, is the obvious place for a consideration
of reform ideas and proposals to begin. But a fair reading of the impact of
money and media coverage of fund-raising on the process warrants a broader
approach. The reform debate must be broadened to consider the presidential
nomination process as a whole, examining changes and trends that date from
the 1970s and 1980s and that now can be seen as having had quite unintended
consequences. Perhaps most importantly, the reform debate needs to move
beyond legislation concerning state- and party-governed formal nomination
processes to consider innovations that approach the presidential nomination
process as a whole from new and non-traditional directions.

Advancing the movement toward campaign finance reform certainly is an
appropriate place to begin in addressing the impact of money and media coverage of fund-raising. Increasingly, Federal Election Commission rulings and
even federal campaign finance reform legislation have become primarily political decisions rather than genuine election reform decisions. Continual tin-
kering with campaign finance laws suffers increasingly from misguided decisions, whether regarding higher contribution limits, new restrictions on
contributions to political parties, or constitutionally questionable limitations
on political activity by interest groups. Moreover, even more seriously flawed
than what campaign finance reform legislation has overtly sought to change is
what it has overlooked. The political realities of the campaign finance reform
debate have resulted in legislation that fails to effectively regulate interest
group activity in presidential campaigns, especially through PACs, and that
leaves unaddressed expenditures by presidential candidates through campaign committees at the federal and state levels prior to their formal announced candidacy. The failure of Congress to design the structure of the FEC
to ensure its effectiveness and to empower it to identify and remedy campaign
finance abuses is perhaps the greatest gap, even in recent campaign finance
legislation. Moreover, the artificial time periods established by the FEC for
regulating presidential nomination campaign contributions and spending,
namely the period dating from a candidate's establishment and registration of
a formal presidential campaign committee, fail to recognize the extended and
even informal character of early and pre-candidacy presidential campaigns.

The overwhelming impact of money and media coverage of fund-raising
on candidate survival, viability, and success in the presidential nomination
process also warrants re-framing the reform debate to encompass the broader
nomination process rather than focusing on campaign finance reform alone.

It must be kept in mind that the formal structure of the reformed nomination process in terms of the proliferation of presidential primaries is the central reality of presidential nomination politics, both for good and for bad. The inadequacies of the current post-reform era presidential nomination process in some instances result from this basic reality and in almost every instance are exacerbated by it. The proliferation of primaries in the 1970s proved to be the first step toward the front-loading of this primary calendar, a trend that began in the 1980s and accelerated in the 1990s. The exhaustive primary calendar certainly created the necessity for candidates to have substantial funding, in itself a factor working against the original objective of the reforms in terms of opening up the nomination process. But far more serious in its consequences was the trend toward front-loading of this formal nomination process, with the large number of early state contests, whether caucuses or primaries, and their rapid-fire pace from late January though early March, making it essential for candidates not only to raise significant funding but to do so prior to the start of the formal campaign. A major direction for reform, therefore, is to adjust the nomination structure, both by altering the pacing of these contests to allow longer intervals between Iowa and New Hampshire, between New Hampshire and the next set of primaries, and in advance of the height of the primary schedule in March, a critical reform priority that would reduce the need for early and substantial pre-candidacy and pre-campaign fund-raising. Introducing greater variety in the types of contests, including more caucuses and perhaps even state conventions as well as primaries, would allow for greater candidate competition, to an extent irrespective of financial resources, providing some opportunity for even modestly funded candidates to compete and for long-shot candidates to have some chance for success.

Most importantly, the extent to which money and media coverage of fund-raising dominate presidential nomination politics, especially during the early campaign, necessitates careful consideration of reforms that go beyond the structure of the formal nomination process itself. There is a need for new venues, beyond the formal delegate selection process, to test candidates and frame the early campaign in which they compete. A more structured and extensive schedule of nomination candidate debates, especially during the pre-election year and during the nomination period itself, would provide a forum for candidate competition and voter attention in addition to the delegate selection process, permitting candidates—regardless of funding—to present their candidacies to voters. Expansion of public funding to include political parties as well as candidates is a further reform direction that could encourage parties to be active in planning and sponsoring opportunities for candidate debates, party meetings, and voter engagement prior to and during the formal nomination process. Indeed, the political parties themselves could be part of this broader reform movement, exploring ways to engage party leaders and elected officials, party activists, and voters in general in the pre-campaign and early campaign nomination process, whether through state conventions, issue forums, or other public gatherings. Such creative new directions in presidential nomination process reform could have an enormous impact, offering candidates with varied levels of advance funding the opportunity to compete effectively, opening the way for a greater variety of candidates and for competition based on ideas and experience as well as funding.

In sum, the reality of presidential nomination politics in the post-reform era is that it has come full circle, only temporarily changing from the political elite-based system that existed prior to reform to a reformed nomination process that remained true to its original intent of openness and responsiveness for a decade or less. The disappointing reality of the presidential nomination process in 2004 and beyond is that the elite-based system of 1968 and before is once again in force, with the original promise of reform devolving to the political and financial elite-centered system that prevails today. The challenge in resurrecting a truly reformed presidential nomination process certainly calls for continuing efforts to achieve campaign finance reform and formal nomination process reform. But at the same time it is essential to broaden the sphere of reform to encompass new and creative avenues for re-configuring the dynamics of the presidential nomination process as a whole. Nothing short of the democratic character of the presidential selection process and the presidency itself, now and for the twenty-first century, is at stake.

Bibliography

Primary Sources

Public Documents

Federal Election Commission. *Federal Election Campaign Laws.* Washington, D.C.: U.S. Government Printing Office, 1997.
———. *Report of Receipts and Disbursements of an Authorized Committee.* Washington, D.C.: Federal Election Commission, 1999.
Federal Register. *Code of Federal Regulations for Federal Elections.* Washington, D.C.: U.S. Government Printing Office, 1999.

Magazines

Barlett, Donald L., and James B. Steele. "Big Money and Politics: Who Gets Hurt? How the Little Guy Gets Crunched." *Time,* 7 February 2000, 38–41.
Duffy, Michael. "The Money Chase." *Time,* 13 March 1995, 93.
Glen, Maxwell. "Front-Loading the Race: Because of the Accelerated Timetable for the 1988 Presidential Nominating Contest, Ample Financial Resources Will Be More Important Than Ever to Candidates." *National Journal,* 29 November 1986, 2882.

Newspapers

Babcock, Charles R. "Robertson Blending Charity and Politics: Tax-Exempt Television Ministry Was Foundation for Campaign." *The Washington Post,* 2 November 1987, sec. A, p. 1.

Balz, Dan. "Bush's Fund-Raising Opens Huge Disparity: Unprecedented Edge May Limit Rivals." *The Washington Post*, 1 July 1999, sec. A, pp. 1, 9.

——. "GOP Process Is Echo of the Past." *The Washington Post*, 8 August 1999, sec. A, p. 1.

Berke, Richard L. "One Way to Break a Tie: Start the Next Race." *The New York Times*, 19 November 2000, sec. 4, pp. 1, 5.

——. "Presidential Hopefuls' First Race Is a Test of Fund-Raising Waters." *The New York Times*, 31 March 1999, sec. A, pp. 1, 19.

——. "Shorter Season Is Already Molding 2000 Race." *The New York Times*, 19 January 1999, sec. A, p. 12.

Brownstein, Ronald. "The Money Machine." *The Los Angeles Times*, 15 November 1987, 14.

Clymer, Adam. "The 2000 Campaign: The Also Rans; Standing on the Sidelines, Analyzing the Reasons Why." *The New York Times*, sec. A, p. 21.

Connolly, Ceci. "Huge Money Chase Marks 2000 Race." *The Washington Post*, 28 February 1999, sec. A, pp. 1, 6, 7.

Connolly, Ceci, and Susan B. Glasser. "Bradley's Campaign Bankroll Nearly Equals Gore's." *The Washington Post*, 1 July 1999, sec. A, pp. 1, 8.

Dionne, E. J., Jr. "13 Candidates Reach 1988, With Plenty To Fret Over." *The New York Times*, 27 December 1987, sec. 4, p. 1.

Edsall, Thomas. "Fund-Raising as Preoccupation: Early Advantage Becomes More Critical." *The Washington Post*, 15 April 1987, sec. A, p. 1.

Feldman, Linda. "The Race Before the Race—It's a Money Thing." *The Christian Science Monitor*, 23 April 1999, sec. USA, p. 2.

Glasser, Susan B. "A Bounce in Bucks for McCain, Bradley: As Poll Ratings Rose, So Did Donations." *The Washington Post*, 30 December 1999, sec. A, pp. 1, 11.

——. "Bush to Set Record for Campaign Donations: Bradley Also Makes a Strong Showing." *The Washington Post*, 30 June 1999, sec. A, pp. 1, 24.

——. "Network That Funded Father Hears from Son." *The Washington Post*, 7 April 1999, sec. A, pp. 1, 8, 9.

——. "A New Conduit for 'Soft Money': Critics Decry Big, Largely Untraceable Donations to Lawmakers' 'Leadership PACs'." *The Washington Post*, 16 May 1999, sec. A, p. 1.

Kuntz, Phil. "Fund-Raising Race Is Also Part of Presidential Contest." *The Wall Street Journal*, 11 March 1999, sec. A, p. 24.

Marcus, Ruth. "Dollars Dictate Field's Early Exits." *The Washington Post*, 21 October 1999, sec. A, pp. 1,14.

——. "Flood of Secret Money Erodes Election Limits." *The Washington Post*, 15 May 2000, sec. A, pp. 1, 6.

Taylor, Paul. "'88 Presidential Campaign Shaping Up as 'Short and Intense.'" *The Washington Post*, 4 January 1987, sec. A, pp. 4–5.

——. "Letter from Among the Money Men: At Democratic Kingmakers' Banquets, the Candidates Were the Entre." *The Washington Post*, 12 January 1987, sec. A, p. 1.

Van Natta, Don, Jr. "Early Rush of Contributions Opened The Floodgates for Bush." *The New York Times*, 30 January 2000, 20.

Secondary Sources

Books

Ackerman, Bruce, and Ian Ayres. *Voting with Dollars: A New Paradigm for Campaign Finance.* New Haven, Conn., and London: Yale University Press, 2002.

Alexander, Herbert E., and Monica Bauer. *Financing the 1988 Election.* Boulder, Colo.: Westview Press, 1991.

Alexander, Herbert E., and Anthony Corrado. *Financing the 1992 Election.* Armonk, N.Y.: M.E. Sharpe, Inc., 1995.

Anderson, Annelise, ed. *Political Money: Deregulating American Politics.* Stanford, Calif.: Hoover Institution Press, 2000.

Arterton, F. Christopher. *Media Politics: The News Strategies of Presidential Campaigns.* Lexington, Mass.: D.C. Heath, 1984.

Association of the Bar of the City of New York, Commission on Campaign Finance Reform. *Dollars and Democracy: A Blueprint for Campaign Finance Reform.* New York: Fordham University Press, 2000.

Bartels, Larry M. *Presidential Primaries and the Dynamics of Public Choice.* Princeton, N.J.: Princeton University Press, 1988.

Bauer, Robert F. *Soft Money Hard Law: A Guide to the New Campaign Finance Law.* Washington, D.C.: Perkins Coie LLP, 2002.

Birnbaum, Jeffrey H. *The Money Men: The Real Story of Fund-raising's Influence on Political Power in America.* New York: Crown Publishers, 2000.

Blumenthal, Sidney. *The Permanent Campaign,* rev. ed. New York: Simon and Schuster, 1982.

Brown, Jr., Clifford W., Lynda W. Powell, and Clyde Wilcox. *Serious Money: Fundraising and Contributing in Presidential Nomination Campaigns.* New York: Cambridge University Press, 1995.

Busch, Andrew E. *Outsiders and Openness in the Presidential Nominating System.* Pittsburgh, Pa.: University of Pittsburgh Press, 1997.

Ceaser, James W., and Andrew E. Busch. *The Perfect Tie: The True Story of the 2000 Presidential Election.* Lanham, Md.: Rowman & Littlefield Publishers, Inc., 2001.

Center for Responsive Politics. *Public Policy and Foundations: The Role of Politicians in Public Charities.* Washington, D.C.: Center for Responsive Politics, 1987.

———. *The Wealth Primary.* Washington, D.C.: Center for Responsive Politics, 1994.

Chirban, John T. *Interviewing in Depth: The Interactive Relational Approach.* Thousand Oaks, Calif.: Sage Publishers, Inc., July 1996.

Clawson, Dan, Alan Neustadtl, and Mark Weller. *Dollars and Votes: How Business Campaign Contributions Subvert Democracy.* Philadelphia: Temple University Press, 1998.

Congressional Quarterly, Inc. *Presidential Elections Since 1789,* 7th ed. Washington, D.C.: Congressional Quarterly Press, 1999.

Cook, Rhodes. *Race for the Presidency: Winning The 2000 Nomination.* Washington, D.C.: Congressional Quarterly Press, 2000.

Corrado, Anthony. *Campaign Finance Reform.* New York: The Century Foundation Press, 2000.

———. *Creative Campaigning: PACs and the Presidential Selection Process.* Boulder, Colo.: Westview Press, Inc., 1992.

———. *Paying for Presidents: Public Financing in National Elections.* New York: The Twentieth Century Fund Press, 1993.

Corrado, Anthony, Thomas E. Mann, Daniel R. Ortiz, Trevor Potter, and Frank J. Sorauf, eds. *Campaign Finance Reform: A Sourcebook.* Washington, D.C.: Brookings Institution Press, 1997.

Cramer, Richard Ben. *What It Takes: The Way to the White House.* New York: Vintage Books, 1992.

Crotty, William, ed. *America's Choice 2000.* Boulder, Colo.: Westview Press, 2001.

Dahl, Robert. *How Democratic Is the American Constitution?* New Haven, Conn., and London: Yale University Press, 2001.

Davies, Philip John. *US Elections Today.* New York: St. Martin's Press, Inc., 1999.

Davis, James W. *U.S. Presidential Primaries and the Caucus—Convention System: A Sourcebook.* Westport, Conn.: Greenwood Press, 1997.

Drew, Elizabeth. *The Corruption of American Politics: What Went Wrong and Why.* Secaucus, N.J.: Core Publishing Group, 1999.

Fallows, James. *Breaking the News: How the Media Undermine American Democracy.* New York: Vintage Books, 1997.

Gais, Thomas. *Improper Influence: Campaign Finance Law, Political Interest Groups, and the Problem of Equality.* Ann Arbor: The University of Michigan Press, 1996.

Gierzynski, Anthony. *Money Rules: Financing Elections in America.* Boulder, Colo.: Westview Press, 2000.

Green, John C., ed. *Financing the 1996 Election.* Armonk, N.Y.: M.E. Sharpe, 1998.

Hadley, Arthur T. *The Invisible Primary.* Englewood Cliffs, N.J.: Prentice-Hall, 1976.

Haskell, John. *Fundamentally Flawed: Understanding and Reforming Presidential Primaries.* Lanham, Md.: Rowman & Littlefield Publishers, Inc., 1996.

Hofstetter, C. Richard. *Bias in the News.* Columbus: Ohio State University Press, 1976.

Jamieson, Kathleen Hall, and Paul Waldman, eds. *Electing the President 2000: The Insiders' View.* Philadelphia: University of Pennsylvania Press, 2001.

Johnson, Dennis W. *No Place for Amateurs: How Political Consultants Are Reshaping American Democracy.* New York: Routledge, 2001.

Kessel, John. *Presidential Campaign Politics,* 4th ed. Pacific Grove, Calif.: Brooks/Cole, 1992.

Koplinski, Brad. *Hats in the Ring: Conversations with Presidential Candidates.* North Bethesda, Md.: Presidential Publishing, 2000.

Mayer, William G. *The Divided Democrats: Ideological Unity, Party Reform, and Presidential Elections.* Boulder, Colo.: Westview, 1996.

Nelson, Michael, ed. *The Elections of 1988.* Washington, D.C.: Congressional Quarterly Press, 1989.

Ornstein, Norman, and Thomas Mann, eds. *The Permanent Campaign and Its Future.* Washington, D.C.: American Enterprise Institute and The Brookings Institution, 2000.

Orren, Gary R., and Nelson W. Polsby, eds. *Media and Momentum: The New Hampshire Primary and Nomination Politics.* Chatham, N.J.: Chatham House Publishers, 1987.

Patterson, Thomas E. *The Mass Media Election: How Americans Choose Their President.* New York: Praeger, 1980.

———. *Out of Order.* New York: Vintage Books, 1994.

Plissner, Martin. *The Control Room: How Television Calls the Shots in Presidential Elections.* New York: The Free Press, 1999.

Polsby, Nelson W., and Aaron Wildavsky. *Presidential Elections: Strategies and Structures of American Politics,* 10th ed. New York and London: Chatham House Publishers, 2000.

Pomper, Gerald M., ed. *The Election of 2000.* New York: Chatham House Publishers, 2001.

Robinson, Michael J., and Margaret A. Sheehan. *Over the Wire and on TV: CBS and UPI in Campaign '80.* New York: Russell Sage Foundation, 1980.

Runkel, David R. *Campaign for President: The Managers Look at '88.* Dover, Mass.: Auburn House Publishing Company, 1989.

Sabato, Larry J., and Joshua J. Scott. *Overtime: The Election 2000 Thriller.* New York: Pearson Education, 2002.

Schier, Steven E. *By Invitation Only: The Rise of Exclusive Politics in the United States.* Pittsburgh, Pa.: The University of Pittsburgh Press, 2000.

Shafer, Byron E., ed. *The State of American Politics.* Lanham, Md.: Rowman & Littlefield Publishers, Inc., 2002.

Sorauf, Frank J. *Money in American Elections.* Glenview, Ill.: Scott Foresman and Company, 1988.

Thurber, James A., and Candice J. Nelson, eds. *Campaign Warriors: Political Consultants in Elections.* Washington, D.C.: Brookings Institution Press, 2000.

———, eds. *Campaigns and Elections American Style.* Boulder, Colo.: Westview Press, 1995.

Wattenberg, Martin. *The Rise of Candidate-Centered Politics: Presidential Elections of the 1980s.* Cambridge, Mass., and London: Harvard University Press, 1991.

Wayne, Stephen J. *The Road to the White House, 2000: The Politics of Presidential Elections, Postelection Edition.* Boston: Bedford/St. Martin's, 2001.

Wayne, Stephen J., and Clyde Wilcox, eds. *The Election of the Century: And What It Tells Us About the Future of American Politics.* Armonk, N.Y.: M.E. Sharp, 2002.

West, Darrell M. *Checkbook Democracy: How Money Corrupts Political Campaigns.* Boston: Northeastern University Press, 2000.

Winebrenner, Hugh. *The Iowa Precinct Caucuses: The Making of a Media Event.* Ames, Iowa State University Press, 1998.

Witcover, Jules. *No Way To Pick a President: How Money and Hired Guns Have Debased American Elections.* New York: Farrar, Straus and Giroux, 1999.

Articles and Book Chapters

Adkins, Randall E., and Andrew J. Dowdle. "The Money Primary: What Influences the Outcome of Pre-Primary Presidential Nomination Fundraising?" *Presidential Studies Quarterly* 32, no. 2 (June 2002): 256–75.

Aldrich, John H. "A Dynamic Model of Presidential Nomination Campaigns." *American Political Science Review* 74 (1980): 651–69.

Birnbaum, Jeffrey H. "The Money Chase." *Fortune* 138, no. 5 (7 September 1998): 96.

———. "Money, Money Everywhere." *Fortune* 140, no. 2 (19 July 1999): 80.

Buell, Emmett H., Jr. "The Invisible Primary." In *In Pursuit of the White House: How We Choose Our Presidential Nominees*, ed. William G. Mayer, 1–43. Chatham, N.J.: Chatham House Publishers, Inc., 1996.

———. "Meeting Expectations? Major Newspaper Coverage of Candidates During the 1988 Exhibition Season." In *Nominating the President*, ed. Emmett H. Buell, Jr. and Lee Sigelman, 150–95. Knoxville: The University of Tennessee Press, 1991.

Cook, Rhodes. "The Nominating Process." In *The Election of 1988*, ed. Michael Nelson, 25–61. Washington, D.C.: Congressional Quarterly Press, 1989.

Corrado, Anthony. "Financing the 1996 Elections." In *The Election of 1996: Reports and Interpretations*, ed. Gerald M. Pomper, 135–71. Chatham, N.J.: Chatham House Publishers, Inc., 1997.

———. "Financing the 2000 Elections." In *The Election of 2000*, ed. Gerald M. Pomper, 92–124. New York: Chatham House Publishers, 2001.

Damore, David F. "A Dynamic Model of Candidate Fundraising: The Case of Presidential Nomination Campaigns." *Political Research Quarterly* 50, no. 2 (June 1997): 343–64.

Hagen, Michael G., and William G. Mayer. "The Modern Politics of Presidential Selection: How Changing the Rules Really Did Change the Game." In *In Pursuit of the White House: How We Choose Our Presidential Nominees*, ed. William G. Mayer, 1–55. New York: Chatham House Publishers, Inc., 2000.

Haskell, John. "Reforming Presidential Primaries: Three Steps for Improving the Campaign Environment." *Presidential Studies Quarterly* 26 (Spring 1996): 380–90.

Haynes, Audrey A., Paul-Henri Gurian, and Stephen M. Nichols. "The Role of Candidate Spending in Presidential Nomination Campaigns." *The Journal of Politics* 59, no. 1 (February 1997): 213–25.

Jones, Charles O. "Nonstop! The Campaigning Presidency and the 2000 Presidential Campaign." *Brookings Review* 18, no. 1 (Winter 2000): 12–15.

Mayer, William G. "Forecasting Presidential Nominations." In *In Pursuit of The White House: How We Choose Our Presidential Nominees*, ed. William G. Mayer, 44–71. Chatham, N.J.: Chatham House Publishers, Inc., 1996.

———. "Perspectives on the Current Presidential Selection Process." In *Nominating Future Presidents*, Advisory Committee on the Presidential Selection Process, Republican National Committee, 114. Washington, D.C.: Republican National Committee, May 2000.

———. "The Presidential Nominations." In *The Election of 2000*, ed. Gerald M. Pomper, 12–45. New York: Chatham House Publishers, 2001.

Norrander, Barbara. "Nomination Choices: Caucus and Primary Outcomes, 1976–1988." *American Journal of Political Science* 37, no. 2 (May 1993): 343–64.

Orren, Gary R., and William G. Mayer. "The Press, Political Parties, and the Public-Private Balance in Elections." In *The Parties Respond: Changes in the American Political System*, ed. L. Sandy Maisel, 204–24. Boulder, Colo.: Westview Press, Inc., 1990.

Patterson, Thomas E. "The Press and Its Missed Assignment." In *The Elections of 1988*, ed. Michael Nelson, 93–109. Washington, D.C.: Congressional Quarterly Press, 1989.

Pomper, Gerald M. "The Presidential Nominations." In *The Election of 1988: Reports and Interpretations*, ed. Gerald M. Pomper, 33–71. Chatham, N.J.: Chatham House Publishers, Inc., 1989.

Robinson, Michael, Clyde Wilcox, and Paul Marshall. "The Presidency: Not for Sale." *Public Opinion* 2 (March/April 1989): 49–53.

Steger, Wayne P. "Do Primary Voters Draw from a Stacked Deck? Presidential Nominations in an Era of Candidate-Centered Campaigns." *Presidential Studies Quarterly* 30, no. 4 (December 2000): 727–53.

Trent, Judith S. "The Beginning and the Early End." In *The 1992 Presidential Campaign: A Communication Perspective*, ed. Robert E. Denton, Jr., 51–75. Westport, Conn.: Praeger Publishers, 1998.

———. "The Early Campaign." In *The 1992 Presidential Campaign: A Communication Perspective*, ed. Robert E. Denton, Jr., 43–64. Westport, Conn.: Praeger Publishers, 1994.

———. "Presidential Surfacing: The Ritualistic and Crucial First Act." *Communication Monographs* 45 (November 1978): 282.

Wald, Kenneth D. "Ministering to the Nation: The Campaigns of Jesse Jackson and Pat Robertson," in *Nominating the President*, ed. Emmett H. Buell, Jr. and Lee Sigelman, 119–49. Knoxville: University of Tennessee Press, 1991.

Wilcox, Clyde. "Financing the 1988 Prenomination Campaign." In *Nominating the President*, ed. Emmett H. Buell, Jr. and Lee Sigelman, 91–118. Knoxville: University of Tennessee Press, 1991.

Wilcox, Clyde, and Wesley Joe. "Dead Law: The Federal Election Finance Regulations, 1974–1996." *PS: Political Science and Politics* 30, no. 1 (March 1998): 14–17.

Index

About the Author

Michael J. Goff is Vice President for Development and College Relations at Loyola College in Maryland and has more than twenty-five years of experience in educational fund-raising. He holds a Ph.D. in Government from Georgetown University and teaches in the Master of Liberal Studies Program and the Department of Political Science at Loyola College in Maryland.